TRUE AND FALSE PATHS
OF SPIRITUAL RESEARCH

TRUE AND FALSE PATHS OF SPIRITUAL RESEARCH

Eleven lectures given in Torquay from 11 to 22 August 1924

REVISED AND TRANSLATED BY PAUL KING WITH
REFERENCE TO EARLIER TRANSLATIONS
BY H. COLLINSON AND A. H. PARKER

INTRODUCTION BY PAUL KING

RUDOLF STEINER

RUDOLF STEINER PRESS

CW 243

Rudolf Steiner Press
Hillside House, The Square
Forest Row, RH18 5ES

www.rudolfsteinerpress.com

Published by Rudolf Steiner Press 2020

Originally published in German under the title *Das Initiaten Bewußtsein. Die wahren und die falschen Wege der geistigen Forschung* (volume 243 in the *Rudolf Steiner Gesamtausgabe* or Collected Works) by Rudolf Steiner Verlag, Dornach. The text is based on shorthand notes that were not reviewed or revised by the speaker. This authorized translation is based on the sixth German edition (2004), edited by Walter Kugler

Published by permission of the Rudolf Steiner Nachlassverwaltung, Dornach

© Rudolf Steiner Nachlassverwaltung, Dornach, Rudolf Steiner Verlag 2004

This translation © Rudolf Steiner Press 2020

A catalogue record for this book is available from the British Library

ISBN 978 1 85584 576 3

Cover by Andrew Morgan Design
Typeset by Symbiosys Technologies, Visakhapatnam, India
Printed and bound by 4Edge Ltd., Essex

CONTENTS

LECTURE 1
TORQUAY, 11 AUGUST 1924
Nature is the Great Illusion. 'Know Thyself'

Why investigate the spiritual worlds at all? The true paths to real
spiritual knowledge. Knowledge of the world in its totality through spiritual
perception within physical facts.

LECTURE 2
TORQUAY, 12 AUGUST 1924
The Three Worlds and their Reflected Images

Differences in consciousness in ancient and modern times.
Creative imagination that occurs naturally in dreaming today.
Further strengthening of the soul-life.

LECTURE 3
TORQUAY, 13 AUGUST 1924
*Form and Substantiality of the Mineral Kingdom in relation to Human
Levels of Consciousness*

The nature of crystallized minerals. Substantiality and metallity of the mineral
world. From spatial consciousness into time consciousness.

EDITOR'S PREFACE

These lectures were given at an International Summer School organized by the Anthroposophical Society in England under the theme of 'Right and Wrong Paths of Spiritual Research'. Marie Steiner gave them the title of 'Initiation Science' for the [German] printed edition published in 1927. She also gave the headings for the individual lectures as well as the section headings within the lectures.

The division of the lecture into three parts comes from the fact that Dr Steiner interrupted each lecture twice to allow the interpreter, George Adams-Kaufmann, to translate.

Introduction

In this cycle of lectures, given during a 'summer school' held in Torquay in August 1924, Steiner is responding to a request to speak about 'true and false paths of spiritual research'. Bearing in mind we are dealing here with spiritual *research* and not just spiritual experiences in general, a 'true' path in this sense is one that leads to genuine and reliable results that advance our knowledge of the human being and the world. A 'false' path is one that uses methods that are inappropriate for the subject, or anachronistic, or occur in a drug-altered or dulled state of consciousness; for although these may involve momentous experiences for the experiencer, they tend to be too subjective or chaotic to be of value for the purposes of knowledge.

By way of analogy consider the following.

Imagine a world in which a group of scientists who have been deaf from birth, decide to make a scientific study of music. They choose a symphony orchestra as the subject of this project. While the musicians play, the researchers film their movements, the expression on their faces, measure the temperature fluctuations in their bodies, etc. They connect monitoring devices to their instruments to measure the vibrational frequency of the strings in the stringed instruments, the air vibrations of the wind instruments, the pressure vibrations in the percussion. Everything is filmed, measured and monitored. All the data are then collated, analysed, and presented in a report of several hundred pages.

But how close have the researchers come to understanding music? And how useful is their study for a general deepening of our knowledge?

This method could be described as a 'false path' for researching music. The most basic requirement for an understanding of music is firstly to listen to it! One must leave the realm of sight and listen one's way into the world of sound, and take it from there. As Steiner says: 'This is the secret to researching other worlds: that we undergo a change in ourselves, even in our forms of consciousness. For we cannot gain access to other worlds by theorizing or by investigation using the same means as we use in ordinary life, but by a metamorphosis, a transformation of our consciousness into other forms of consciousness.'

But the approach of the deaf scientists in our analogy is very close to the approach usually taken by our present physical science when it comes to researching non-physical phenomena. To research meditation, for instance, monitoring electrodes are attached to a meditator's head and body and the meditative process is assessed according to brainwaves and breath rate, etc. The essential component—namely *consciousness* (the 'music')—is not investigated directly. The scientific approach is 'deaf' to it.

So the problem here for our present scientists is that non-physical phenomena, even when conceded to exist, cannot be measured by physical means. The only technology that can explore consciousness is consciousness itself. And, as Steiner describes in these lectures, consciousness—or certain levels of it—is also the means by which we enter the spiritual world.

Fortunately, this 'consciousness technology' can be developed. Through rigorous self-training in specific meditation and concentration, and regular work on 'detoxifying' one's thoughts, feelings, and actions, consciousness can be developed to a point where it can enter the spiritual world in a stable and reliable way. When this is achieved, spiritual research becomes possible.

This naturally poses a great challenge for any would-be scientist. Scientific training today does not usually include serious schooling in meditation and work on one's character! But in the future (perhaps in a century or two?), we can hope that scientific training will come to incorporate something of the ancient mysteries, so that study of the spiritual world will be integrated with study of the physical world, and the students trained in developing a consciousness that is capable of spiritual research.

Individuals who are already able to investigate it, report that the realm of consciousness is vast. Each condition of consciousness is like a whole world in itself ('We must familiarize ourselves with the fact that other consciousnesses enable us to look into other worlds which are not the world of our everyday existence'). And a change of consciousness brings one into a different 'place' ('But we are now once again somewhere else because the condition of our consciousness has altered...'). In the lectures Steiner shows a variety of entry points to certain conditions of consciousness and the spiritual realms they connect with: for example, by focusing on various parts of the body, on certain metals, or on different stages in our biography.

But why research the spiritual at all? What's the point?

From a purely materialist perspective there is naturally no point at all—what's the point in investigating what doesn't exist? But if we see things from a broader spiritual standpoint, then everything in the material world has 'precipitated' out of the spiritual and can only be understood fully when the spiritual laws of its being are taken into account. Child development, for example, involves not just physical growth and brain development, but also a gradual unfolding of the child's non-material members-of-being, of the etheric and astral body. By understanding this unfolding—which can only be done by means of spiritual science and spiritual research—we can design an education for the child that supports this development, rather than undermines it and perhaps leads to compromised health in later life.

The importance of initiation science for medicine is almost self-evident. Steiner describes how understanding certain organs requires entering into a particular condition of consciousness that opens us up to the nature of these organs at a cosmic level. It also indicates the possible cure when the organs are sick. Steiner speaks in these lectures about how, for example, certain digestive disorders are associated with the patient being drawn unconsciously and too strongly into the realm where human souls wander in their first phase after death. For our present way of thinking this is an extremely bizarre notion. And yet, insight of this kind can also lead to a cure, which Steiner describes in the lecture.

Initiation science can also give insight into the nature, for example, of the plant and the cosmic influences that promote its healthy growth. In agriculture and horticulture such knowledge is important to ensure healthy and vibrant crops for healthy and vibrant food.

Initiation science may even have the potential to develop alternative energies that are not harmful to the environment and are even health-promoting! This alone would be quite a 'point' for researching the non-physical worlds.

Since the Enlightenment, humanity has been steadily developing its modern mode of clear rational thinking. This achievement has led to the deep penetration and investigation of the physical world that is characteristic of our age. The next evolutionary step, however, is to take this clear logical thinking and apply it to the non-physical world, so that our understanding of the physical can be extended into the super-physical. This requires more than just experiencing the spiritual world; it requires the training mentioned above to the point where it can not only perceive the spiritual, but also understand what it perceives and can *formulate this into thoughts* so that someone else, who does not necessarily have spiritual perception themselves, can also comprehend it. Then the research becomes valuable to all who are prepared to study it.

Without the spiritual dimension, life and the cosmos become pretty meaningless. Peoples with a strong spirituality tend to have a rich culture. Without nourishment from the spirit, culture becomes impoverished and in our civilization is replaced by mere entertainment and human-unfriendly technology. In fact, it seems to me that if we are to have a future at all, we must find the spirit, embrace it, and integrate it into our physical lives. This is perhaps the greatest challenge of our time.

'The significance of the great turning point of our age lies in the fact that the world presents a picture of destruction, of increasing chaos; but in this chaos, in this terrible fury of human passions that casts darkness over everything and would finally bring it all into decadence, there is revealed, to those who have insight, the impulse of the spiritual powers who stand behind it all and are ready to lead humanity into a new spirituality. And the right preparation for anthroposophical spiritual science consists in listening to the voice of the spirit that is sounding into our materialistic existence.'

We need to *listen* to 'the music'.

Paul King
May 2020

LECTURE 1

11 AUGUST 1924

Nature is the Great Illusion
'Know Thyself'

Why investigate spiritual worlds at all?

I HAVE been asked to speak in these lectures about the paths leading to the supersensory world, to spiritual life and to super-sensory knowledge. These paths can combine with those taken in such a magnificent and positive way by the modern age which have increased our knowledge of the sensory physical world. For reality can be apprehended only by the person who is able to reinforce the remarkable discoveries which the natural and historical sciences have added to our stock of knowledge in recent times, with insight derived from the spiritual world.

Wherever the external world confronts us it is in truth both spiritual and physical; behind every physical phenomenon will be found, in some form or other, a spiritual agent which is the real protagonist. And there is never any kind of spiritual entity that leads an empty, idle existence, just passing time in boredom, but every spiritual entity wherever it may be found will also be active right into the physical level at some time and some place.

I propose to discuss in these lectures how the world in which man lives may be known in its totality, on the one hand through a consideration of his physical environment and, on the other hand, through the perception of the spiritual. In this way I hope to indicate the true and erroneous methods of attaining such knowledge.

Before touching tomorrow on the actual subject matter of these lectures, I should like to offer a brief introduction so that you can have some idea of what to expect from them and what purpose I have in view. They are concerned in the first place with bringing home to us the question: why do we undertake spiritual investigation at all? Why, as thinking, feeling, practical persons, are we not satisfied with accepting the phenomenal world as it is and taking an active part in it? Why do we strive at all to attain knowledge of a spiritual world?

In this context I should like to refer to an ancient perception, an old saying that embraces a truth ever more widely accepted and which, inherited from the earliest days of human thinking and aspiration, is still found today when we inquire into the nature of the world. Without in any way using these ancient, unfamiliar views as a basis, I would like nevertheless to call attention to them whenever appropriate.

From the East there echoes across thousands of years the saying: the world that we perceive with our senses is *maya*, the Great Illusion. And if, as man has always felt during the course of his development, the world is *maya*, then he must transcend the 'Great Illusion' to find ultimate truth.

But why did man look upon this world that he sees with his eyes, hears with his ears, and perceives with his other senses, as *maya*? Why, precisely in the earliest times when people were nearer to the spirit than they are today, did the mystery centres arise, centres that were dedicated to the cultivation of science, religion, art and practical living, whose aim was to point the way to truth and reality, in contradistinction to that which, purely in the external world, was the Great Illusion, the source of man's knowledge and activity? How is one to account for those outstanding sages who trained their neophytes in the ancient, holy Mysteries and sought to lead them from illusion to truth? This question can only be answered if one reviews man more dispassionately, from a more detached angle.

'Know thyself!'[1]—such is another ancient saying that comes down to us from the past. From the fusion of these two sayings—'The world is *maya*,' from the East, and 'Know thyself!', from ancient Greece—there first arose the quest for spiritual knowledge amongst later humanity. But in the ancient Mysteries, too, the quest for truth and reality had its origin in this twofold perception that, in the final analysis, the world is illusion and that man must attain to self-knowledge.

But it is only through life itself that man can come to terms with this question, not through thinking alone, but through the will and through full participation in the reality immediately accessible to us as human beings. Neither in full consciousness, nor in clear understanding, but with deep feeling, every human being the world over can say to themselves: 'You yourself cannot be like the outer world that you see and hear.'

This feeling goes deep. One must reflect upon the implication of these words: 'You cannot be like the external world that you perceive with your five senses.' When we look at the plants we see the first green shoots emerge from the root in springtime; they blossom in summer and towards autumn they ripen and bear fruit. We see them grow, fade and die; the duration of their life-cycle is a single year. We see, too, how many plants absorb 'hardness' from the soil, if I can put it that way, permeate themselves with 'hardness' and form a tree trunk. On the way here yesterday evening by road we saw many extremely old plants which had absorbed quantities of these hardening substances in order that their life-cycle should not be limited to a single year, but should be extended over a longer period of time and thus would bear new growing-points again and again on their stems. And the human being is able to observe how these plants grow, fade and die.

And we observe the animals. We see them come into being and pass away. It is even the same with the mineral kingdom. We observe the mineral deposits in mighty majestic mountain ranges. And modern scientific knowledge has also come to realize that even these majestic mountains come into being and pass away. And finally we turn to some conception such as the Ptolemaic or Copernican system, for example, or some conception borrowed from the ancient or later Mysteries, and we conclude as follows: all that I see in the majesty of the stars, all that rays down to me from sun and moon with their wondrous and complex orbits, all this, too, comes into being and passes away. But apart from coming into being and passing away, the kingdom of nature has other attributes. These are such that, if he is to know himself, man should not assume that he is the same as everything that comes into being and passes away—the plants, minerals, sun, moon and stars.

Man then comes to the conclusion: I bear within me some quality that is different from anything I see and hear around me. I must find the truth of my own being. I cannot find it in anything that I see and hear.

In all the ancient Mysteries human beings felt this urge to discover the reality of their inner being, whereas all the transient phenomena of space and time were felt to be an expression of the Great Illusion. And so, in order to arrive at an understanding of man's inner being, they looked for something other than what was revealed by the outer senses. And this 'something other' was experienced as a spiritual world. And how to find the right path to this spiritual world will be the subject of these lectures.

You can easily imagine that man's initial impulse will be to want to follow the same approach he is wont to follow in exploring the sense-world. He will simply transfer the method of sense-perception to his exploration of the spiritual world. If, however, investigation into the sense-world is subject to illusion, then we can expect the potential for illusion to be greater, not less, if the methods for investigating this sense-world are also applied to the spiritual world. And, in effect, this is what happens, as we shall see. If we research the spiritual world in the same way as we do the sense-world, the illusion cannot be reduced but must increase. And by extending sensory research into the spiritual world, we simply become absorbed in a greater and more compelling illusion.

And again, if we harbour vague, indistinct mystical feelings about the spirit, dream-fantasies about it, the spiritual will simply remain unknown to us. We just believe but have no real knowledge. If we are content simply to adopt this course, the spiritual will not become better known to us but progressively more unknown. Thus man may follow two false paths, as it were.

On the one hand, he pursues the same line of enquiry in relation to the spiritual as he does to the sense-world. And the sense-world presents him in the first place with illusion. If he tries to take the same approach with the spiritual world—as the ordinary spiritualists sometimes do—then he arrives not at a lesser illusion but at an even greater one.

On the other hand he can follow the other way of approach. In this case no attempt is made to investigate the spiritual world along clear, deeply penetrating lines, but through belief and mystical feelings. That way the spiritual world remains a closed book. No matter how hard we pursue this path of vague inklings and mystical feeling we will know ever less and less about the spiritual world. Neither path leads us into the spiritual world. In the first instance the illusion is magnified, in the second, our ignorance. As against these two erroneous paths we must find the right path.

The true paths to real spiritual knowledge

We must bear in mind how impossibly difficult it is to get from a knowledge of the Great Illusion in the sense I have indicated to a knowledge of the true self; and furthermore, if one intends to prepare oneself for a true, authentic approach to spiritual understanding, how impossible it is, in a state of illusion, to overcome all these nebulous feelings about the true self and come to a clear perception of reality.

Let us look quite impartially at what is involved here. A materialist can never feel such deep admiration and respect for the recent scientific discoveries of Darwin, Huxley, Spencer[2] and others as someone who has insight into the spiritual world. For these individuals, and many others since the time of Giordano Bruno[2], spared no effort in order to gain insight into what the ancient Mysteries considered to be the world of *maya*. One does not have to accept the theories advanced by Darwin, Huxley, Spencer, Copernicus, Galileo[2] and the rest. Let others theorize what they will about the universe, we have no intention of being drawn into their arguments. But we must recognize the tremendous impetus given by all these individuals to the detailed, factual study of specific organs in man, animal and plant, or of some particular enigma relating to the mineral kingdom. Just imagine how much we have learned in recent times about the functions of the glands, nerves, heart, brain, lungs, liver and so on, as a result of their stimulating researches. They deserve our greatest respect and admiration. But in real life this knowledge can take us only to a certain point. Let me give you three examples to illustrate my point.

We can follow in extraordinary detail how the very first cells in the human ovum develop; how they gradually develop into a human embryo, how the various organs evolve step by step, and how from tiny peripheral organs the complex heart and circulatory system are built up. All this can be demonstrated. We can follow the organic growth of the plant from root to blossom and seed and from this factual information we can construct a theory of the world that extends to the stars. Our astronomers and astrophysicists have already done this. They construct a theory of the cosmos showing how the world emerges from a stellar-nebular system which assumed a progressively more definite structure, was capable of evolving life, and so on.

But despite all this theorizing, we come ultimately face to face once again with the essential being of man, the problem of how to respond to the injunction, 'Know thyself!' If we know only the self that is limited to a knowledge of the minerals, plants, animals, and human glandular and circulatory systems, then what do we know? We know only the world man enters at birth and leaves at death. Nothing more. But, in the depths of our being, we sense that this is not our true and final limit. And so, in face of all the knowledge that the external world yields in such majesty and perfection, we must answer from our innermost being: all this is what you assume only between birth and death. But what are you in your essential being? The moment the question of knowledge of man and nature takes a religious turn, the human being whose organs can only apprehend the world of the Great Illusion becomes stuck. The injunction, 'Know thyself, so that you may know in your innermost being whence you come and whither you go,' this problem of cognition, looked at from a religious standpoint, remains unanswered.

On entering the Mystery Schools the neophyte was left in no doubt that however much he may have learned through sense-observation, this information could offer no answer to the great riddle of human nature when approached from a religious point of view.

Furthermore, though we may observe very precisely how the human face is formed, or how an individual moves their arms and hands, how they walk and stand, or however much we may train ourselves to have the finest sense for the form of an animal or a plant insofar as we can know these through sense-observation—directly we try to give artistic expression to this feeling, to what we have perceived, we are again faced with an unanswerable problem.

For how have people since ancient times given artistic expression to what they know of the world? It was the Mysteries in earlier ages that gave the impetus for this. Their knowledge of nature and its various aspects was related to the existing level of understanding, but at the same time it was deepened by spiritual insight.

One need only look back to ancient Greece. Today a sculptor or painter works from a model—at least this was the practice until recently. He sets out to copy or imitate something. The Greek artist did not work in this way, although he is assumed to have done so; rather, he sensed the spiritual human form within himself. In sculpture, if he wished to portray an arm in movement, he was aware that what he saw externally in a model was informed by a spiritual content, that every material object has been created according to the spirit, and in his work he strove to create according to that spirit.

Even as late as the Renaissance a painter did not use a model; it served only as a stimulus. He knew intuitively what activated hand or arm and expressed this in his rendering of movement. He expressed how the human being lives inwardly with the spirit. Merely looking at the external and superficial aspects of the Great Illusion, of *maya*, merely copying the model, leaves us stuck where we are: not *in* the human being but *in front of* him. From the standpoint of art, if we fail to transcend the world of illusion, we are faced with the formidable enigma of human nature and no answer is vouchsafed us.

And again, on entering the ancient Mysteries, it was made clear to the neophyte who was about to be initiated: if you remain within the world of *maya*, you will be unable to penetrate the essential being of man or of any other kingdom of Nature. You cannot become an artist. In the sphere of art too it was found necessary to remind the neophyte of the clear injunction, 'Know thyself,' and then he began to feel the need for spiritual knowledge.

But, you will say, there are some thoroughly materialistic sculptors and painters. They also achieve something and know very well how to draw forth the secrets from their model and invest their figures and materials with these secrets. That is indeed so, but where does this ability come from? People fail to realize that this ability has not come from the artists themselves. They owe it to earlier artists who in their turn had it from their predecessors. It is through tradition. But they are unwilling to admit this because they claim they owe everything to themselves. They know how the old masters worked and imitate them. But the earliest of the old masters learned their secret from the spiritual insights of the Mysteries. The earliest painters and sculptors received it from the Mysteries. Raphael and Michelangelo[3] learned it from those who still drew on these Mysteries.

But true art must be created out of the spiritual. There is no other solution. As soon as we touch upon the problem of man, any perception of the Great Illusion, of *maya*, has no answer to the riddle of life, to the riddle of man. If we are to return to the fountain-head of art and artistic creativity we must recover insight into the spiritual world.

Now a third example. The botanist or zoologist can gain wonderfully detailed knowledge of the form of every available plant. The biochemist can describe the processes that take place in plant life. He can also learn how foodstuffs are transmuted in the organs of digestion and the blood, and are carried to the nervous system. A highly intelligent anatomist, physiologist, botanist or geologist can cover a wide field of the world of the Great Illusion, but if he intends to use this knowledge for purposes of healing or medical treatment, if he wishes to press forward from the outer, or even the inner constitution of man to his essential being, he cannot do it.

You will say: but there are doctors aplenty who are materialists and have no interest in the spiritual world. They treat patients in accordance with the methods of natural science and yet they cure people.

That is so, but why? They are able to affect cures because they too have behind them a tradition based upon an old world-conception. Old remedies were derived from the Mysteries, but they all shared a remarkable characteristic. If you look at an old prescription, you will find that it is highly complicated. It makes considerable demands upon those who prepare it and who apply it to the particular purpose laid down by tradition. If, ladies and gentlemen,* you had gone to an old physician and asked how such a prescription was made up, he would never have replied: first I make chemical experiments and ascertain whether the materials behave in such and such a way; then I try it out on the patients and note the results. Such an idea would never have occurred to him. People have no idea of the circumstances prevailing in earlier epochs. He would have replied: I live in a laboratory (if I may call it that) that is arranged on the basis of the Mystery teachings, and when I light upon a remedy I owe it to the Gods. He was quite clear on this point, that through the whole atmosphere created in his laboratory he was in close communication with the spiritual world. Spiritual beings were just as present to him as human beings are to us. He was aware that through the influence of spiritual beings in the spiritual world he could be more than he would be without their influence. And he proceeded to make up his complicated prescriptions, not from natural knowledge, but as the Gods indicated. It was known within the Mysteries that, in order to understand man, one could not remain stuck in illusion, but had to penetrate through to the truth of the divine world.

With all their knowledge of the external world, people today are further from the truth of the divine world than the ancients were with their Mysteries. But the way back must be found again.

From this third example it is evident that if we seek to heal, even though equipped with the widest possible knowledge of nature (that is, of the Great Illusion), we still stand with unanswered questions in the face of human life and the riddle of man. If we wish to understand man from the standpoint of *maya*, the 'Great Illusion,' to the standpoint of 'Know thyself', which is demanded for the purposes of healing, then we shall be unable to advance a single step further in our understanding.

---

*Translator's footnote: 'ladies and gentlemen' is the English rendering I have used for Steiner's phrase *meine sehr verehrten Anwesenden*, which translates literally as 'my esteemed those-who-are-present'.

And so, in the light of these examples, we can say: anyone who wishes to bridge the gap between the world of the Great Illusion, of *maya,* and the 'Know thyself', will realize, the moment they approach the human being with religious feeling, or as a creative artist, a healer or doctor, that they stand before a void if their sole starting point is the world of illusion. They are powerless unless they find a form of knowledge that transcends the knowledge of external nature, which is knowledge of *maya,* the Great Illusion.

Knowledge of the world in its totality through spiritual perception within physical facts

Let us now draw a comparison between the way in which people sought to reach a comprehensive knowledge of the world out of the spirit of the Mysteries, and the way in which this is attempted today. We shall then be in a position to find our bearings in relation to the paths leading to this comprehensive knowledge.

The world and its essential nature were spoken of in a very different way a few thousand years ago from how authorities speak today. Let us look back to the epoch a few thousand years ago, when a brilliant and majestic knowledge flourished in the Mysteries of the Near East. We will attempt to look more closely into the nature of this knowledge by giving a brief description of its characteristics.

In ancient Chaldea, the following was taught: man's soul forces reach their maximum potentiality when he directs the eye of the spirit to the wonderful contrast between the life of sleep (his consciousness is dimmed, he is oblivious of his environment) and his waking life (he is clear-sighted, he is aware of the world around him). These alternating conditions of sleep and waking were experienced differently thousands of years ago. Sleep was less unconscious, waking life not so fully conscious. In sleep man was aware of mighty, ever-changing picture formations, of the weaving swell of cosmic life. He was in the midst of 'beingness' when he slept.

The dimming of consciousness during sleep is a consequence of human evolution. A few thousand years ago waking life was not as clear and lucid as it is today. Objects had no clearly defined contours; they were blurred. They still rayed out all kinds of spiritual qualities. There was not the same abrupt transition between sleeping and waking. The people of that epoch were still able to distinguish these two states, and the environment of their waking life was called *Apsu*. That was the world of waking.

The life of the weaving swell of movement experienced during sleep, this realm that blurred the clear distinction between the minerals, plants and animals of waking life, was called *Tiamat*.

Now the Chaldean Mystery Schools taught that when man was weaving in Tiamat during sleep, he was closer to truth and reality than when he lived his waking life amongst minerals, plants and animals. Tiamat was more primordial, more closely related to the world of man than Apsu. Apsu was more unknown. Tiamat represented something that lay closer to man than Apsu. But in the course of time Tiamat underwent changes and this was brought to the notice of the neophytes in the Mystery Schools. From the weaving life of Tiamat emerged demoniacal forms, horse-like shapes with human heads, leonine forms with the heads of angels. These arose out of the warp and weft of Tiamat and these demoniacal forms became hostile to man.

Then there appeared in the world a mighty Being, *Ea*. Anyone today who has a feeling for the quality of the sounds of language can sense how the conjunction of these two vowels points to that powerful Being who, according to these old Mystery teachings, stood at man's side to help him when the demons of Tiamat grew strong. *Ea* or *Ia*, became later—if one anticipates the particle that indicates something existing, 'Soph'—Soph-Ea, Sophia. 'Ea' is what we designate with the abstract word *wisdom;* 'Ia' is the Wisdom that holds sway in all things. 'Soph' is a particle that signifies roughly a state of being. Sophia, Sophea, Sopheia, is the all-prevailing, omnipresent Wisdom who sent to mankind her son, then known as Marduk, later called Michael—the Michael who holds sway from the hierarchy of the Archangels. He is the same Being as Marduk, the son of Ea, Wisdom—Marduk-Michael.

According to the Mystery teachings Marduk-Michael was great and powerful, and all the demoniacal beings such as horses with human heads and lion forms with angels' heads—all these surging, weaving, demoniacal forms, conjoined as the mighty Tiamat, were arrayed against him. Marduk-Michael was powerful enough to command the storm-wind that sweeps through the world. All that Tiamat embodied was seen as a living reality, and rightly so, for they experienced it as real beings. All these demons together were envisaged as the adversary, a powerful dragon which embodied all the demonic powers born out of Tiamat, the night. And this dragon-being, breathing fire and fury, advanced upon Marduk-Michael. Michael first smote him with various weapons and then drove the full force of his storm-wind into the dragon's entrails so that Tiamat burst, rolled asunder, and was scattered over all the world. And so Marduk-Michael was able to create [out of him] the Heavens above and the Earth beneath. Thus arose the Above and the Below.

Such was the teaching of the Mysteries: that the great son of Ea, Wisdom, has vanquished Tiamat and has fashioned from one part of him the Heavens above and from the other the Earth below. And if you lift up your eyes to the stars, O man, you will see one part of what Marduk-Michael formed in the Heavens out of the fearful abyss of Tiamat, for the benefit of mankind. And if you look below, where the plants grow out of the mineral-rich earth, where the animals take form, you will find the other part which the son of Ea, of Wisdom, has reshaped for the benefit of mankind.

Thus the ancient Chaldeans looked back to a formative process in the world that arose out of *being*. They experienced it all as a living reality. The demonic forms that populated the night, the weaving, surging beings of Tiamat, had been transformed by Marduk-Michael into the stars above and the Earth below. All the demons had been transformed by Marduk-Michael into shining stars; all that grows out of the Earth was the reshaped skin and tissue of Tiamat—this is the form in which the people of ancient times pictured what they were aware of through the old attributes of soul. This they accounted as knowledge.

Then, in conditions of great secrecy, certain priests prepared their pupils, strengthening their soul powers for a particular mystery. And once the neophytes had developed the necessary strength of soul, they were in a position to understand what is taught to children today in their first elementary lessons: that the sun stands still, the earth turns on its axis, that worlds are formed from nebulae. This natural scientific knowledge that children today are taught at school, was then a great secret. On the other hand, the teaching that was given openly was that concerning the deeds of Marduk-Michael which I have just described to you. In our schools and universities today— and they lay no claim to secrecy—and even in our primary schools the Copernican system and astro-physics are taught, subjects which, in ancient times, only the sages were able or permitted to undertake, and then only after long preparation. What every schoolchild knows today could, in those days, only be known by Initiates. Today all this is part of the school curriculum.

There was an epoch dating still further back than the epoch of the ancient Chaldean Mysteries, when people only spoke of such things as I have just described—of Ea, of Marduk-Michael, of Apsu and Tiamat. They abhorred everything taught by these 'eccentric' Mystery teachers about the movements of the stars or of the sun, and who wished to study only what is external and visible, and not the invisible which was evident to humanity albeit in the form of the ancient clairvoyance. They rejected the knowledge which the old Initiate-teachers and their pupils had acquired.

Then came the time when the primeval wisdom gradually spread from the East, and both forms of knowledge were valued. People valued the expression of the beings of the spiritual worlds, the deeds of Marduk-Michael, for example; and equally they treasured what we could draw on the board like this (Steiner draws)—the sun in the centre and the planetary bodies revolving round it in cycles and epicycles.

Then, in the course of time, insight into the spiritual worlds, the worlds of demons and gods, was lost and intellectual knowledge was developed, the knowledge which we prize so highly today and which reached its zenith in the early years of our epoch. We are now living in an age in which the spiritual is despised as much as the material world was despised in ancient times by those for whom the spiritual was self-evident. We need to get used to a time when we will again be in a position to accept side by side with the teachings of astronomers, astrophysicists, zoologists and botanists, a knowledge of spiritual realities derived from spiritual insights. That time has arrived and we must be ready to meet it if we are to accomplish what the age requires and gain access once more to religion, art, healing, and so on.

Just as in ancient times spirituality shone amongst people while the material world was despised, to be followed by an epoch when material knowledge was accepted and the spiritual suppressed; just as people were in error in ancient times by living solely in the spiritual and despising the outer world; and just as in an age when people valued materiality and were in error by despising spirituality—so now the time must come when we need to transform our vast, comprehensive knowledge of the external world, so deserving of admiration, into a renewed knowledge of the Mystery teachings.

Since the material science of today has torn itself away from primal spirituality piece by piece, so that nothing remains on earth of the ancient edifice except, at most, a few fragments like those we dig up from ancient buildings, we must once again recover the spiritual; but there must be a full and clear understanding of everything we bring to light when we delve into the history of past epochs. We must find our way back to the spiritual through a new deepening of religious feeling, through a new artistic expression, through a new art of healing, and through a new knowledge of the spirit that permeates the being of man, and so on.

These are three examples which I have given you today in the hope of renewing the Mysteries which can give us an understanding of the totality of the world's being and of human activity for the welfare of humanity with regard to this totality, and not just in the one-sidedness of material reality.

LECTURE 2

12 AUGUST 1924

The Three Worlds
and their Reflected Images

Differences in consciousness in ancient and modern times

IF we wish to develop an understanding of spiritual research we must first of all have a clear idea about the different states of consciousness which it is possible for the human soul to experience. In his normal life on earth today man finds himself in a specific state of consciousness which is characterized by the fact that he experiences a clear distinction between waking and sleeping. This state of consciousness, though not coinciding in time, corresponds approximately with the passage of the sun round the earth, or rather, with a revolution of the earth on its axis. At the present time, however, this correspondence has been disrupted to some extent. If we look back into the not very distant past with its ordered system of life, we find that people worked approximately from sunrise to sunset and slept from sunset to sunrise.

In our age this has been somewhat disrupted. I have even known people who reverse this situation entirely by sleeping during the day and staying awake at night. I have often enquired into the reason for this. The people concerned who, for the most part were poets and writers, told me that it was all part of poetic creativity. Yet when I came across them at night I never found them writing poetry!

Now I wish to emphasize, ladies and gentlemen, that the most important thing for the consciousness of today is the fact that we are awake during the hours of sunlight, or for a period that is as long as this time, and that we sleep for a period equivalent to the hours of night. Many, many other things are bound up with a consciousness with this mode of experience, amongst them that we attach special value to sense-perceptions. We regard sense-perceptions as the prime reality. And when we turn from sense-perceptions to thoughts, we regard them as 'mere thoughts', as something not as real as the reality of sense-perceptions.

Nowadays we regard a chair as something real. You can set it down on the floor; you can hear the noise it makes. You know that you can sit on it. But the *thought* of the chair is not regarded as real. If you bash a thought that you believe to be in your head, you hear nothing. Nor do you believe—and rightly so, given the present constitution of man—that you could sit down on the thought of a chair. You would be far from pleased if only thoughts of chairs were provided in this hall!

And many other things are connected with this experience of consciousness, a consciousness that follows the sun. Circumstances were different for those whose life-pattern was ordered and directed by the Mysteries, by the Chaldean Mysteries for example, of which I spoke yesterday. Those people lived quite differently in their consciousness from how people do today.

We can look at an external phenomenon which can illustrate for us this difference between the consciousness of people then and people today. According to our calendar we reckon 365 days in a year; this is not quite accurate however. If we continued to reckon 365 days in a year over the centuries, we would eventually get out of step with the sun. We would lag behind the positions of the sun. We therefore intercalate a day every four years. Thus, over relatively long periods of time, we return approximately to congruency with the sun.

How did the Chaldeans deal with this problem in the very early days? Not the way we do. For long periods they used a calculation similar to ours, but they arrived at it in a different way. Because they calculated 360 days to the year they were obliged to intercalate a whole 'leap month' every six years, whereas we reckon a leap year, with an additional day, every four years. So they had six years of 12 months each, followed by a year of 13 months.

Modern scholars have noted these facts. But they are unaware that this chronological difference is bound up with profound changes in human consciousness. These Chaldeans who intercalated a leap month every six years instead of an extra leap day every four years, had a completely different outlook on the world from ourselves. Why is this? It is because they did not experience the difference between day and night in the same way as we do. As I mentioned yesterday, their daytime experience was not as clear and vivid as ours. If someone with our present-day consciousness comes into this hall and looks around, they will, of course, see the people in the audience here in sharply defined outlines, some closer together, others further apart and so on.

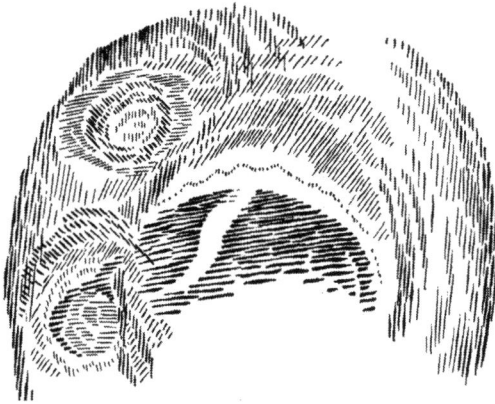

[Earth—dark blue
Snow, Euphrates—white
Air—green
Funnel—violet
yellow
red
light blue]

Erde - dunkel blau
Schnee, Euphrat - weiss
Luft - grün
Rohr - lila
gelb
rot
hell blau

This was not the case amongst those who received their inspiration from the Chaldean Mysteries; they saw things very differently. In those days they saw a person sitting, for example, not as we see him now, for that was rare at that time, but surrounded by an auric cloud which was regarded as part of him. And whilst we, in our prosaic way, see each individual in sharply defined outlines sitting on their chair, and the whole so clear-cut that we can easily count how many people are here, the old Chaldeans would have seen each block of chairs to the right and left of the gangway surrounded by a kind of auric cloud, drifting like patches of mist—here a cloud, there a cloud, and then darker areas, and these darker areas would have indicated the human beings.

This kind of visual experience would still have been known in the earliest Chaldean times, though not in later periods. By day the ancient Chaldeans would have seen only the dark areas of this nebulous image. At night they would have seen something very similar, even in a condition of sleep, for their sleep was not as deep as ours; it was more dreamlike. Today, if someone were asleep and you were all sitting here, they would not see anything of you at all. In olden times people did not sleep so deeply; they would have seen a dreamy form of the auric cloud to the right and left with the people inside it as light forms; during the day these were dark in the auric cloud, and were light during the night.

Thus the difference in the perception of conditions by day and by night was not as marked in those times as it is today. And so they did not experience the difference between the sun high in the sky and the sun that was absent during the night. They saw the sun by day as a luminous sphere surrounded by a magnificent aura which I could draw like this (see diagram). They pictured to themselves the following: below was the earth (dark blue); everywhere above the earth there was water, and higher still were the snows considered to be the source of the Euphrates. Above all this, they thought, was the air (green), and in the heights was the sun, travelling from East to West and surrounded by a most beautiful aura.

Then they imagined the existence of something that today we might call a kind of tube; in the evening the sun descended into this tube and emerged again in the morning (violet). But they actually saw the sun in this tube. The night sun was seen approximately as follows: a luminous, greenish-blue centre, surrounded by a reddish-yellow halo. That was the image they had of the sun. In the morning the sun emerged from the tube, luminous in the centre and surrounded by a halo. It travelled across the vault of heaven, slipped into the tube in the West, became dark, but had an aura that projected beyond the tube, and then descended further like that. People spoke of a tube or hollow space because to them the sun was dark or black. They described things exactly as they saw them. So, when they looked up to the sun-filled sky, they did not see such a definite difference between day and night as we do.

But, by contrast, there was something else that people saw very strongly in those times. They looked back at their childhood; and when they looked back to the first six or seven years they perceived how, during those years, they were still positively immersed in the divine element in which they had lived before descending to earth. Then, between the seventh and fourteenth year, they saw how they partially emerged from this spiritual auric egg until the process was finally completed in their twenties. It was only at this age [i.e. the twenties] that they really felt themselves to be earth beings. And then they saw the difference between day and night somewhat more strongly.

They saw in their own being a development taking place that ran in cycles of six or seven years. This connected them with the passage of the moon, not the sun. The moon's phases of 28 days connected them with what they experienced in their own life through the number six or seven. And they felt that a moon cycle of one month was equivalent in a human life to a period of 28 years, of four times seven years. They expressed this in their calculation of time by inserting an intercalary month every seventh year[4]. Their calculations were based on the moon, not the sun.

And they did not see external nature as we do today. Today, when we are awake, we see nature unspiritually, with sharp contours. At that time people saw external nature by day and by night, albeit not with sharp contours, but spiritually and aurically. Today we see everything by day, and by night, nothing. This is shown by the importance we attribute to the sun which brings about the alternation of day and night.

In the Mystery-wisdom of the ancient Chaldeans the emphasis was placed not on the sun but on the moon because its phases were a faithful reflection of their own growth to maturity. They paid closer attention to the human being and his development. They felt themselves very differently at each stage—as a child, a youth, an adult—in a way we no longer experience today. Today when we look back [on our childhood] there seems to be very little difference between the first seven years and the second seven years. Nowadays children are so very clever that we don't know how to get on with them! Special methods of education will have to be devised in order to cope with them. They are as clever as grown-ups and everyone seems equally clever, whatever their age.

This was definitely not the case in ancient Chaldea. At that time little children's nature was such that they were still immersed in the divine-spiritual element; when they grew up they remembered this relationship, and knew that they had only later become earthly beings, after having emerged from the auric egg. So their calculations were based not on the sun but on the moon, on the phases presented by the moon in the heavens and ordered according to the number seven. This is what they calculated by. Therefore every seventh year they intercalated a leap month, a period related to the moon.

But this outward sign in the evolution of civilizations, the fact that we intercalate an additional day every four years whereas the Chaldeans intercalated an additional month every seven years, indicates that in reality, though their day consciousness was not sharply divided from their night consciousness, they experienced great differences in their states of consciousness during their successive life-periods.

Today, when we wake in the morning and rub the sleep from our eyes, we say: 'I have slept.' The ancient Chaldeans felt that they awoke in their twenty-first or twenty-second year; then they began to see the world clearly and said: 'I have been asleep up to this moment.' They believed that they preserved a waking consciousness up to their fiftieth year and that in old age they did not fall asleep again but entered into a much brighter conscious life. For this reason the old men were looked upon as sages who, with the consciousness acquired since the age of 20, now entered the realm of sleep, but became highly clairvoyant there.

Thus the old Chaldeans knew three states of consciousness. We experience two, with the addition of a third which we characterize as a dream condition: waking, sleeping, dreaming. A Chaldean did not experience these three conditions from day to day; he experienced a dull, sleeping condition of consciousness up to his twenties, then a condition where he lived more consciously in the world, a waking condition, up to his fifties. And then a condition where it was said of him: he is taking his earthly consciousness into the spiritual world; he has arrived at the stage when he knows much more than other people.

Those advanced in years were looked up to as sages. This no longer happens. Today they are regarded as old fogies who have become weak-minded. This is the great difference that strikes right into the inner constitution of human existence.

We must be quite clear about this difference for it is enormously important for the being of man. We do not survey the world simply through one state of consciousness. We learn to know the world only when we understand the form of consciousness which, for example, was common to the children of ancient Chaldea. It resembled our own dream state, though it was far more active, capable of stimulating the individual to action. Today it would be considered a pathological condition. What is pathological today was the [normal] condition of consciousness for the ancient Chaldean child. The condition of waking consciousness that we find so prosaic today was unknown in those times. I use the term 'prosaic' (*philiströs*) advisedly, for the fact, ladies and gentlemen, that we have everyone in their physical contours is prosaic. Perceiving people in sharply-defined contours, and even to paint them with sharp outlines, is prosaic. This would not be readily admitted, of course, but it is so. In ancient Chaldea this situation did not yet exist; man was perceived both as a physical entity and as endowed with an aura, as I have described. And in old age people saw beyond the physical into the human soul. This was a third state of consciousness which is extinguished today. It may be compared to the state of dreamless sleep.

If we look at the situation historically, we find that we encounter states of consciousness very different from our own, and that differ more and more the further back we go. By comparison, our normal states of consciousness today are nothing much to boast of. We set no store on what a person may experience in dreamless sleep because, as a rule, he has little to relate. There are few, very few, today who can tell us anything of their experiences in dreamless sleep. Dream life, it is said, is fantasy; and only waking consciousness is regarded as respectable and reliable.

This was not the situation with the ancient Chaldeans. The child-like condition of consciousness with its lively dream life that led to positive action, was considered to be one where the children were still half living in pre-earthly life, and when they spoke they said something that belonged to divine worlds. People listened to them because they knew the children had brought a wealth of information with them from the spiritual world. Children were regarded in a completely different way in those times.

Then followed the state of consciousness when they were already earthly beings, but in their auras they remained soul beings. Then came the consciousness of old age. When people listened to the old men, they were aware that they were receiving communications from the spiritual world, about what was happening in the spiritual world. And of those who rose ever higher in the Mysteries it was said that in their fifties they overcame the purely solar element and entered into the spiritual world; from Sun-heroes they became Fathers who were in communion with the spiritual home of mankind.

So I wanted to indicate for you, from a historical perspective, that mankind passes through various states of consciousness.

Creative imagination that occurs naturally in dreaming today

In exploring the states of consciousness let us set aside for a moment the dreamless sleep of present-day man and examine the ordinary waking state with which you are familiar when you say: I am fully conscious, I see objects around me, hear other people speak to me, converse with them and so on.

And let us take the second condition, known to all of you when you imagine yourself to be asleep, when dreams arise which are often so unsettling or so marvellously liberating that if you are in a normal healthy state you have to say: these things are not part of ordinary, everyday life; they rise up, living and weaving out of some kind of natural fantasy, and throng towards us in the most varied ways. Prosaic individuals will pay little attention to dreams. Superstitious individuals will interpret them in an external way. The poetically endowed person, who is neither prosaic nor superstitious, still pays attention to this wonderful weaving life of dreams. For out of the natural depths of man there rises something which does not have the sort of significance that superstitious people think it does, but shows that the sleeping human being has experiences that rise up naturally like mists or clouds, just as mountains rise up and after long ages disappear again. It is just that in dream life this all happens quickly, whereas in the cosmos structures arise and disappear slowly.

Dreams have another peculiarity. We may dream of snakes all around us, even of snakes that touch our body. People who recklessly take cocaine, for example, can have this dream-experience of snakes in a particularly intense way. Those who succumb to the vice of cocaine-use have a dream perception of snakes crawling out of every cranny of their body, even when they are awake.

When we observe our own life we realize that such dreams indicate some internal disturbance. Dreams about snakes point to some digestive disorder. The coils of the intestines are symbolized in the dream as the writhing of snakes.

Or someone might dream they are going for a walk and come to a place where a white post stands—a white post or stone pillar which is damaged at the top. In their dream they feel uneasy about this damaged top. They wake up to find they have toothache! Unconsciously they feel the urge to hold one of their teeth. (I am referring to present-day man; the man of ancient times was above such things.) The typical man of today decides to go to the dentist and have the decayed tooth filled. What is the explanation of this? This whole experience associated with a painful tooth, indicating some organic disturbance, is symbolized in a picture. The tooth becomes a 'white post' that shows signs of damage or decay. In the dream picture we become aware of something that is actually situated within our organism.

Or again, we have a vivid dream that we are in a room where we can't breathe. In the dream we become disturbed, which is [the basis of] all dream life. Then suddenly—we had not noticed it before—we catch sight of a stove in the corner which is very hot. The room is overheated. Ah, now we know in the dream why we can't breathe: the room is too hot. We wake up with palpitations and a racing pulse. Our circulation, which had become irregular, was symbolized externally in the dream. There is something going on in ourselves [in our own organism]; we become aware of it, but not in the way we would during the day. We become aware of it in symbolic pictures. Or we may dream that outside the window there is bright sunshine. The sunlight disturbs us and we become uneasy, though normally we would welcome the sunshine. We wake up and find a neighbour's house is on fire. An external event is not depicted as it actually is, but is clothed in a completely different, symbolic form. Thus we see that a natural creative imagination is at work in dreams; external things are expressed in them.

But we can go further. The dream can rouse itself, so to speak, to the point of taking on its own inner meaning and being. We may dream of something which, although certainly represented in the dream in pictures, cannot be related to anything in the external world. When that point is reached in gradual stages, we say that a totally different world has come to expression in our dreams; quite other beings are active there: we encounter demonic or also beautiful elf-like beings. Thus it is not only our usual sense-perceptible world as it exists both externally and internally for us that appears in dream pictures, but a wholly different world can also push in upon us. Human beings can dream of the supersensory world in the form of sense-derived images.

Thus present-day human consciousness has a dream life alongside our ordinary waking life. And we have to say that, indeed, it is the disposition to dreaming that makes us poets. People who are unable to dream will always remain inferior poets. For in order to be a poet, or any kind of artist in general, one must be able to translate the natural stuff of dreams into the imaginative fantasy of waking life.

Anyone, for example, whose dreams draw their symbolism from external objects as in the dream where sunshine pouring into a room symbolized a neighbour's house on fire, will feel next day an urge to compose. He is a musician. Someone who experiences the palpitation of their heart as an overheated stove will feel impelled next day to turn to modelling or architectural design. He is an architect, sculptor or painter. These things are connected; they are associated in ordinary consciousness in the way I have described.

But now we can go further. As I have described in my books, *Knowledge of the Higher Worlds* and *Occult Science—An Outline*[5], this ordinary consciousness can be developed by undertaking certain spiritual exercises—we will speak of them later—so that by concentrating on certain precise concepts and linguistic relationships, our whole inner life of thinking, feeling and will is made more active. Through these exercises thoughts become virtually tangible realities and feelings living entities. I will have to describe this later.

Then begins the first stage of modern Initiation. What happens is that we continue to dream in waking life. But at this point misunderstandings may easily arise. We set little store by the dreams of someone who quite naturally daydreams during the day. But an individual who, in spite of his daydreaming, is as awake as anyone else, yet can *go on dreaming* because he has made his feeling and thinking far more active than others, such an individual is starting to become an initiate. When he has reached this stage, the following takes place. Because he is a sensible person—no less sober and sensible than others, doesn't get up to crazy tricks during the day because he is dreaming—he sees his fellow human beings, on the one hand, as they appear to normal consciousness, the shape of their nose, the colour of their eyes, their tidy or untidy hair and so on. On the other hand, he begins to dream something else around them, but now something that is true: he dreams their aura, and begins to see spiritually the inner spiritual meaning of the actions between people. He begins to have dreams in full waking consciousness that are meaningful and correspond with reality. His dreaming does not cease when he wakes up; it continues through the day and is transformed in sleep. But it is meaningful. What he sees in people is their true soul nature. What he sees in people's actions is spiritually genuine. He lives in an activity that is otherwise associated with mere reminiscences or ordinary dreams. But these dreams are a spiritual reality.

A second state of consciousness is now added to the first. Waking dreams become a form of perception higher than the normal perception of everyday life. In full waking consciousness a higher reality has been added to the reality of everyday life. In ordinary dreaming something of reality is lost; it gives us only fantastical shreds. But in waking dreams, as I have described them, which permeate everything—permeate the individual human form, animals and plants, and through which the deeds of people are seen to be full of meaning, thereby revealing their spiritual content—all this adds something to everyday reality and enriches it.

To the perception of ordinary consciousness is added a second element. We begin to see the world completely differently. This other way of seeing is most striking when we look at the animal kingdom. The animal world now appears to us in such a way that we say to ourselves: What was I actually seeing before? I was only seeing a part of this world. What I saw before was definitely not everything of the animal. I only saw its external aspect. Now a whole new world is added. In each animal species, in lions, tigers, and all the various genera, lies something that is akin to man, that really resembles man. Each species becomes something completely unique. This is difficult to illustrate by comparison with a human being, but please try in the following way.

Imagine that you enhance your body, so to speak, by tying a string to each finger of both hands and that to the end of each string at a fixed distance you attach a ball painted with various coloured figures. So you now have ten strings. Now you learn a spectacularly adroit finger game in which you manipulate the strings with your fingers so that the balls are agitated in all directions. Now you do the same with your toes—tie a thread to each toe, attached to a ball covered with figures. Now practise leaping in the air and working your toes so skilfully that something wonderful is created out of this form. Thus each finger will have become longer with a painted ball at its tip, and every toe the same.

Imagine that you can see all this as being connected to your human form and the whole under the control of the soul. Each ball is a separate entity, but the moment you survey it all, you have the impression that it forms a composite whole. All these balls and strings are not as connected to yourself as your fingers and toes are, but you control it all. If you begin to control things in the way I have indicated, then you will see the lion-soul above and the individual lions attached to it like the balls, the whole forming a unity. Previously, if you had looked at the 20 balls lying there, they would have represented a world unto themselves. Now you add the human being, add the inner activity, and it becomes a completely new situation.

The same applies to your mode of perception. You see the individual lions moving about separately: this is like the balls moving around. Then you see the lion-soul endowed with self-consciousness which, in the spiritual world, resembles a human being; and you see the individual lions as though suspended like the moving balls, you see the individual lions emerging everywhere from the self-consciousness of the lion. You have ascended to a completely new being.

And in this way you ascend to completely new beings for everything in the animal kingdom. Animals have something akin to man in their make-up, a soul nature, but this is not in the world in which man has his soul nature. As you go through life you emphatically bear your soul with its self-consciousness wherever you go. You can confront anyone you meet with your self-consciousness. This the lion cannot do. But there is a second world. This borders on this realm where we confront others with our self-consciousness. In the spiritual world the lion-souls do precisely the same. To them the individual lions are so many balls dangling at the end of a string. Consequently, when we see the true nature of the animal kingdom with our newly acquired consciousness, we get something of a shock. A second world has been added.

And now we say to ourselves: As human beings we are also actually in that world, but we carry it down into the normal world of earth. The animal leaves something of itself behind—its group-soul or species-soul—and only moves about on the earth with the part that goes about on four legs. We drag down to the earth what the animal leaves behind in the spiritual world and acquire in consequence a different bodily form from the animal. What lives within us belongs also to this higher world, but as human beings we drag it down to earth.

So, as you see, we become acquainted with a completely different world that we perceive initially through the animals. But we need a different consciousness: we must awaken our dream-consciousness, then we can gain insight into what is in the animal kingdom. Those who can do this call this second world the soul-world, the soul-plane or astral plane, as distinct from the physical plane. We reach this astral plane or astral world, in contrast to the physical world, through a different consciousness. We must familiarize ourselves with the fact that other consciousnesses enable us to look into other worlds which are not the world of our everyday existence.

Further strengthening of the soul-life

We can strengthen and vitalize our soul-life still further. We can not only practise concentration and meditation, as described in the books I have mentioned, we can also strive to expel again this reinforced soul-content. After the most strenuous endeavours to fortify the soul-life, after strengthening thinking and feeling, we reach a point when we are able to dampen it all down again and even finally to reduce it to nothing. We have then brought about what we can call empty consciousness.

Now, if we empty our normal consciousness, we fall asleep. This can be demonstrated experimentally. We take someone and then remove all visual stimuli so that the subject is in darkness. Then we remove all auditory stimuli so that the person is enveloped in silence. Then we try to eliminate all other sense-impressions, and the subject will gradually fall asleep.

This does not happen if we have first strengthened our thinking and feeling. It will then be possible to empty our consciousness by an act of will and still remain awake. We do nothing but remain awake through an act of will. We do not fall asleep. But we no longer have the sense-world before us. We are no longer filled with our ordinary thoughts and memories—we are in a condition of empty consciousness. But now a real spiritual world at once enters into this empty consciousness. Just as our ordinary consciousness is filled with the colours, sounds and the rich gradations of warmth in the sense-world, so a spiritual world enters and fills this empty consciousness. Only when we have awoken and emptied our consciousness are we surrounded by a spiritual world.

Once again we can perceive in a surprisingly intense way this new consciousness and its connection with a spiritual world through something in external nature. Just as we become aware of the next higher level of consciousness through our different perception of the animal kingdom, so we are now able to perceive this different and new level of consciousness through the completely different attributes that we see in the earth's plant kingdom.

How does the plant kingdom appear to normal consciousness? We walk on the earth and see the wealth of colour and the greenness of the plant world growing out of the mineral earth. We rejoice in the blue and gold, the red and white of the blossoms, and in the living green. We delight in the beauty of the plant world spread out before us like a carpet. We are filled with joy and the heart leaps up as we behold the earth clothed in this brilliant, many-coloured garment of flowers and plants.

Then we lift our eyes to the dazzling sun and the blue vault of heaven. We see nothing out of the ordinary, just what is usually to be seen on a cloudy or clear day, which you are all familiar with. We are not initially aware of any connection between the earth and the heavens, between looking down upon the flower-bedecked fields and up at the sky.

But we can go further. Let us assume we have felt intense joy at the sight of this carpet of flowers spread out before us. We wait on a beautiful day until the fall of night. We now lift our eyes to the canopy of heaven and see the stars, arrayed in their manifold shining constellations, spread out across the sky. And now a new joyous exultation of soul begins, something that works down from above and sends inward jubilation into our soul.

By day then, we can look down upon the growing plant-cover of the earth as something that fills our heart with inward joy and exultation. We can then look up at night and see the canopy of heaven that appeared so blue by day now studded with shining twinkling stars. We rejoice inwardly at what is revealed to our soul. This is the response of our ordinary consciousness.

If we have developed a consciousness that is empty but awake, and into which the spiritual world has found an entry, we can then say to ourselves when by day we survey the plant-cover, and by night we look up at the glittering stars: Yes, during the day, what covers the earth as a carpet of colour enchanted us, filled us with an inner jubilation. But what did we really see by day? Then at night we look up to a sky glittering with stars. To this empty waking consciousness, the consciousness emptied of all earthly content, the stars do more than merely shine and sparkle: they assume the most varied forms. The star-shine ceases, and there above us is wondrous *being*. Growing weaving life is spread out above us, great and powerful and sublime. And we stand there understanding in reverence, reverent in understanding. We have reached a middle stage of Initiation and say to ourselves: The real origin of the plants is there above. The true being of the plants is what previously shone down to us only in separate points in the stars. It seems as if now for the first time we see the true plant world there above. It is as though the violet had not revealed itself to us, but rather, in a violet-flower filled with morning dew, we saw not the violet itself but only the sparkling of the single dewdrop. In looking at a single star we see the single twinkling dewdrop. In truth, however, a mighty weaving world lies behind it, full of being. This is what we look up to. We now know what the plant world really is; it is not on the earth at all but out in the cosmos, and is grand and mighty and sublime. And what is it that we saw by day in the many-coloured carpet of flowers? What is it? It is the reflected image of what is above.

And we now know that the cosmos with its weaving life of forms and beings is reflected on the surface of the earth. When we look into a mirror we see ourselves reflected and we know that the reflection is only of our outer form, not of our soul. The heavens are not reflected on the earth so definitely, but in such a way that they are mirrored in the yellow, green, blue, red and white of plant colours. They are a reflected image, the faint, shadowy reflection of the heavens.

And we have come to know a new world. There above, plants are 'human'—beings endowed with self-consciousness. And so, to the physical world and astral world, we can add a third, the actual spiritual world. The stars are like the cosmic dewdrops of this world, and the plants are its reflected image. What they are on earth is not everything that they are; in their manifestation here they are not even an entity, just a reflection in relation to the endlessly manifold richness, the intense reality that is there above in the actual spiritual world, from where the separate stars shine out like cosmic dew. We have a third world, the actual spiritual world, and we now know that the magnificent world of plants is just a reflection of this world.

And now we discover that, as human beings, we bear within us what is the real being of the plants there above. We bring down into this mirrored life on earth what the plants leave behind in the world of spirit. Plants remain above in spirit-land; they send down to the earth their reflected images. And the earth fills these [images] with matter, with earthly substance. We human beings [on the other hand] bring our soul-nature, which also belongs to that higher world, into this world of images. We are not just reflected images, but also soul realities here on earth. On earth we live in three worlds: in the physical world, where animal self-consciousness is not to be found; at the same time we live in a second world in which animal self-consciousness *is* present, the astral world, but we bring this astral world with us down into the physical world. We also live in a third world, the spiritual world, where the true plant-being lives. The plant-beings send only their reflected images down to earth, whereas we bring down our soul in all reality.

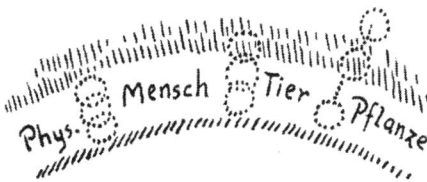

[*Phys. Man Animal Plant*]

And now we can say: a being that possesses body, soul and spirit here on earth is a human being. A being with body and soul here on earth, but whose spirit lives in a second world bordering on this one, and therefore is less real in the physical world, is animal. A being with only body in the physical world, soul in the second world, and spirit in the third world, so that the body is only a reflection of the spirit that is filled out with earthly matter, is plant.

Thus in nature we recognize three worlds. We know that the human being bears these three worlds within himself. We feel the plants reaching up, as it were, to the stars. As we look at the plants we say to ourselves: here is a being which manifests only its reflected image on earth, an image without its essential being. The more we direct our gaze to the stars at night, the more we see the plant's true being there above. Nature only becomes a totality when we look from earth to the stars, when we regard the cosmos as one with the earth.

Then we look back at ourselves as human beings and say: what in the plants reaches up to the heavens, we have pulled together within ourselves here on earth. We bear within ourselves the physical, astral and spiritual worlds.

To see this clearly, to grow upwards with nature even to the heavens, to grow inwards into the human being to the point where the heavens reveal themselves to us—this is what it means to undertake the first steps in spiritual research.

LECTURE 3

13 AUGUST 1924

Form and Substantiality of the Mineral Kingdom
in relation to Human Levels of Consciousness

The nature of crystallized minerals

Yesterday I attempted to give some idea of the inner experiences of the soul when, through [spiritual] training, through soul exercises, the human being develops higher levels of consciousness. And I tried to show how the chaotic, disordered experiences of dream life during sleep, typical of normal consciousness, can be transformed into fully conscious, exact waking experiences. [And I showed] how we can thus attain a level of consciousness which, in a certain sense, most closely borders on our normal consciousness, by perceiving for the first time, for example, the animal kingdom in its totality, and how this reaches up into a higher world of soul, into the astral world.

I then tried to show how the plant-cover of the earth appears in its totality when, at a further level of consciousness that is based on full waking consciousness, but a consciousness that is empty with regard to the physical sense-world—how with this [second] level of consciousness we attain to the world of stars and there for the first time learn the truth about the plant-cover of the earth. We then realize that the plants we see growing out of the earth are a reflected image of something majestic and stupendous and which we see externally only in the shining world of stars, much like the drops of dew on plants on earth. I would like to express it by saying that what reaches towards the heavens in the wide expanses of cosmic space, gains the quality of 'being-ness', gains form, gains colour, even gains a tonal quality, when we lift ourselves towards it in this way with empty consciousness. Then we can look back upon the earth and perceive the truth about the plant world: that it is a reflected image of cosmic being, of cosmic events, and so on.

I should like to draw your attention to a peculiar phenomenon when we observe the world of stars on the one hand and the world of plants on the other. I should like to describe these things, ladies and gentlemen, entirely from [my own] inner experience, just as they present themselves. My description will not be based on any tradition, literary or otherwise, but I will describe things as they present themselves to direct spiritual experience and research. But first of all I should like to point out a peculiarity that arises for anyone who explores the spiritual in the way I have described.

Let us visualize the following picture (see drawing on page 36): above us is the world of stars, below is the earth. The point from which we start our enquiry we call our point of observation. At the second level of consciousness, a consciousness that sees a link between the world of stars and of plants in the manner already described, we perceive clearly that the archetypal forms are there above, that they are mirrored in the earth, not as ordinary reflections but in the form of living plants reflected in the mirror of the earth. This is what one sees. We can describe it by saying: cosmic life is there above, and the earth as a mirror below. And of course these plants do not arise as lifeless, unreal, shadowy images, but like a real reflection created by the earth. But we always have the feeling that the earth has to be there below, there has to be a mirror, so that what is in the cosmos can sprout forth out of the earth. Without the earth, upon which we stand and move, there would be no plants. And just as a mirror intercepts the light and offers it resistance—for otherwise it could not reflect—so the earth must act as a reflecting medium for the plants to come into being.

But we can now go further by making a transition from this second level of consciousness that I described yesterday, a consciousness of waking emptiness, by developing an inner strength of soul that is not usually valued as a force of knowledge: the force of love towards all things and beings. If, having entered into this realm that is so differently constituted, where the cosmos no longer appears bright with stars but as a revelation of being, we permeate ourselves completely with this power of love; if, having entered the spiritual ocean, so to speak, of the universe, we can preserve the spiritual, soul and physical organization that we have as a gift from the earth; if we can hold on to ourselves and extend immeasurably the power of love and devotion to all beings—then we develop our insight and understanding more and more. We then develop the capacity to perceive clairvoyantly not only the animal and plant kingdoms, but also the mineral kingdom and especially that part of the mineral kingdom which is crystalline in structure. Mineral crystals become a wonderful field of research and observation for those who wish to penetrate into the higher spiritual worlds.

When we are fully acquainted with the animal and plant kingdoms, we are then in a position to approach the crystallized mineral world. Once more we feel impelled to turn our attention from the mineral crystalline element on earth to a contemplation of the cosmos. And again in the expanses of the cosmos we see 'being', in the same way as we see what lies behind the plant kingdom. But our whole perception is different. We experience something completely different when our gaze starts with the crystallized mineral than when we start from the plant world. We again become aware of 'being-ness' in the cosmos (see drawing on page 36); and once more we say to ourselves: what we see here below in the earth as the crystallized mineral, is brought about by a living, spiritual principle in the widths of the cosmos.

But, in its influences on the earth (arrows from above) it is not reflected in the earth or by means of the earth. That, you see, is the crucial point. When we raise ourselves from the mineral to the cosmos and look back at the earth, the earth is no longer a mirror for the mineral. It is as though the earth were not there at all. It vanishes from our sight. We cannot say, as we did of the plants: the earth is there below and reflects. No, it doesn't reflect; it behaves as though it were not there at all. When we have concentrated on a perception like this that arises from the crystallized mineral, when we have turned our gaze to cosmic space and then look back, then below us is what at first is a frightening and terrible abyss, a void. We must wait. We must hold on to our presence of mind. The period of waiting should not be too prolonged. If we wait too long our fear becomes gigantic because we feel we have lost the ground under our feet. This is a feeling which is wholly foreign to us, which comes to expression as enormous fear if we do not keep our presence of mind and actively pierce through this void.

We must look through the earth which is not there. We have to look beyond it because it is not there. Then we are obliged to gaze not only on that aspect of the mineral kingdom which is above us, but also on the entire surroundings. The earth must be as though extinguished. We must see the same below as above, the same west-wards as eastwards (see drawing).

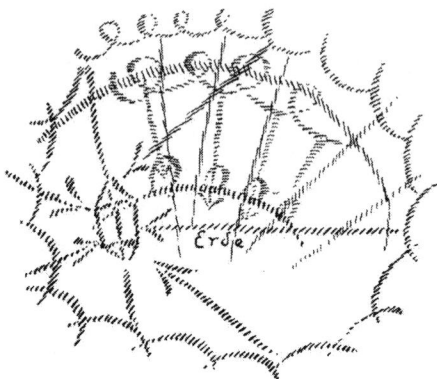

[earth]

We then experience a current of cosmic energy from below, in contrast to the cosmic energy of the plants which streams down from above. And when we look out and see a current coming from one direction, then [we see] another current coming from the opposite side. On all sides we see cosmic currents coming together. They converge there below us. In the case of the plants this stream of cosmic energy flows down from above (I have drawn it here in green), the earth offers resistance and the plants grow up out of the earth. But when we look at a current for the mineral realm, we have here an opposite current, and through the coming together of these, the form of the mineral kingdom takes shape. Here there is another current, and there an opposite current, and so on. Through the free meeting of these converging currents out of the cosmic All, the mineral kingdom arises. The earth is not a mirror for this crystallized mineral. In this case everything is mirrored in its own element.

If you find a quartz crystal in the mountains, it is usually set upright; but the earthly element only has a disturbing effect here, for ahrimanic powers work on it negatively. In reality, the quartz is formed by spiritual elements shooting in and converging from all sides, reflecting in each other, and there you see the crystal floating freely in the spiritual cosmos. And we can see in every crystal, perfectly fashioned from all sides, a little world in itself.

Now there are many types of crystal formation—the cube, octahedron, tetrahedron, dodecahedron, rhomboid, monoclinic, triclinic—every conceivable kind of structure. When we examine them we see how the currents [of cosmic energy] interact and converge to form the quartz crystal, a hexagonal prism terminating in a hexagonal pyramid; or a salt crystal possibly in the shape of a cube; or a pyrites crystal in the shape of a dodecahedron. Each of these crystals is formed in the way I have described. And we must say to ourselves: there are so many kinds of formed cosmic current, indeed so many cosmic worlds; there is not just one world but as many worlds in cosmic space as there are crystals in the earth. We are gazing into an immeasurable number of worlds.

We look at the salt crystal and say: out there in the universe there is 'being-ness' (*Wesenhaftes*); the salt crystal is a manifestation for us of something that permeates the whole of cosmic space as 'being-ness', a world in itself. Then we look at a pyrites crystal, also cuboid or dodecahedral, and say to ourselves: there is something out there in the universe that fills all space; and a crystal is the expression for us, the manifestation, of a whole world. We are gazing on many beings, each of which is a world unto itself. As human beings standing here on earth we say to ourselves: the earth-sphere is the meeting-point of the deeds of many worlds. In all that we think and do here on earth, the thoughts and deeds of the greatest diversity of beings flow together. The infinite variety of crystal forms reveals a multitude of beings whose activities come to expression in the mathematical-spatial forms of crystals. In crystals we recognize the presence of the Gods.

As an expression of reverence, of adoration even, towards the universe, it is far more important to allow the wondrous secrets of this universe to work on our souls than to know things theoretically with the head. Anthroposophy should lead to this feeling of oneself in the universe. Through anthroposophy human beings should be able to perceive in every crystal the weaving and working of a god in the universe. Then the whole human soul is filled with cosmic content, not just the head with thoughts. Anthroposophy exists least of all to fill our heads with thoughts; it is there to enlighten the whole human being with regard to the universe, and to fill us with reverence and devotion towards it. Into every object and every event in the world there should flow what I would like to call an inner soul-service of the human being. And this service is to become knowledge and understanding.

Substantiality and metallity* of the mineral world

At first, when we stand in this way facing the cosmic All, and gaze into what is taking shape towards the earth out of the crystallized mineral world, it is a satisfying sight. But this quickly gives way to the state of anxiety and fear I mentioned earlier. Before sensing this crystallized world borne by the gods, we are filled with fear. This fear is initially extinguished when we perceive this god-borne crystallized world; but after a time the fear returns, for we have a strange feeling, the feeling that everything that is taking shape there as the crystal, supports us only partially.

Let us take the example of the two kinds of crystal already mentioned: a salt crystal and a pyrites, a metal crystal. The pyrites gives us the feeling we could build on it, it supports us. When we look at the salt crystal on the other hand, it feels as though we could fall right through it, as though it would not support us.

In brief then: the fear we previously had of falling because the earth had become a void, returns partially in relation to certain forms. A moral element now mixes in with this feeling. This sensation of

---

*Translator's note: *Metallität* (metallity) is a word coined by Steiner. I take it to mean something like 'the quintessential quality intrinsic to metals, quintessential 'metal-ness'. As Steiner uses this as a neologism, I have kept it in the text as 'metallity'.

fear has definite moral implications. The moment we feel this fear for the second time, we become aware in ourselves not only of all the sins we have committed in our past lives, but also of all those we are still potentially capable of and could still commit.

All this is like weights hanging on us, trying to plunge us into the abyss that opens up before us due to the mineral crystals, and which we fear to fall into. At this point we must be able to come to a further feeling, a further experience. Everything we go through here requires courage, courage that arises by saying to ourselves: you have something in you that will let you fall neither upwards nor downwards, neither to the right nor left: you have a firm centre within your own being.

Oh, ladies and gentlemen, never in the whole course of life do we need more confidence, more inner courage than at the moment when, confronted with the crystallized mineral world, the leaden weight of our egotistical deeds (*Egoismen*)—for egotistical deeds are always a sin—weighs upon the soul. That transparent void, over which we are suspended and could fall into, now holds a terrible warning for us. If we hold on to our courage we can say to ourselves: a droplet of the divine is within me; I cannot perish, for I partake of the divine essence. If this becomes an experience for us and not mere theory, then we have the courage to hang on to ourselves and to go further.

We now learn something else about the mineral kingdom. Hitherto we had known the crystallized being of the minerals. Now we become aware of their 'substantiality', their 'metallity', that which permeates itself inwardly with matter. First the form, now the matter that permeates it. And we realize how we are supported in different ways in the cosmos by certain representative basic metals. For the first time we begin to understand how man is related to the cosmos. We get to know the different 'metallities', the 'substantialities' of the mineral being. We really begin to feel in ourselves that centre-point which I have just mentioned (see drawing, page 42).

Now, for what I am about to say, I have to use words that refer to material things, but you need to understand it non-materially. When we speak of the heart or head, the materialistically thinking person of today has the physical heart or head in mind. But these are of course also spiritual; they have been formed out of the spirit. And so when we look spiritually at man in his totality, as an entity consisting of body, soul, and spirit, we have the clear impression that his centre of gravity lies in the heart. This centre prevents him from plunging down or flying off, from being pushed to left or right, and holds him steady. If we retain the courage I mentioned, we reach a stage where we find ourselves firmly held and supported in the universe.

But what does it mean to find ourselves held and supported in the universe?

When a person loses consciousness, they are not held. If they have an intense feeling of inner pain so that they feel themselves inwardly more intensely than in ordinary life—for pain is an intensification of inner feeling— then this is again not normal consciousness. Pain drives out normal consciousness. In ordinary life between birth and death man lives in a kind of intermediate state of consciousness. This is what we must maintain ourselves with. But if this consciousness becomes too thin, we lose consciousness. If it becomes too thick, too dense, too conscious in itself, pain ensues. The dissolving into a void when we faint, or being too compacted in pain, are the aberrations on both sides of consciousness. This describes exactly our feeling with regard to the crystallized mineral world before we have its metallity, its substantiality—the feeling that we could swoon at any moment and dissolve into the universe, [on the one hand,] or break down with pain, [on the other].

Then we get the feeling that, physically speaking, it is where the heart muscles are situated that everything converges which gives us a stable hold. And if we have developed our consciousness to the level already indicated, we then perceive that everything that sustains our earthly consciousness, our ordinary waking consciousness, all that keeps it 'normal' (if I may use this ugly, prosaic word,) is gold, *aurum*, which is spread in extremely rarefied form over the world, and works more directly upon the heart than upon any other organ.

Whereas previously we perceived the formation, the crystallization, of the mineral element, we now perceive its inner substantiality, its metallity. We feel in what way this metallic nature works upon man himself.

Outwardly we see the crystal, that forms the metallic element, in mineral form. But we know inwardly that the forces of gold which extend throughout the whole cosmos in extremely rarefied dosage, sustain our heart and thereby maintain our normal consciousness in daily life. And so we can say: gold works upon the human heart (see diagram on page 42).

We can now begin our research. We can learn—by calling to mind the qualities of metallic gold, by concentrating on its colour, its hardness, its substantiality, and making this a real inner experience— that gold is related to the heart. Then we can bring this to a stage where, by concentrating on other metals, on iron and its properties, for example, we discover what effect iron has upon us. Gold has an infinitely harmonizing effect; we attain inner balance through its influence. If, after becoming familiar with all its aspects, we concentrate intently on iron, forgetting the entire universe and concentrating solely on iron itself, so that in our soul life we become inwardly merged, as it were, with iron, become identified with iron, experience ourselves as iron, then we feel as if our consciousness were rising up from the heart. We still have full clarity of consciousness, but feel our consciousness rising from the heart to the throat, to the larynx. If we have done our [spiritual] exercises sufficiently, this is not harmful. If we have not yet done the exercises sufficiently, a slight feeling of faintness comes over us. As our consciousness rises we get to know this slight faintness either by actually fainting or by developing inner activity, a powerful strength of consciousness. Then we gradually transpose ourselves into this ascending consciousness and, by the sort of method I have described, we come to the world I spoke about yesterday, where we see the group-souls of the animals. By concentrating on the metallity of iron we have now entered the astral world.

When we engage with the *form* of the metals, we come to the beings of the gods. When we engage with the metals' *substantiality* and *metallity*, we enter the astral world, the soul world. We feel our consciousness rising upward to the larynx and we emerge into a new sphere of consciousness. We realize that we owe this shift of consciousness to our concentration on iron, and we feel that we are no longer the same person as before. If we attain this state in full, precise consciousness, we feel we are no longer the same person: we have become etheric. We have risen out of ourselves and become etheric. The earth has vanished; it no longer interests us. But we ascend into the planetary spheres which are now our abode, so to speak. Thus we withdraw more and more away from ourselves and into the universe. The path from gold to iron is the path out into the universe.

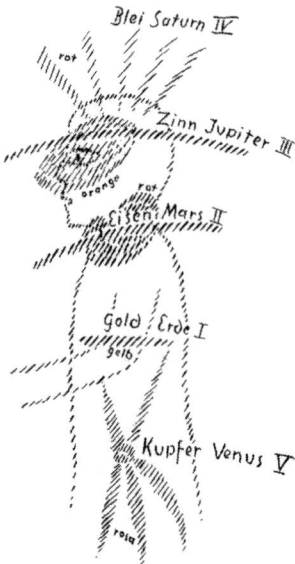

We can go further. Now, in the same way as I described it for gold and iron, we can concentrate on another metal, for example on tin, on its metallity, its colour and consistency and so on, so that with our consciousness we become tin entirely. We feel that our consciousness rises even higher. But if we undergo this without preparation, without the necessary exercises, we feel we will become strongly unconscious, with only a small spark of consciousness left. But if we have done the exercises, we can hold ourselves in this state of diminished consciousness and feel how we withdraw still further from the body. We are now slipping further out. We feel our consciousness rise to the region of the eyes (see drawing). We feel ourselves to be out in the widths of the universe, but still within the realm of stars. But the earth begins to become

[lead Saturn IV
red
tin Jupiter III
orange red
iron Mars II
gold Earth I
yellow
copper Venus V
pink]

visible as a distant star, and we think to ourselves: you have left your body down there on earth, you have risen into the cosmos and share in the life of the stars.

But, you see, all this is by no means a simple matter. What I have described to you, what we experience when we follow the path of initiation—namely, that we feel we have a form of consciousness in the larynx, that we have consciousness in the base of the skull and in the forehead—shows that all these [forms of consciousness] are actually present in us all the time. All of you sitting here have these consciousnesses within you, you are just not aware of it. How can this be? Well, the human is not a simple being. If, at the moment you were to become conscious of your whole larynx organization, you could get rid of your brain, get rid of your sense organs, and develop your consciousness as a human being only in your larynx and what relates to it, you would always have this slight subconscious feeling of faintness. And indeed you do have it; it is just overlaid by ordinary heart consciousness, by gold consciousness. This consciousness I have described is in all of you; it is in part of your human make-up. A part of your being lives in the stars and is not on the earth at all.

Tin consciousness lies even further out in the cosmos (see diagram: orange). It is simply not true that you only live on the earth. You live on earth because you have a heart. The heart holds together your consciousness on earth. What is situated in the larynx (iron: red) lives out in the cosmos. And still further out is what lies in the head above the eyes (tin). Iron reaches as far as Mars; tin as far as Jupiter. You are on the earth only by virtue of gold. You are always in the universe, it is just that heart consciousness veils this from you.

If our concentration is now focused on lead or some similar metal, and again on its substantiality and metallity, then we go out of ourselves completely. You are left in no doubt that your physical body and etheric body are left down on earth. They are something alien down there. They have as little to do with you as a stone lying on a rock bed. Consciousness has risen out of you here (out of the top of the head: red). A minute dosage of lead is always present in the universe. This consciousness at the top [of the head] reaches far out; and with regard to this consciousness which is always present in the human being in the cranium, we are always in a state of complete insensibility.

Just think of the illusion in which man lives. When he is sitting at his desk drawing up accounts or writing articles, he believes he is thinking with his head. But this is simply not true. His head is not on the earth at all; it is only on the earth in its external manifestation.

The head extends from the throat out into the universe. The universe merely reveals itself in the head. What brings it about on earth that you are an earthly being between birth and death, is the heart. Whether you write good or bad articles, whether your accounts cheat other people or not—this comes from the heart. The best thoughts you can have all come out of the heart. It is just an illusion to imagine that man's head lives on the earth. The head is actually in a permanent state of insensibility. And that is why it can be so extraordinarily painful in a way that other organs are not. Let me take this point a little further. When, in our present state, we try to find the reasons for this, we are continually threatened in a spiritual direction (*geistwärts*) with our head being shattered into the cosmos, with our whole consciousness dissolving upwards, disintegrating into a powerful insensibility. This is all held together by the heart.

The human being actually lives in such a way that we can say: in the larynx (iron) we unfold the consciousness I described to you as reaching to the animal realm, to the archetypes behind the animal kingdom. In ordinary life we are just not aware of it; but it is there, where we are always looking up to the stars. We bear this consciousness always within us. Up here [pointing to diagram] is the consciousness of the archetypes of the plant kingdom, and here below are their reflected images (see drawing, page 36). And right at the top, where lead consciousness is situated, which reaches to Saturn, our head knows nothing of the articles we write, for we write those with the heart. But the head is fully aware of everything I have described to you today, of everything that is above this (see diagram on page 36). So someone can be sitting writing earthly things—and it comes out of the heart. Meanwhile their head can be occupied with the way in which a god reveals itself in pyrites, in a salt crystal, or in a crystal of quartz.

When initiate consciousness surveys the audience seated here, it is evident that your hearts are listening to what I am saying, but your three superimposed consciousnesses are in the cosmos. Things take place there that are of a completely different nature from what is in ordinary earthly consciousness. In the cosmos, principally in what happens and constantly radiates out from there, there live the living threads that spin the karma of each individual, and so on.

In this way, as you see, we gradually come to understand the human being through the universe. We have got to know the human being who is indeed related to the outer world, who is constantly under threat outwardly of splitting up, of falling into unconsciousness, and is held together by the heart.

From spatial consciousness into time consciousness

Spiritually we move in a completely different direction when we concentrate on certain other kinds of metallity. We can follow the same procedure with copper as we did with iron, tin, and lead. We can meditate on the metallic nature of copper, merge as it were with copper, become copper in our soul life, with its colour and consistency, its curiously ribbed surface—in short, with everything that we can experience in our soul through the metallity of copper. Then we do not have the feeling of passing over into unconsciousness, but the opposite happens. We have the feeling that something is filling our whole inner being. We become inwardly more sensitive than we otherwise are. We have the feeling that this copper on which we are meditating, fills us from top to bottom, right into our finger tips, everywhere, right into our skin. It fills us. It fills us with something. And we feel this 'something' with which it fills us as radiating out from here (see diagram on page 42, pink). It then streams from this centre-point that is below the heart into the whole body. It is as though we had a second body, a second man in us. We feel inwardly compressed. A slight pain begins and increases. Everything inside feels under pressure.

But again we penetrate all this with initiate feeling, and we feel the presence of a second man within us. And this experience has important implications, for we can say to ourselves: you walk about with this normal self (*Mensch*) which you have received through birth and upbringing, with which you see the world through your eyes, with which you hear, with which you feel objects; but, through the training and exercises you have done, you have brought this second man, who is pressing in you, to the point of being able to perceive. This second man is indeed a strange being: he does not possess eyes and ears that are separate, but is entirely eye and ear, so to speak; he is like a sense organ. He has very subtle powers of perception, and so perceives things that we do not normally perceive. The world becomes suddenly enriched.

Just as a snake can slough off its skin, so it is possible for a short period that might last only a few seconds—a great deal can be experienced here in a few seconds—for this second man that has developed as the 'copper man' in us, so to speak, to withdraw from the body and move about freely in the spiritual world. He can be separated from the body, even though this is painful; even though the pain increases, he is separable.

We can leave [our body]. And when we are separated from the body we can experience more than when we are still inside it. Once we have reached the point when we can relinquish the body, we are then able to follow a person who has died into the world into which they pass after a few days. So someone has passed through the portal of death, and all the associations we as an earthly being had towards this person, cease. They are cremated or buried. They are no longer on the earth.

When we leave the body with this second man that I have just described, we are able to follow the soul of those who have died; we remain together with it. And then we experience that the soul in the first years or decades after death re-lives in reverse order its life on earth. This is a fact that can be observed. We stay with the soul, and then we see what the person experienced on earth in the days before their death; they experience it in reverse order, the last thing first, the penultimate thing second, and so on. Everything is re-lived backwards. This re-living backwards to the moment of the person's birth lasts for a third of the time they lived. If the person died aged 60, they re-live this reverse order for approximately 20 years. And we can follow this.

We can now learn something curious about man's experiences in the period immediately following death. During this backward review we do not experience things in the same way as we experienced them here on earth. Forgive me if I use a fairly forceful example. Let's assume that three years before your death you gave someone a box on the ear—I will use this strong example. You were angry with them and your anger boiled over. (I realize, of course, that no-one sitting here would do such a thing, but I'm taking a strong example.) So, let's assume you are angry with them, your anger boils over, and you cause this other person physical and emotional pain. This gave you some satisfaction. You felt justified in having punished them.

Now, when you go back through your life [after death] and come to this episode—which you will do after a year—you do not re-experience *your* anger, but the physical and emotional pain that *the other person* experienced. You live right into the other person, and receive the boxed ear in your soul. You have to really feel the physical pain. And the same applies to all [our] actions: you experience them exactly as others experienced them. We can accompany the human soul through all this.

You see, the ancient Chaldeans, who received their cultural impulses from the mystery teachings, knew more about these things in the times I have been talking about than we do today. There was something very remarkable about these Chaldeans: they did not so much live out of the heart, but they lived really out of the larynx. The consciousness natural to them was a kind of iron consciousness. Their experience was out in the universe. The earth did not seem so hard and solid to them as it does to us. But when, at particularly favourable times, they lived, for example, on Mars, in communion with the beings of Mars, there came a moment of time when beings came over from the moon and brought with them other beings such as those we perceive when we are in the second man I described above. And so, in a roundabout way out in the universe, the Chaldeans learned of sublime truths relating to life after death. They received their instruction out in the universe.

This is no longer necessary for us today; we can follow the dead without intermediary help. We can follow them as they live through their experiences in reverse sequence and also turned around. And the strange thing is that when we go out of our body with this second man, we feel ourselves to be in a world that is far, far more real than our earthly world. This earthly world and everything we experience in it seems to us like shadows in contrast to the dense, intense reality (*anspruchsvolle Wirklichkeit*) into which we now enter.

When, in the way described, we accompany one who has died, we feel everything to be twice or three times heavier, three times brighter, three times louder—everything far more real; and the whole physical world strikes us as really very shadowy. To anyone who is associated with the world of the dead through initiate consciousness, the physical world becomes like a sum of paintings, and it is quite possible that an initiate who is called upon to associate a good deal with the dead in this way, would say to you: You are all just paintings. You are not real. You are just painted sitting on your chairs. For true reality is only discovered on the other side of existence. There everything is far more real. It is possible to experience this reality, ladies and gentlemen.

Perhaps some of you can recall the figure of Strader in my Mystery Dramas[6]. This character is drawn from life. Strader is not a photographic portrait, but an artistic or poetic one of a personality who lived in the last third of the nineteenth century and on into the twentieth. In real life this individual interested me deeply as a personality. He began life as a Capuchin monk, then changed course and became a philosopher, and stayed for a time in the monastery at Dornach. I re-worked and re-cast this personality that interested me so much in life into Strader in the Mystery Dramas—but he is not the same, only similar.

Then came the fourth Drama. In the fourth Mystery Drama, you will remember, Strader dies. I had to let him die; I would not have been able to develop Strader further. It would not have been possible to bring him into a fifth Mystery. I could not have put pen to paper if I had tried to develop his character further. Why was this? Well, the real individual, who had been a Capuchin monk and become a philosopher, had meanwhile actually died. And due to the interest I had in this personality, I was able to follow him into the other world. There he seemed far more real. What could still be written in the physical world was now of less interest than what could be experienced with this personality when I followed him after death.

Then a strange thing happened. A few anthroposophists tumbled to the fact—some people can be very astute—that Strader was to some extent a portrait of this man. They investigated further, discovered unpublished manuscripts and all sorts of interesting things which the man had left behind. They brought them to me expecting me to light up with jubilation and interest. I could not find the slightest interest in them. What did interest me, on the other hand, was what this man was doing now after his death. That is far more real. By comparison, everything related to the external world which he had left behind was of no significance.

People were surprised that I showed so little interest after they had been at such pains to gather the information. I had no use for it then, nor do I need it now. The fact is that earthly reality becomes an illusion in comparison with the mighty reality we encounter when we follow an individual after death. There the soul is in a world that we can experience for ourselves when, as I described, we are filled with the second man who can leave the physical body, if only for a short time. But much can be experienced in a short time.

So this world that borders directly on our physical sense-world really exists, in which the dead live more directly, so to speak, which we experience as being far more real because we experience it with the human being who strides out into it. Now we do not lose consciousness, we are now more densely within our consciousness. If we rise in consciousness above the heart, our consciousness becomes thinner; we come close to unconsciousness. If we move below the heart, our consciousness condenses; we enter worlds that are very real. We just have to be able to endure it. They press on us, they hurt. But if we push in with the necessary courage, we do get in. (See drawing on page 42.)

So we have our ordinary daily consciousness in the heart (I), a second consciousness in the larynx (II), a third consciousness in the region of the eyes (III), a fourth consciousness at the top of the head (IV) that leads us right out into the cosmos, and a fifth consciousness (V) that does not lead us out into the worlds of space but backwards into time. We go into time. When we enter this fifth consciousness we travel a path in time—the same path that the one who has died travels in backward order. We have stepped out of space into time.

So you see, everything depends on transposing ourselves into different states of consciousness. When we do this we get to know entire worlds. Here on earth we live in *one* world because we have *one* consciousness and are asleep to our other states of consciousness. If we are not asleep to them but transpose ourselves into these other states of consciousness, then we experience other worlds.

This is the secret to researching other worlds: that we undergo a change in ourselves, even in our forms of consciousness. For we cannot gain access to other worlds by theorizing or by investigation using the same means as we use in ordinary life, but by a metamorphosis, a transformation of our consciousness into other forms of consciousness.

LECTURE 4

The Secret of Research into other Realms
through the Metamorphosis of Consciousness

The connection of metallity with other states of consciousness

I HAVE spoken about the form, substantiality and metallity of the mineral kingdom in so far as they are related to the different levels of consciousness in the human being. Before broadening my observations to include certain metallic substances, I need to say the following.

One could easily believe from what I have said that I was recommending the ingestion of these substances as a kind of nutriment to bring about states of consciousness that diverge from the normal. When the methods are spoken about for finding the path into the spiritual world, and the inner schooling and intimate training are discussed which one must undergo, people often say: Yes, I would really like to know something of other worlds, of other states of consciousness, but it is so difficult to do these exercises; they take so much time.

Nevertheless people make a start on the exercises. But then life comes along with all its habits that we are so reluctant to give up. Then the inner enthusiasm and inner intensity for the exercises is gradually lost. The whole thing becomes a bit blurry in our soul life, and then people don't manage anything. They find it extremely uncomfortable to have to exercise the soul in this way. If they then hear that certain, shall we say, metallities are connected with other states of consciousness, they easily say: Yes, that's more comfortable. For example, if, in order to accompany someone who has died, all I needed to do was ingest a small quantity of copper, why shouldn't I just take some copper in order to attain the state of consciousness that would enable me to accompany the one who has died through their whole soul life?

The idea becomes even trickier when people hear that in the ancient mysteries things not so dissimilar from this were actually done; that in the ancient mysteries—albeit under the strict and constant supervision of initiates—such things were indeed practised. When people also hear about this they say: why shouldn't these ancient methods be revived? But they fail to take into account here that the human body in its innermost structure was completely different in those ancient times from what it is now.

So what was it that was present or, better put, was *not* present in people in ancient times, including the ancient Chaldaean period that we have been discussing over the past few days?

You see, what was lacking in them was our present intellectuality. People did not think out of themselves the way we do today, but received their thoughts as inspiration. In the same way that we are aware that we do not make the red of a rose, but that the rose makes an impression on us [from without], so the people of ancient times were aware that the thoughts of things also came into them, were inspired into them. And this was because the bodily nature was completely different in those ancient times. The bodily nature, right into the constitution of the blood, was different.

And so it happened that in those times metals such as we have been discussing were administered to people in what today we would call a high-potency homoeopathic dose in order to support their soul exercises. But, you see, the whole body at that time was different. Now let us suppose that someone in those ancient Chaldaean times we have been discussing, was given high-potency copper and instructed, before he took the copper—this was always the case—to do specific soul exercises; this person did not have to do this training for days but for *years* before he was administered with high-potency copper. Then, because of the completely different bodily constitution, when copper was administered he had learnt through his training how this highly rarefied, highly potentized substance pulsating in his blood worked in the upper part [of his body]. He discovered that when, after careful training, he received copper, he experienced inwardly that the words he spoke became in a certain sense warmer—became warmer because he himself became warm in his larynx and in the nerves that go from the larynx to the brain.

Now, all this rested on the fact that, because of his different physical make-up, the human being in those times was able to develop a subtle sensitivity for what was happening in him in this way. If you give someone highly potentized copper today, it also has an effect of course. But the effect is that the larynx becomes sick, and nothing else. We have to take cognizance of this difference between the ancient and the modern organization of people, then we will not have the desire and wish to put ourselves into different states of consciousness by ingesting [substances], which was usual in ancient times and still often practised even in the Middle Ages.

The only valid method today is for the individual to acquaint themselves in soul, as I described yesterday, with the nature and essential being of copper; for them to develop a subtle feeling for the colour of copper in its natural state, for its colour when burnished; a feeling for how copper operates in copper sulphate, as an oxide, and so on. If someone develops a feeling in this way, meditates and concentrates on it, then the feeling acts on the newer man in the proper way.

Now you could say: Yes, but you have written a book, *Knowledge of the Higher Worlds*, and there is nothing in there about transposing oneself into copper in this way. Indeed, that is so. But there are other things in the book. And it *is* actually in the book in principle, just not for copper but for other things. The book describes how one should enter into the nature of crystals, of plants and so on. These elementary exercises are given there[7]. Granted it does not say that we should get to know the nature of copper, for in that case we would need to write a library, not just a book. But it is also not necessary, because exercises are given in the book, for example exercises in self-confidence, concentration exercises on specific subjects. They correspond to what I have just described concerning the nature of copper. It does not say to look at the nature of copper, but it says to choose a simple subject and endeavour to concentrate on it every morning and evening. This is the same, just in different words, as saying 'concentrate on the essential nature of copper'. A content is given for the soul [to work on] which we could also have taken from the realm of metallities.

If I say to someone, 'You should concentrate every morning and evening on a specific soul-content, for example "Wisdom radiates in Light" (*Im Lichte strahlt Weisheit*),' it will have an effect, if he really does it, in his soul. It works in the same way as if I had said, 'Get to know copper in all its aspects, and concentrate on copper.' It is just that the one case proceeds from the moral aspect and the other case from the physical, chemical aspect. And for someone who is not a chemist it is much better to enter the spiritual world on the moral path.

So we see how these things need to relate to one another, for to take a path into the spiritual worlds that imitated the ways of the ancient mysteries would be completely wrong for the modern person. The proper way today is one that substitutes external physical nature with a more moral, soul-oriented approach. For all our connections and relationships with nature have changed under the influence of the evolution of our human bodily nature. The make-up of the blood, tissue fluids, our physical constitution, are all different today from what they were in the people of ancient Chaldaea. Our body is different.

Anatomists are not able prove this. Firstly, modern anatomists work mainly with cadavers. And recently at a science congress a cry went up on behalf of science: 'Give us cadavers!'—anatomists feel they have too few cadavers to be able to research all the secrets [of life]—and it would be very difficult to get hold of Chaldaean cadavers to research these things! [And secondly, using their unsubtle techniques, anatomists would find nothing.] Things have to be investigated by spiritual means.

So we have a bodily nature that is different from the ancients. And because of this, there is something very particular we have to note. We are also capable today of producing highly potentized substances—metals for example. But why do we do this? It is precisely a deeper insight into the being of nature that gives us the necessary orientation and direction. When we really understand the human body, we know that it is changed by each of the metals I have mentioned—tin, copper, lead, and so on. And I have indicated this effect as a change in states of consciousness.

But there are also changes in our human body during normal life, if I may use that philistine expression. Let us say, for example, that we have a change in the area from which, as I mentioned yesterday, the copper-effect radiates out (see diagram, page 56). A change of this kind comes to expression in all sorts of disorders in the organs of digestion, disorders of the metabolic-limb system, disorders in the parts of the human being that are primarily concerned with metabolism, digestion, with distribution of nutrients in the body. But every such disturbance in the human organism, which we call illness, is also connected with the inducement of a different state of consciousness. We just have to be aware of the full significance of this.

What does it mean to have a sick organ? I said yesterday that in ordinary life the human being today has his waking conscious state by virtue of the heart. Other parts of the human organism have different states, but these do not come to consciousness. The area of your larynx, and everything that connects the larynx with the brain, has a constant condition of consciousness that is closest to ordinary consciousness, as I described yesterday. The region down here, the area of the digestive organs, has a constant condition of consciousness that leads us along the time-line that the deceased pass through after death (see diagram, page 56). The human being is always participating in this. Every individual experiences the life of those he knew after they have passed through the portal of death. But he experiences them below his heart, not in his heart. That is why he is not aware of it and it remains in the subconscious, the unconscious.

Now when a disorder arises in the same area in which we are constantly experiencing the life of the deceased after their death, when, in other words, a disorder arises in the digestion, then the state of consciousness down there is changed. We get a consciousness below the heart that is too strong. What does it mean, for example, to have a certain kind of stomach complaint? In physical life it naturally means what doctors describe physically. And what I am presenting here has nothing whatever against physical medicine. Medicine is fully recognized and respected. In anthroposophy we do not take a dilettante, amateur or charlatan-like stance that rejects physical medicine, criticizing and preaching against it. We give it full recognition. But alongside having what physical medicine describes, a person with a certain kind of stomach illness becomes more suited to following the life immediately after death of people who have died. So what can we say here from a spiritual point of view?

Naturally, to begin with, we describe the illness in physical terms so that the right medication can be given and so on. But in spiritual terms we could say: The person has an urge to accompany people he has known and who have died. But he is unable to go down and enter into the consciousness below his heart. He is unaware that he is going into the region of the dead. This is the spiritual aspect of the illness. We are ill in our stomach because we are too much with the dead. But the moment one is with the dead too much, the dead also have an over-strong effect. A great deal comes into us from the world which I described yesterday as being more real than the physical world. And if you have a pair of scales with the fulcrum here (Dr Steiner draws on the blackboard), the scale-pans here, and the scales go down too far [on one side], and you want to establish a balance again, you have to put more weight on the other side. When the scales are out of balance, you need more weight on the opposite side.

So let us assume that someone has developed such a sensitive consciousness under their heart—but they are unconscious of it—that they accompany the dead too strongly: this is like one side of the scales going down too far, and is too strong. We need to put more weight on the opposite side. How do we do this?

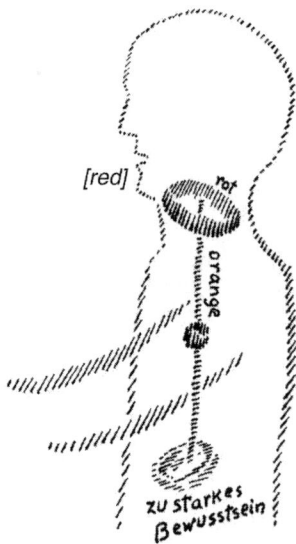

[overly strong consciousness]

If we have a consciousness that is too strong here (pointing to diagram on page 56), we have to weaken the consciousness here (red), because the heart is the fulcrum of the scales (orange). So we need to reduce consciousness here in this region. How do we do this? We administer copper. I mentioned that the modern human body is organized such that copper has an effect on the larynx. But the organs of digestion and the organs of the larynx relate to one another like two sides of the scales. We can regulate the one by means of the other. If we give the person an appropriate dosage of copper, he then, to the benefit of his own health, tends once more to by-pass the region of the dead, whereas otherwise he tended to remain there. This is the spiritual aspect of healing.

For this reason we need to realize today that all substances, all substantialities, have a physical and a moral side. The physical side could be used by the ancient initiates on their pupils after a long period of training, as I described. It is not permissible in modern times to use it in this way. Today moral substance belongs to the realm of soul development, and physical substance belongs to the doctor. With regard to the moral side, it is a matter simply of someone who knows the physical side also having the possibility to penetrate [so] deeply into this physical side of substance that it supports his understanding of the moral side as well.

Where modern practical knowledge is concerned, all this must be confined strictly to the area of a spiritual path. The physical aspect of the substantiality of things belongs to the physician; the moral aspect is an integral part of soul-development. For, human organisms have fundamentally changed since the times I have been speaking about. The same intimate relation that used to exist between knowledge of the moral and knowledge of the physical aspects of the different substances has been lost for a time and it must be established once more. (I shall have more to say presently about the loss of this relationship.) At the same time, the connection between physical medical science and moral science must, even when it is re-established, be different from what it was in past ages. It must return, but in a different form. Upon the knowledge of such things as these depends the ability to distinguish between true and false methods of finding the way into the spiritual world.

Changes in the relation to knowledge and science in the course of history

In order to throw a little more light on what we have considered so far, we must now turn our attention to the changes that have occurred over long periods of time in respect of man's whole attitude towards knowledge. Turning away from the present, we will look back upon the evolution of humanity and observe how very differently people used to speak about everything connected with research and learning. Today when we contemplate all the marvellous progress that has been made in recent times in our knowledge of the forces of heat and electricity, and of living organisms, we speak of 'Nature'; we speak of natural history and natural science and in England of natural philosophy.

When we look at what is taught in schools, even in primary schools, under the term 'Nature,' we find that it is something extraordinarily abstract. It is a kind of summary of 'natural laws'—that is the expression used—something really quite abstract, that the children are supposed to learn. And the abstractness of it all also comes to expression in life. Even the most enthusiastic student of natural science feels this. In botany, for example, they have to learn scores of names of plants and plant species by heart, or of animals and animal species in zoology. They then forget them, but have to learn them again for the examinations. After the examination they forget them altogether, just looking them up in a reference book if needed. And it couldn't really be said that someone today has the same relation to their botanical or zoological studies as they might have, for example, towards someone they love. This is certainly not the case today.

Nature now is something floating in a kind of mist. It is all laws: laws of gravity, laws of heat, laws of light, laws of electricity, laws of magnetism, laws of steam and water, equilibrium and disturbance of equilibrium. Natural science is what we know about rocks and plants. Natural science is also what people say we [still] do not know about the life and inner constitution of the organs of plants and animals and of the human being. In short, it is a lot of what we know today and also a lot of what we say we don't know. That is natural science or natural philosophy today.

It is not something you can take warmly by the hand because everything in it is vague, conceived in a thin and abstract way. We are making great efforts today to master this abstraction we call Nature. It is fair to say that quite a few people have become somewhat indifferent towards this abstraction. We maintain a benevolent neutrality towards it unless we belong to the youth of today who are raising a strong opposition to what is being taught in schools as natural science. We profess a benevolent neutrality. Things were not always like this. I should like to describe the attitude towards knowledge [that existed] some centuries ago.

If we go back to the ninth, tenth, and eleventh, and even to the twelfth and thirteenth centuries—though then it was very much less the case—we find individuals whom we should describe today as learned men of science; for in terms of that period they were supremely learned. They were teachers in the wonderful school of Chartres[8] during the eleventh and twelfth centuries, and among them we find Bernardus Sylvestris, Bernard of Chartres, Alanus ab Insulis.[8] Personalities such as these were a type of initiate who lived among the people at that time, were a type of individual who knew a great deal about the mysteries of existence. Such a type for instance—and he was a great initiate of the Middle Ages—was Joachim of Flora[8], or again, another great personality of that period was known to the world as John of Auville[8]. I mention these few, to which many more could be added, in order to take us back into that period, in order to characterize the mood, the attitude, in those days towards knowledge.

If we stand before one of these personalities in soul and hear them speak about nature, it is something totally different from how we speak of nature today. If we meet a botanist or anatomist or histologist today, we seldom have the feeling that the physiognomy they present us with bears any traces in it of the secrets of the mysteries of pathological anatomy or zoology. When we come across such a pathology anatomist or histologist or even a physician today, we are more likely have the feeling that their physiognomy comes from a pleasant dance they were at somewhere the day before. We are more likely to see things like this revealed in their physiognomy than any experiences they have gathered from the mysteries of nature.

It was a very different thing to look into the eyes of a Joachim of Flora, or an Alanus ab Insulis, or a Bernardus Sylvestris, who lived in an age I have just described. There was something tragic in their faces which seemed to say: We live in an age that has lost much. A tragic sorrow was visible there, a sorrow born out of the depths of their knowledge.

Or again, if we had seen the fingers of these individuals, the sort of fingers which people today would call 'nervous,' we could have seen that they were a living witness to the fact that these individuals wanted to delve into the ancient secrets, the loss of which was expressed in their faces. We should have noticed that something was working in these individuals that wanted to revive what had been there in ancient times. Sometimes they succeeded. Sometimes they succeeded in conjuring up a picture, even if only a shadow-picture, of the ancient days for their pupils.

We can imagine to ourselves—and what I am telling you is not a poetic image, ladies and gentlemen, but a reality—we can picture to ourselves the school of Chartres where the wonderful cathedral still stands today, and Alanus ab Insulis speaking to his pupils. He would say: 'Natura!—a being we no longer comprehend, who eludes us when we try to draw near to her. Humanity has developed forces that draw it towards other things, but which are no longer capable of grasping nature in the way it was grasped by knowledgeable people in ancient times. For Natura was a great and powerful spirit-being who was active everywhere: where rocks took shape in the mountains, where plants grew out of the earth, where stars sparkled in the heavens. An immeasurably great being was at work everywhere, who revealed herself in the sublime form of a woman. The ancients saw her with their [clairvoyant] sight. From their descriptions we can still form an idea of what Natura was like: this activity and weaving in everything that surrounds us, that lives and weaves in all warmth, in all phenomena of light and colour, in all life. But if we try to approach her, she eludes us. For the goddess Natura is living and weaving in all things. A goddess, a divine spiritual being who, people realized, can only be known in her true being if we can behold her directly.'

A personality like Alanus ab Insulis was still able in the twelfth century to bring pictures like this clearly before the souls of his pupils in the school of Chartres. But because these teachers saw the goddess Natura dissolving in a mist along with the inner vitality of everything that today we find as dead, abstract laws of nature—because she evades us, sorrow and tragedy were written on their faces.

Then again, there were men like Brunetto Latini, the great teacher of Dante[9]. Due to a particular karmic incident, Brunetto Latini[9] received a kind of sunstroke during his travels which produced a change in his state of consciousness. This was a far more important event for him than the sufferings he endured by being exiled from his native home by the Guelphs. Through this change in his consciousness he became aware of the goddess Natura, and described her in his book, *Tesoretto*. In a living Imagination-picture, he describes vividly how on his homeward way to his native city of Florence he comes to a desolate forest, and how in the midst of this desolate forest there is a hill where the goddess Natura is working. She explains to him the meaning of thinking, feeling and will in the human soul. The goddess explains to him the true nature of the four temperaments in man, and of the five senses.

This was a genuine soul-spiritual teaching, a reality, which he experienced on his homeward journey from Spain to his native Florence, under the influence of a pathological condition. After he had experienced all this, he saw the weaving life of the four elements of fire, earth, water and air; he saw the weaving life of the planets; and the soul's journey through the starry heavens. He saw all this under the influence of a spiritual teaching given to him by the goddess Natura.

An individual of that period could describe such things with a vividness of language that is barely possible today. But at the same time it was felt that the others, the ancients, had known it all in quite a different way, and that in later times this knowledge slipped out of reach. One would even have to be in a muted, pathological state to look into these mysteries now.

But there was a tremendous urge in these men to conjure up again something like the real form of the goddess Natura. So you see, when we trace back this path in humanity's feeling, in humanity's thinking with regard to knowledge, we have the feeling that, yes, we also stand before Natura, but we refer to her with a name that is something entirely abstract, a mere collection of laws. We are proud when we are able to classify these laws with a certain amount of inner cohesion. Then we go back a few centuries. We see there a living relationship between man and a divine being who was real and alive and whose activity was behind all the phenomena [we see around us]—the rising and setting of the sun, the warming of the rocks, the warming of the plants—and who brought the whole living warp and weft of the world into activity. Just think what an utterly different kind of science that is! It was a science that contained the deeds of the goddess Natura. The mood of the students—they were mainly of the Cistercian order—as they came out of Chartres was certainly very different from the mood of students coming out of classes today. It was very different—more vital, alive, and full of reality. And the descriptions given by such people as Brunetto Latini, the great teacher of Dante, were also full of vitality and reality.

The vital reality of these things can be seen in all the glorious pictures and figures painted by Dante in his *Divina Commedia*, for they arose out of the living descriptions given by his teacher, Brunetto Latini, whose initiation had taken place through a karmic event; just as much else of what was taught in Chartres and other schools like it originated from initiates like Joachim of Flora, and others.

The expression 'Natura' was not used at that time in the abstract way that we use it; it stood for something that really exists and is at work in everything perceived by the senses, but that retreats and slips away from us. And there was something else. Imagine—and again I am not describing a poetical fancy but something absolutely real— that you had sat for some years as a student of Alanus ab Insulis, taking part in everything that went on. The students had been dismissed from their work, and you were walking alone with Alanus ab Insulis, discussing events. What might you have experienced?

Such a conversation might have taken a particular turn. You might have spoken of the goddess Natura who was manifest everywhere in the physical world but who was always eluding you. Alanus ab Insulis, if he had been warmed by this conversation soul-to-soul, might have tapped you on the shoulder and said: 'Ah, if only we still had the condition of sleep that the ancients had! Then we would behold the other side, the hidden side of the goddess Natura. But when we sleep we fall into unconsciousness precisely where for the ancients the other side of Nature was revealed. If we could still sleep the clairvoyant sleep of the ancients, we should know the goddess Natura!' Alanus ab Insulis would have tapped us on the shoulder and spoken in this way.

Or perhaps you might have been talking intimately in this way with Joachim of Flora; and presently he would have said: 'Yes, it is hard for us, whose sleep is so poor in content and completely subdues our consciousness, to learn to know the other side of Natura, the great goddess, who creates and weaves in all creating and fashioning. The ancients knew both sides of her. And do you know'—he would have said to you— 'the ancients did not use the name Natura. This being whose existence we only feel rather than know, was not, to them, the goddess Natura. They called her by another name: they called her Proserpina [Persephone]. That is the truth.'

This was still known in those days. The abstract [notion of] nature which we have as ideas, is the transformation of what I have just described. And what lived in the souls of such men as Bernardus Sylvestris, Alanus ab Insulis, John of Auville, and above all in Brunetto Latini, was the transformation of what the ancients had seen as Proserpina, the daughter of Demeter. Demeter—the entire universe, Proserpina! It is totally prosaic when in place of Proserpina we use the new word 'Nature'—Nature who can only live half her life in the upper world—that is, when she turns her physical and sensory aspect towards human beings—and half her life descended into the regions which human beings reach with sleep, but which, because our sleep today has become empty of reality, we no longer reach [consciously].

Our own natural science, although due to its abstractness today we are unable to recognize it as such, is an echo of what lived in the ancient Greek myth of Proserpina. The fact that the men of sorrowful countenance were aware of this and that it could still be known in their day, shows how greatly the paths of knowledge have changed since those times. As I said in the earlier part of my lecture, we can only get the right feeling, the right colouring for these things when we look back at the whole manner in which knowledge was approached, and its whole character; not in order to rehabilitate the ancient knowledge, but for the sake of awakening a feeling for what once existed. It is for this reason that I am describing these things.

Pictures of Ancient Times

If we can hold in our minds the words that could still be spoken by Joachim of Flora, or John of Auville (while patting us on the shoulder long ago in the Middle Ages)—'What we regard as nature today, or what vanishes from us because we cannot reach it on the other side of life, this was once known as Proserpina'—and if this myth of Proserpina (for it has survived only as a myth) arises again in our souls, then the images evoked by this myth awaken images of still earlier relationships. These are pictures from the time when people experienced not abstract nature, not the goddess Natura felt in tragic mood, but saw the brightly radiant goddess on the one side, and the tragic goddess on the other: Proserpina and Persephoneia.

How did she appear in those ancient days when she was fully alive? For it was not during the time when Plato[10] was writing his philosophy, nor when Socrates[10] was imparting his philosophy by the spoken word—no, not in those times. It was in far more ancient times, when knowledge was something tremendously alive, even more alive than in the brilliant days of Greek culture.

Let us try to bring a picture before our souls, and to awaken in this picture what knowledge really was in the course of human evolution, so as to throw the right light on what we have already considered from the standpoint of the present, and will consider further in the course of these lectures. Let us try to envisage the nature of the mysteries into which the Greek philosopher, Heraclitus[10] was initiated, who was called Heraclitus the Dark, or the obscure, because in later years a darkness of soul had descended on all that he had received from these mysteries. In our mind's eye, let us paint a picture of that particular period of the mysteries' development, which Greek culture drew from above all for its imagination and the shaping of its mythology. And let us picture to ourselves the mysteries of Ephesus, into which Heraclitus had been initiated.

A most ancient and primordial knowledge still held sway in Ephesus, and was preserved right on into the days of Homer, and indeed was still to be found there, though in a somewhat weaker form, when Heraclitus received his initiation. These ancient mysteries existed as intensely living realities, and strong and powerful influences of initiation flowed in that temple, where, on the eastern side stood the well-known statue of the goddess Diana, the goddess of fertility, who, in sculptural form, brings to expression the teeming fertility that is everywhere in nature. The greatest secrets of existence, the profoundest spiritual secrets, were clothed in human words in conversations that were held immediately after participation in the mysteries, when those involved had received their mighty impulses from the ritual and its specific details, in the temple at Ephesus. These were profound conversations. They took place as the participants of the ritual came out of the temple, and at a time when the outer world is most inviting of such things: in the evening twilight. They would follow the path leading from the doorway of the temple to a grove with wonderful walks and thickly growing deep-green trees, and where the paths leading in different directions from Ephesus lost themselves in the beauty of the scenery. I should like to offer you a somewhat imperfect picture of conversations of this kind.

It would happen that one who was an initiate in the mysteries of those times would come into conversation with a pupil who could be either male or female. For we should note that the idea of the equality of the sexes in those days, though it very soon waned, was a far more real and living thing than it is today. So we can speak just as much of female pupils at Ephesus as of male. In these conversations there was always an especially living appreciation of the myth of Persephone in its most spiritual aspect.

But how was such a conversation about the Proserpina myth conducted?

First of all there was the teacher, the priest-initiate, who, out of the impulses he had received, could speak about the secrets of the world of forms, the secrets of the things taking place between the different beings of that world; and he would say something like the following, speaking to his neophyte out of his knowledge as an initiate: 'See, we are walking through the twilight. Sleep, which reveals the divine world, which makes it visible, will soon come to us. Consider yourself in your whole human form. Below us are the plants; all around us is twilight and the deep greens and evening shadows of the wonderful grove. The first twinkling stars are already beginning to appear above us. Gaze upon all this. Behold its majesty and its sublimity, and behold too the budding, quickening quality of life both above and below. Then, behold yourself. Think how in you a whole universe lives and weaves; how everything within you that is in constant circulation, that has its existence in every process taking place within you, is truly a pleroma, a fullness, of the transformations and workings of beings which never cease for a single instant. Feel how you yourself are an entire world, a world greater in mystery and in splendour—though spatially smaller—than the universe which your gaze can survey from earth to the stars. Feel it! Feel how, as a human being, you are yourself a world, a world of greater fullness than the world you behold with your eyes and comprehend with your thoughts. Feel this world within, inside your skin.

'And then sense how you are now looking out from your own world into the world that extends from the earth to the stars. And you will soon be wrapped in sleep. Then you will not be in your body, not in your own world; you will then be in the world that you see now stretching from the earth to the stars. You will then be out of your body with your soul-spiritual part. Then you will be living in the radiance of the stars and the exhalations of the earth. Then you will think with star-radiance. Then you will be living in your outer world, and will look back at what you are as a world in yourself.'

It was still possible in those days for a teacher to speak in this way to a pupil since the waking vision of things was not so clear and defined as it is today. Neither was sleep-life as yet wholly darkened; it was still saturated with experience upon experience; and if one wished to point to those sleep-experiences, to that state of being received by and cradled in sleep, one would have said : 'You are now enveloped by Prosperpina or Persephone or Kore. Kore lives in the stars. Kore lives in the rays of the sun and in the moonbeams. Kore lives in the growing plants. Everywhere Persephone is working; it is she who lives in all things, for she has woven the garment of which all this is composed. And behind it all is Demeter her mother, for whom Persephone has woven this raiment which you see as the outer world.' One would not have used the word ' nature,' but would have spoken, or rather one did speak, of Persephone or Kore.

And continuing the dialogue with his pupil, the teacher went on: 'If someone were to remain awake for a longer period than you, then, whilst you were asleep, they would perceive what appears outwardly as the form of Prosperpina in plants, in mountains, in clouds and stars, exactly as you do now. For illusion lies in the manner of our seeing. It is not Proserpina who is the illusion, it is not her creative activities in mountains, plants, clouds and stars that are illusory, but how you see them; that is the illusion. You will soon fall asleep. Through your eyes, through those wonderful riddles of your existence, Kore-Persephone will enter into you.'

These things were described so vividly because they were experienced so vividly; so that while falling asleep, the sleeper did not merely feel that his sense of sight was being extinguished, or his sense of hearing; he did not merely feel that he was ceasing to be aware of things, but he felt Persephone sinking down through his eyes, into his physical body and his etheric body, which, while he slept, were forsaken by his soul- and spirit-nature.

When we are awake, we are in the upper world; when we sleep, we are in the underworld. Persephone entered through the eyes of the sleeper into the physical and etheric bodies. She was there with Pluto [or Hades], the ruler of the state of sleep, within the physical and etheric bodies. The sleeping neophyte, who, through the instruction he had received, now understood clearly how Kore entered into him through the gateway of his eyes, experienced during his sleep all the united activity of Pluto and Persephone that took place within his physical and etheric bodies; for by his understanding of the entrance of Persephone he transformed it into living actuality and thus experienced the deeds of Pluto and Persephone in his sleep. And whilst the neophyte experienced this, his teacher had corresponding experiences that were related to the world of forms.

Then, when the teacher and pupil met again, they had both experienced certain mysteries. Then they were able to speak about a plant, or a tree. The teacher would describe how forms arose, because while he slept this had revealed itself to him. He went deeply into the forms of leaves, of stems, into the whole configuration of the world—into those formations which, so to say, tend to sink downwards from above. And perhaps the pupil had experienced it from the other side, and so was able to understand what his teacher said when he spoke of the secrets of chlorophyll, and the secrets of sap that rises from below upwards and spreads itself out in the plant. In this way the conversation would have a wonderful completeness, since it included so vividly and comprehensively the goddess Proserpina in the underworld, revealing herself to people while they slept, and revealing her secrets in their souls.

And so in those ancient times the pupil learned from the teacher, and the teacher from the pupil. For on the one side there were revelations that were of spirit and soul, and on the other side revelations that were of soul and spirit. And a conversation that took place in this way between human beings, in human community, in shared human experience, resulted in the very highest knowledge.

In entering into and experiencing this wonderful knowledge, and with the first light of dawn when they saw the morning star rising in the East and sending its beams into the green darkness of the wooded glades whose dim perspectives were so full of wonder—in experiencing these heights of knowledge they knew that they had passed a brief hour or two in the realm we call the realm of nature, and had been re-invigorated there. This all came together in the conversation. They knew quite clearly that they had had converse with Persephone. They knew that everything which afterwards became embodied in the myth of Persephone was in reality the great secret of humanity's knowledge of nature.

I have been able to give only an inadequate description of the magical atmosphere surrounding these conversations, conversations that were bound up with the mysteries of Ephesus. There was a real magic in them. Persephone-knowledge lived in them with a vividness that was later dimmed down to the abstraction of 'nature' we have today, and which laid those lines of tragedy upon the countenances of such men as Joachim of Flora.

We can only understand the paths leading to the spiritual nature of man and the spiritual nature of the cosmos when we draw attention to, and characterize, not only the separate states of consciousness that the human being can attain, but also how, during the course of human development, these states of consciousness have gradually metamorphosed; when we see how different knowledge once was, in what a different fashion knowledge lived in the intimate and wonderful conversations that took place between those coming out of the temple of Ephesus; and again, when we see how different were the conversations that were conducted with individuals like Joachim of Flora or Alanus ab Insulis; and how different today is the knowledge we must strive to attain once more in order to return from the Outer to the Inner, from the Above to the Below, back from the Inner to the Outer, and from the Below to the Above, with true spiritual understanding.

LECTURE 5

The Inner Enlivening of the Soul through the Qualities of Metals

The copper condition of the human being

I HAVE tried to indicate how the human being can attain to states of consciousness other than those of ordinary life, and how the historical course of human evolution shows that man, in his knowledge and activity, has not always lived in the condition of consciousness that is natural to him today. I then tried to direct your gaze to the conditions of consciousness existing in people of knowledge from the tenth to the twelfth century in connection with the way in which knowledge was cultivated at that time, for instance in the school of Chartres; and I pointed to how this gave rise, in a personality like Brunetto Latini, the great teacher of Dante, to a form of understanding that does not belong to the present-day condition of consciousness.

I also tried yesterday to direct your gaze still farther back to the particular way in which people related to the universe, for example in the mysteries of Ephesus. We see there that people lived in entirely different conditions of consciousness, which, however, bore some resemblance to the everyday and scientific consciousness of modern times.

Today I want to continue the considerations we have been looking at initially as a kind of episode in history. I spoke about how the metallic nature, the real substantiality of the mineral, is related to man and to his conditions of consciousness. From man's relationship to the metal copper, I made clear the state of consciousness that can be attained in the way I described, and which makes it possible to follow the experiences of the so-called dead beyond the moment when they pass through the portal of death.

Now we must realize that it was knowledge of this kind (which I described the day before yesterday) that Brunetto Latini entered into in the semi-pathological condition resulting from his sunstroke. Indeed, everything he describes, everything that came to him through the inspiration of the goddess Natura, can be attained by this kind of consciousness that is able to follow the experiences of the dead during the years immediately following their death, and which is in fact closely allied to our everyday consciousness. As I said, it is a far more real condition. We stand there within a world that presses in on us more strongly, shines more strongly, carries out everything more strongly than our usual physical world. Only because this is so is it possible for us to participate in the experiences of one who has recently passed through the gate of death.

But this world also has another very particular attribute. When we find ourselves in this world with the condition of consciousness I have described, we can no longer view our everyday experiences, [no longer view] everything that we undergo in ordinary life; but rather what we see of our own life is only what took place immediately before we entered earthly life, we see what we went through while still in the spiritual world before entering earthly life. We must therefore say that in this condition of consciousness we are, for the human being, not in the same world in which we usually find ourselves.

Let us try to form a graphic picture of this. A person is born at a certain point in time (Steiner draws on the board). If, when they are forty years old, they attain to what we might call the copper condition of consciousness—you will understand what this means from yesterday's lecture—they do not live with their knowledge in the present time, nor indeed in the period of their thirty-fifth or thirtieth years, but they can only go back to their experiences in the spiritual world immediately before birth. A person can do this with regard to themselves and also with regard to other people, but they cannot lay hold of the everyday existence in which they presently are. This applies, however, only for human beings.

Where animals are concerned we do not see them as they are in the physical world, we do not see their physical nature, but we look into the world immediately above and perceive what I have called the species- or genus-soul. We see, as it were, the aura of the animal species. When we look out into the world we find that it is changed, and we learn to know something that is of great significance for humanity but is entirely ignored in the present materialistic age.

If, with everything we can learn today up to the highest science of any university faculty, we come into the presence of that being who still exists as the goddess Natura—that being of whom the teachers of the school of Chartres, Bernardus Sylvestris, Alanus ab Insulis and others, spoke in such a living way—if we come into the presence of this being, we feel that we are ignorant despite all our modern learning. Then we say to ourselves: 'What I have learnt from the science and learning of the present day only relates to the world in which I live between birth and death. It is already no longer true when I enter with my consciousness into even just the next spiritual world, where I can follow the experiences of the dead beyond death.'

We learn chemistry, but what we learn in chemistry is applicable only to the world we live in between birth and death. The whole of chemistry has no meaning in the world where the dead are to be found. Everything we learn here in the physical world has no significance for that other world; it exists there only as a memory. The new world in which we find ourselves immediately opens before us, and we feel that the everyday world in which we have learned so many things fades away. The other world opens up.

Now let us suppose that in the world we live in between birth and death we have a mountain. In this world, the mountain is decidedly dense. At first we look at it from a distance; it reflects back to us the light it receives from the sun. We see its various formations, its contours. Then we walk towards it and get closer and closer. We feel it offers us resistance when we walk on it. It makes the impression on us of something real. Then we are in that other world. Everything that was solid now seemingly ceases to have any significance, and there is something as though emerging from the mountain, growing larger and larger, that makes the impression on us of another reality.

And further, in the world of everyday life we see cloud above the mountain. We are convinced that it is up there as condensed vapour. It also ceases to have its reality. And again, something entirely different emerges from this cloud. What we now see emerging unites with the gradually disappearing cloud and mountain, and something new arises, a new reality is there that is not merely nebulous, but has form. And this is the case with everything. We see many things here, a number of people, for example. The moment we enter the spiritual world, all the sharp contours vanish. And ladies, we must grow accustomed to the idea that all our beautiful clothes are no longer to be seen there. Instead, from everything that is sitting here, there arises a soul-spiritual aspect. But what comes from the surroundings is what mysteriously holds sway in the air and in the entire environment. That is what approaches. A new world arises. And it is in this world that the dead are after death.

But now we become aware of something else. If this world we have now entered into did not also exist everywhere where the world is that we see between birth and death, we should, as human beings, have no eyes, no ears, no senses at all. For the world that the chemist and the physicist describe cannot give us senses. We would be entirely without senses, blind and deaf.

This was the astonishing thing that happened to Brunetto Latini when he travelled from Spain to the neighbourhood of his home in Florence, and suffered the slight sunstroke which was the cause of his entering this other world. Brunetto Latini's experience was this: 'Your senses are given to you by this other world. As a human being you would have no senses if this other world did not permeate the ordinary world which you usually see. So you stand here as man because your senses are set into your body in connection with this second world.'

In all ages this second world was called the world of elements. It makes no sense in that world to talk of oxygen, hydrogen, nitrogen and so on. We can speak of these only between birth and death. In the other world it only makes sense to speak of the elements: of earth, water, air, fire, light, and so on. For the real essence of hydrogen, oxygen, and so on, has absolutely no relation to our senses.

All that the chemist finds out about the scent of a violet or of asa-foetida,[11] that the one has a very pleasant scent and the other an exceedingly disagreeable one, everything that is chemically analysed here and the nomenclature given to substances, has no meaning in this second world. On the other hand, everything that works there as scent or smell is imbued with spirit. In that world, into which the dead enter immediately after their death, we would have to call it 'of the nature of air' (*luftförmig*), but a differentiated air, an air every-where imbued with spirit. Thus our senses have their roots in the world of the elements, in the world where it makes sense to speak of earth, water, fire, air.

You see, here we have a correct thought in contrast to a false one. What is the attitude of a modern philosopher who, according to himself, is rational and has overcome the naiveté of the views of earlier ages? He says: 'These earlier conceptions were crude. In those days people spoke only of the coarse elements, of earth, water, air, fire. We know that there are seventy or eighty elements, not only four or five.'

Now, if an ancient Greek were resurrected—as he was in Greece, not in a modern incarnation—and had to hear this, he would say: 'Yes, of course you have oxygen, hydrogen and so on; these are your elements. But you have forgotten what we had in our four elements. You no longer perceive it. You no longer know about it. But with your seventy-two or seventy-five elements the senses would never have come into being, for they arise out of the four elements. We therefore had a better knowledge of the human being. We knew how his external, peripheral nature that is permeated by senses, was developed.'

We can only form a true estimate of the impressions received by individuals of former times who came close to initiation, such as Brunetto Latini, when we look at the effect these had on their inner being, when we look at the astonishment and surprise, how their soul was stirred and caught up by them. Of course, if someone has believed up to now that what they see with their eyes and hear with their ears is real, and then realizes that this reality could not even have produced an eye or an ear, but that behind this reality there must exist what I have described, they are naturally deeply shaken by the experience.

Again, the essential thing is to realize that we cannot come to knowledge of this kind if we stay within the dead concepts of nature that we have in ordinary life. When we enter this other world everything immediately comes alive. We say to ourselves: the mountain as we knew it is a dead thing. We did not know that there was something alive in it. But there *is* something alive there; now we are aware of it. Previously we thought of the cloud as dead, but now the living element in it appears which we did not see before. Everything comes alive. But within this living weaving a 'being-ness' is likewise revealed.

In that world we no longer squeeze natural laws out of our brain, but stand face to face with a spiritual being, the goddess Natura, who tells us these things, shows them to us, communicates real things to us. We are enlightened about the facts of our environment by a being of a supersensory world. We step out of the abstractness of the laws of the [physical] world and into a sphere of 'being-ness', where instead of formulating natural laws as the result of experimentation and cognition, we feel ourselves in the presence of beings of a different world, beings who instruct us because they know what we, as human beings, have yet to learn.

In this way we enter the spiritual world by a true path. We then realize that if we had senses alone, if only the eye was there with its visual nerves, the nose with its olfactory nerves, the ear with its auditory nerves, and if these nerves were simply united with each other further back, it would not occur to us that such things exist as oxygen, hydrogen, nitrogen, and so on, that all the things exist that we as humans perceive between birth and death. We would look out into the world of the elements; everywhere we would perceive earth, water, air, fire. Further differentiations of the solid-earthly, the fluid-watery elements, would be of as little interest to us as small change to a millionaire. We would simply have no interest in them. From the nerves emanating from our senses we have knowledge, as sensory beings, of the world of the elements. The moment we become aware of what I have just spoken about, we also become aware of the significance of the fact that in us as human beings the nerves and senses, as they go further back, become more differentiated, more perfected, and develop something internally as the brain. Because of this we do not enter more deeply into ourselves but go more out of ourselves and add to the nature of the four elements—earth, fire, air, and water—everything else that we learn to know between birth and death.

[orange, red]

But this whole brain that is heaped up through the elaborations of the visual, auditory and other nerves as they run backwards, this whole brain that is so valuable to us as human beings, only has significance between birth and death. That which is so particularly elaborated in the human cranium is only significant for earthly life; so far as the spiritual world is concerned it is of no importance at all.

This is why we must shut out the brain when we wish to enter even the first of the spiritual spheres that border on our world. The brain must be shut out. It is a terrible disturbance for higher perception. But even having shut out the brain we must still live in the senses, but now receiving impressions in the senses from the awakened spiritual element; then we receive Imaginations. In the ordinary course of events the senses perceive sense-pictures in the external physical world, and the brain transforms these pictures into abstract thoughts—dead, abstract thoughts. When we shut out the brain we live once more in the senses and perceive everything in Imaginations. We become aware of this. We also then realize that entry into the deeper strata of life is bound up with the development of states of consciousness that are higher and more spiritual than those of ordinary life.

Our senses, situated on the surface of our physical being—eyes, ears, and so on—perceive this world of the elements all the time (see drawing, red), and they perceive the dead in this world years after they have died. That all this is obliterated in ordinary life is due to the fact that behind the senses lies the brain (orange). So here (referring to drawing) is a person with their brain, their senses. The outer senses on the surface of their being look into the spiritual world and behold the dead in the years after their death. But the brain obliterates it all, obliterates earth, water, fire, air; and the person, as they stand there, perceives in sharp contours all that exists as the physical world they live in between birth and death. A world of a quite different kind is there. It is obliterated by the brain, and we look on the world that is known to us as the world of ordinary consciousness.

And so we have the kind of meditation I spoke about yesterday for the modern human being. For people of ancient times such meditation also consisted of the consumption of metallic substances, as discussed in the last lecture. Thus entry into the next higher state of consciousness entails shutting out brain consciousness and sinking with the spirit into the consciousness possessed by the eyes, ears and so on. Animals also have this, for in them the brain has not developed physically behind the senses. But animals do not have an ego-endowed soul, and so cannot dive down with their spirit into their senses. They dive down only with an unrefined soul element, and therefore do not see what humans can see in their environment when they dive down with their spirit into the senses. Animals perceive in the same way, but their perception is lower, non-individualized.

The mystery of Mercury

I ask you, ladies and gentlemen, to take what I am about to say concerning 'metallity'—that is, the real substantiality of the mineral world—with the same caution I mentioned yesterday when I said that the inner enlivening of the soul through the qualities of the metallic nature—that is to say, the development of an inner communion with the metallic nature in a moral sense—belongs, for the modern person, to actual spiritual development. The introduction of metallity into the human organism is a matter for the doctor. And so I ask you to take everything I have yet to say about the mysteries of other metals with this same reservation as for the metals I have already spoken about.

The mystery of mercury has particular significance primarily for those who view the world spiritually, that is to say, those who can look at physical nature, physical substances in such a way that they see the active spiritual element working behind them. The actual metal mercury is only one part of what in spiritual science is known as the mercurial principle. Everything that is metallic and fluid is mercurial, it is just that in our present condition of nature there is only one metal, quicksilver, that is both metallic and fluid and therefore mercurial. But this is only *one* individual from the mercurial genus. When we speak of the mercurial principle in spiritual science, we are speaking in a general sense, considering quicksilver as the representative metal. A mystery of great significance lies behind this quicksilver or mercury. Its effect upon humans is to shut out from them the effects they experience from the physical world, and also from the elemental world I have just described.

As human beings we stand in the world in such a way that we have formed organs like our brain out of the physical world. Many other organs have been built up from the physical world as well, in particular many of the glandular organs that are so essential to physical life. Further, many organs—I have already spoken about the senses— have developed out of the world I described as the second condition of consciousness. Copper and iron take us into this second world. But things are different with mercury.

Mercury has to exist in the universe. And in highly rarefied dosage it is indeed everywhere. We live, if I may express it so, in an atmosphere of mercury. But the moment we absorb more than this normal mercury, our organism begins to attempt to shut out all the organs that are derived from the physical world and the world of the elements. The human astral body is stimulated, as it were, to make use only of those organs that are derived from the world of stars. Hence, directly the consciousness is concentrated on the metallic nature of mercury, on the metallic-fluid principle, on the strangely intangible quality of the mercurial element that is nevertheless related to the human being, we become inwardly filled with a 'third man.'

We saw that through our relationship to copper the human being is filled with a 'second man' that pulls and pushes us, and is able to leave the physical body and then follow the dead in the early years of their after-death existence. Quicksilver immediately attracts to itself everything that calls into existence within us a far, far denser inner soul organism. With all that arises within us through quicksilver, we feel as if we are taking hold of the whole metabolism of our organs. When we experience the strong metallic influence of quicksilver we feel how the fluids flow through the various vessels, and we are suddenly caught up by this.

This is not something that could be described as particularly wonderful or pleasant, for we feel as though we have no brain, no senses. We feel as though everything within us is in activity and movement, is swarming and tingling with weaving life. Everything in us is suddenly lively and active. And we feel this inner liveliness to be associated with a liveliness outside.

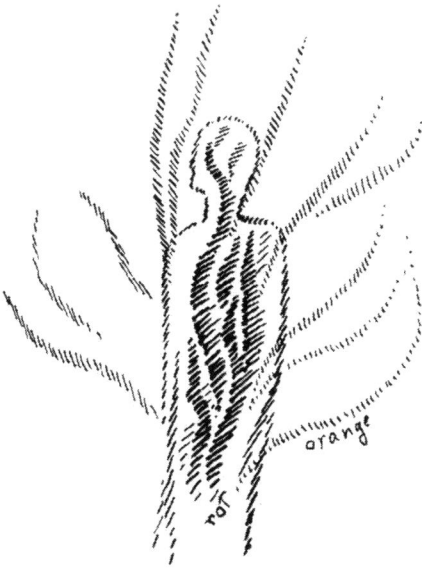

[words in diagram: red orange]

All this, undergone consciously through training the soul in the way I described, can be roughly represented in a diagram like this (see drawing to left). Through the influence of the quicksilver impulse we cease to feel the brain; it becomes a hole. This is good for the perception of the spiritual world since the brain is of no use for that. Other organs are also not yet felt. What we do feel, however, is movement passing through the whole organism (red). All these movements hurt initially, are painful as though we were inwardly weary.

These movements are connected everywhere with external movements (orange). The inner activity is connected with an outer activity. We have the impression that we have left the earth and the world of elements; they are all below us. They smoke and steam. But spiritual beings live in this vaporous, airy, steaming movement. Divine Natura of whom Brunetto Latini speaks so vividly has turned round.

As I said yesterday, Natura is the same as the Greek Persephone. Previously she turned her countenance more towards the earth and illuminated for us those things that are still connected with the earthly, such as the first periods of our life after death. Now she turns round and we have the earthly and elemental beneath us, and above us the world of stars. Just as on earth we were surrounded by plants and animals, our environment now is the world of the stars. But we do not now feel: what a little squirt I am in face of this world of stars! We feel our size in relation to the world of stars to be the same as it is in relation to our immediate environment on earth. For we have also become big. We have grown in size into the world of stars. But the stars are not as we saw them with our eyes on earth: they reveal themselves as colonies of spiritual beings. We are once again in the world which I described as being called forth in us as a result of our relationship with the metallic nature of tin. There is an inner relationship between mercury and tin. Mercury takes hold of a certain part of our being, lifts it out of the rest of our being, and bears this part into that spiritual world whose external, physical manifestation is the world of stars.

But we are now once again somewhere else because the condition of our consciousness has altered; it is not now determined by the senses or the brain but by what the metallity of mercury has lifted out of our organism. We are in an entirely different world. We are now in the world of stars. But I could put it differently: the expression 'the world of stars' is the spatial aspect; but in reality we journey in this condition of consciousness out of the world in which we exist spatially between birth and death, and are now in the world where we live between death and a new birth.

The mystery of mercury is indeed that mercury bears us out of the world we live in as physical beings of sense into the world in which we live between death and a new birth. This is because mercury, quicksilver, has an inner relationship to the part of our being that is not derived from this earth but is borne into us from the world in which we live between death and a new birth. The circulation of fluids that we now experience is not of this physical world, but is determined out of the world we pass through between death and a new birth.

And now we become aware of something else, again something that Brunetto Latini perceived under the influence of the goddess Natura. We become aware that we live within our circulation of fluids, but that this is connected with the circulation of fluids in the whole cosmos. We have passed out of ourselves into the realm we live in between death and rebirth. Now we learn to know the nature of this circulation of fluids, we learn to know how our temperament has been formed in this inner activity, in this realm we pass through between death and rebirth—formed in such a way that we have become either sanguine, choleric, melancholic, or phlegmatic beings. We have a deeper understanding of our being than we have as sense-beings. If in life our nature is phlegmatic, for example, we must say to ourselves that our phlegma is determined by what we experienced between our last death and our present birth. It is the same with the choleric, the melancholic, and the sanguine temperaments.

But something else is mingled in this temperament that has its physical expression in the circulation of the fluids. Just think for a moment what we have in this circulation. If we proceed like an anatomist or physiologist, what we have before us is something physical. But the physical is only an expression of the spiritual, and the spiritual element connected with this circulation of fluids is not of the earthly world: it is of the world that works into us between death and a new birth. So that when we consider our temperament—and what amazed Brunetto Latini most of all was the illumination he received from the goddess Natura with regard to the temperaments—when we study temperaments, we can say that these temperaments that have their root in the circulation of fluids, are given their stamp by our life between death and rebirth. If we now go deeper we find that intermingled with all this is what we call karma, the trials of destiny.

If we look at this remarkable metallic fluid of mercury in its physical state, we only really get to know it properly when we realize that its mystery lies in the fact that in a single drop of liquid mercury a profound and far-reaching connection is revealed to the initiate: for this drop is able to draw the spiritual element in human beings into the organs whose formation and origin lie in the life between death and rebirth.

Thus everything in the world is interwoven and interconnected. The physical is only illusion, a physical illusion. For the physical, the spiritual is just an illusion, an abstract illusion. The truth is that physical is interwoven with spiritual, and spiritual with physical. If we observe a disorder that arises in the human organism, and find it to be due to trouble in those organs that are actually formed out of the land we live in between death and rebirth, then we must awaken forces in the human organism that can cure the disorder.

Suppose a doctor sees that a man has a defect in his circulatory system, in the circulation that receives its impulses from the life between death and rebirth. He is confronted with a sick man whose circulatory system has torn itself away from the spiritual world. That is the phenomenon; the diagnosis is a spiritual one. The spiritual element in relation to the physical diagnosis is always to be taken in the sense I explained yesterday. I emphasize this again to avoid misunderstandings. The diagnosis is that the man's circulatory system has torn itself away too strongly from the spiritual world we pass through between death and a new birth.

So what can we do?

Therapeutically we must introduce, in the appropriate way, a metallity into the body that brings the circulation of the fluids back into contact with the spiritual world. This is how mercury works on us. Mercury works on the human organism in such a way that it brings those organs which can only be formed out of the spiritual world, back into contact with that spiritual world when they have torn themselves away from it. Here we see the essential, although at the same time somewhat dangerous, connection that exists between knowledge of the states of consciousness in the human being and the understanding of diseases. The one passes over into the other.

These things played a very great role in the ancient mysteries. And they shed light on subjects like the one we discussed yesterday. Think of it: in an age when humanity had long since lost the spiritual vision that recognized the goddess Natura as a teacher of the secrets of nature, Brunetto Latini, the teacher of Dante, returns from his ambassadorial post in Spain in a state of agitation. He reaches the neighbourhood of his own city where he is further agitated by news of the fate of his own party, the Guelph party. He does all this in a state that produces a slight sunstroke in him. In short, the metallic nature of mercury worked upon him out of his environment.

For what does it mean when we say we have slight sunstroke? It means we have been affected by the mercury that exists everywhere in highly rarefied form in our surroundings in the cosmos. This was what affected Brunetto Latini. And as a result, in an age when it was otherwise impossible for people to approach the spiritual world in this way, it became possible for him to do so.

This shows you that in the human being as he stands before us there is something that is related not only to what is presented to us by the scientific researcher, not only to what is presented to us by one who can follow the dead in the early years of their after-death existence, but that in the human being as it lives in us, there is a relation to something far more sublime, something entirely spiritual in the way we experience it between death and a new birth. We can grasp the form of the liver, the form of the lungs, by the means of ordinary science. With the next kind of knowledge we can understand the structure of the sense organs, but the approach of our modern physics lacks subtlety here. But we can never really understand the unique nature of the circulation of the upright human being, nor the mysteries of the metals, if we do not approach them with initiation science. This means that without initiation science we can never understand the nature of diseases in the sense I have described, because the physical attributes of the metals do not help. If you understand the physical properties of the metals, it is possible to heal the brain. But you cannot heal the circulation of fluids. But even what I have just said is not strictly accurate, because it is only the coarsest part of the brain that you can heal. For there is a circulation of fluids in the brain also; and therefore in reality one cannot really heal brain trouble with metals, only with spiritual knowledge.

You may say: 'Yes, but why is it then that modern medicine can heal nevertheless?' Modern medical science heals through the traditions that still remain for it from olden times. A remnant remains of what the ancients knew with regard to the spiritual element in metals. This is made use of; but it is mixed up with what has been discovered by purely physical means and which is not much help. If materialism were ever to be victorious and all the rest forgotten, no remedy discovered by purely physical means would help any more.

We are already standing at the point in human evolution where, because the ancient traditions stemming from primeval clairvoyance are gradually disappearing, the spiritual must be found in a new way.

The mystery of Silver

The mystery behind the metallity of silver is again of a very special kind. Whereas we can say that behind copper there is the cosmic impulse that conjures up the first 'higher human' into the human being; and that behind mercury there is a second force that conjures up a second human who is related to the world of stars and thereby to the spiritual world in which we live between death and a new birth; when it comes to the metallity of silver we must say something completely different.

When we intensify and heighten our relationship to silver in the way we saw with regard to the metallities of copper and mercury, we turn to a still deeper organization within ourselves. With mercury we turned to the vascular system, which brings us into connection with a circulation in the whole cosmos, with the spirituality of the cosmos. By intensifying our relationship to silver, we bring ourselves into direct contact with what sends its forces and impulses to us from earlier lives on earth.

So we can say: if we concentrate on the special properties of silver (and it is often a long time before results are obtained), we draw together within ourselves not only the forces connected with the circulation of fluids through the vessels, but also the forces that cause warmth to flow through the circulation of the blood. Then a truth becomes clear to us: that in the warmth circulating in our blood—which actually makes us human beings in the first place because we sense a certain warmth in ourselves and thus also blood-substance and even blood-spirituality—in this blood-warmth the forces are active that work in from former incarnations. And in our relationship to silver we have a direct expression of something that can have an effect on the warmth impulse of the blood. This therefore also expresses what leads us spiritually to earlier earth lives.

Just think—in silver we have the metallity which draws our attention, as it were, to elements in us in this earthly life which have come over from earlier incarnations. For our blood circulation, with its marvellous differentiations of temperature, does not come from this physical world. Nor does it come from the world of the elements which I have described to you. Nor does it come only from the world of stars. The course and direction of blood circulation is derived from the world of the stars; but in the actual warmth of the blood, whose pulsations permeate our life, there works the force that flows from earlier lives on earth. It is directly to this force [of former lives] that we appeal when we turn to the forces of silver as they relate to the human being. Thus the mystery of silver is connected with repeated lives on earth.

Silver is one of the most startling examples of the fact that spirituality is everywhere, even in the physical. Those who can look on silver with the right eyes know that silver is the gods' external sign for the cycles of human lives on earth. Hence the mystery of silver is also bound up with reproduction and all the secrets relating to it, because it is through the processes of reproduction that our human being is carried from life to life. The spiritual being that existed in previous earthly lives enters physical life once more through the process of reproduction. But this is the same mystery as the mystery of the blood. And the secret, the mystery of the blood, is the mystery of silver. We can say here that the mystery of our blood-warmth is the mystery of silver.

Again the current of knowledge leads us from our normal condition to pathological conditions. Bear in mind that the blood should not receive its warmth from the world of the present but from the worlds we passed through in earlier incarnations. Now suppose that the warmth of someone's blood is compromised by the present world, that it is not receiving impulses from what connects it by a spiritual thread to earlier incarnations. Then those pathological conditions appear which, we can say, arise because everything that is connected with our blood-warmth has torn itself away from what it actually needs to be connected with, from earlier earth lives.

What is fever? In a spiritual sense, fever is the result of the separation of the human organization from its normal integration in the continuing effects of previous lives on earth. If in a case of illness the doctor is able to diagnose that the external world has worked upon an individual in such a way that it threatens to wrench their organization away from earlier earth-lives, then the doctor will have recourse to a therapy using silver. A very good example can be cited here from Dr Wegman's Clinic in Arlesheim.[12] A condition that can arise spiritually in the way I described, where, as the result of external circumstances, the blood system of the human organism suddenly threatens to tear away from former earthly lives—this condition can arise very suddenly. A short while ago in the Clinic, there was a particular case of an 'occult fever' as it is called in materialistic medicine—a sudden and wholly unexpected high temperature in a convalescent patient. Dr Wegman suddenly found herself faced with this case. Acting out of her inspired medical knowledge she immediately administered a silver cure. When she told me about it the whole case showed itself in its wonderful connection with the cosmos. We see here how things play to-and-fro in their connection with human evolution and its spirituality on the one hand, and with what leads to pathology, but then to therapy, on the other.

How is it then that the initiate can have an overview of former earthly lives? So long as we are connected [to previous lives] in the way we are in ordinary life, where through our karma we just march on with previous lives having their effect, we cannot see our previous lives. Here we are in our present life. We are connected with our previous lives; they work into our present. They work in such a way that, under their influence, we work out our karma; we march through the world according to our karma. But we cannot look back [on our earlier incarnations] with ordinary consciousness. If we want to look back we must first sever the thread for short moments, must tear ourselves loose from it. When we have torn ourselves loose, when our previous earthly lives have become objective, then we can look back at them. We must of course attain the ability—I will speak of this later on—to attach the thread again and restore normality. If we cannot attach the thread once more we become mentally disturbed, not an initiate.

So here we have a phenomenon that occurs in the course of spiritual development: the disruption of the spiritual threads that link us to our former earthly lives. This can happen abnormally, in a pathological way, in the case of disease. Sickness is the abnormal occurrence of something which, in a higher sphere, must be brought about normally for spiritual vision, for other states of consciousness. Just as other organs of the body have special states of consciousness that I have already spoken about, so the blood also has a special consciousness of its own. Now if the blood, separated from the rest of the human organism, gives itself up to its own consciousness, if it emancipates itself from the rest of the organism, it looks back in this abnormal state into previous earthly lives. But this all remains subconscious. To look back consciously, the thread must first be broken. To look back pathologically, the thread does not need to break.

Silver proves to be a wonderful remedy in all diseases that can be traced back to karma, and so the study of the mystery of silver leads us deeply into other cosmic mysteries.

We have now spoken of all the metallities that are connected with various conditions of human consciousness. In the next lecture we will continue our study of these conditions of consciousness and of the relationship we can establish through them to other worlds. In other words, we will continue on the right path to spirituality.

LECTURE 6

16 AUGUST 1924

Initiation Science

Waking and dream consciousness

I HAVE spoken of different states of consciousness which it is possible to develop out of the forces of the human soul. What we call initiation science depends on the fact that our knowledge of the world is formed through these different states of consciousness.

Today we will try to form an idea of how, through these states of consciousness, the human being can relate to the world. First of all we need to bear in mind that as far as the life of present-day civilization is concerned, in everything that humanity today recognizes as reality, as existence, there is only one state of consciousness: that of *waking life*. But we can say that apart from this there are two other states of consciousness for humanity in the present world cycle; but these cannot be regarded initially as reliable for the purposes of knowledge. There is the condition of dream consciousness in which at present we only experience reminiscences of events of the day or small glimpses from the spiritual life. But in ordinary dream these reminiscences, as well as the glimpses or the revelations from the spiritual world, are so garbled, so submersed in all kinds of distorted imagery and symbolism, that no knowledge can be obtained from them.

If with the help of initiation science we try to answer the question: 'Where are we really living when we dream?' the answer will be somewhat as follows. As human beings here in ordinary life, we have, in the first place, our physical body, the body perceived by the senses and studied by the sciences of anatomy, physiology and biology. This is the first member of our human constitution, the member which everybody thinks they know, but about which, as we shall see, they really know least of all in our age.

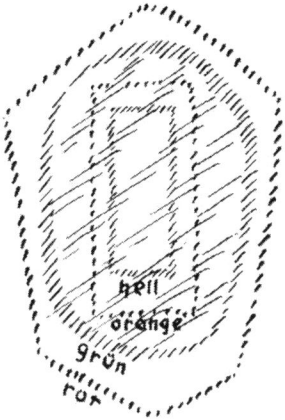

[from top downwards: light, orange, green, red]

A second member of the human being's constitution is the etheric body, of which a more detailed description is given in my books, *Theosophy* and *Occult Science*. The etheric body, or body of formative forces, is a subtle structure that cannot be seen with the eyes but can only be perceived once we have developed the first condition of consciousness I spoke about previously, that consciousness which is able to follow the dead in the first years of their after-death existence. This etheric body, or body of formative forces (orange) is much more intimately bound up with the cosmos than the physical body, whose whole organization is more independent.

Then we have a third member of our human constitution which of course we can give any name we like, but using an ancient terminology we call it the astral body (green). This is a structure that cannot be perceived with the senses; neither can it be perceived in the same way as the etheric body. If we were to try to perceive the astral body using the forces of cognition we use to perceive external nature today, or with the forces of cognition I described as those of the next higher consciousness by which we are able to follow the existence of the dead, we should see nothing but a void, a non-existence, where the astral body is.

So we can say (pointing to the board): Human beings bear within themselves the physical body that is perceptible to the senses, and the etheric body. The etheric body (orange) is perceptible to Imagination; it becomes perceptible through the forces we can acquire by the practice of meditation and concentration in the way pointed out.

But if we approach the human astral body with all these forces, we become aware of nothing but a void, a spatial nothing, like a hole enclosed on all sides in space (green). Only when we reach the empty consciousness I described—that is, when in a fully waking state we can confront the world in such a way that we perceive nothing at all of its sense nature, our thinking and memories are silent, and yet we nevertheless perceive a world—only then does this void fill with content, and we know that in it we have our first spiritual principle: the human astral body.

A further member of the human organization is the ego itself (red). We only perceive the ego when empty consciousness is developed further and further.

When we dream, the situation is that our our physical body and etheric body (or body of formative forces) lie in bed and are separated from the astral body and ego which are in the spiritual world. But we cannot perceive with the astral body and ego if we only possess ordinary consciousness. How is it that we receive external impressions in the ordinary world between birth and death? It is because we have eyes and ears implanted in the physical body. Human constitution in the present epoch of world evolution is such that in ordinary life we have no corresponding organs—no eyes or ears—in the astral body or ego. Hence when we pass out of our physical and etheric bodies and into dreaming, it is the same as if we had a physical body in the physical world with no eyes or ears, and everything around us were dark and silent. But the astral body and ego need not remain without organs for ever, without eyes and ears—but of a soul-nature, of course. Precisely the soul-training discussed in my books is able to bring about the formation of these organs—soul eyes, soul ears, and so on—in the astral body and ego. Then it becomes possible for us, with initiation sight, to see into the spiritual world. We pass out of our physical and etheric bodies and perceive the spiritual, just as in the physical and etheric bodies we perceive the physical and, in a certain sense, also the etheric. This is what happens to one who has attained to initiation.

Now what is the situation with the ordinary dreamer? Try to picture as clearly as you can the process of falling asleep. The physical body (see drawing, light) and etheric body (orange) remain lying in bed, while the astral body (green) and the ego (red) leave. (I naturally have to draw this diagrammatically.) At the moment when this happens, the astral body is still vibrating completely in unison with the physical and etheric bodies. The astral body leaves, but it has participated in all the inner activity of the eyes and ears, and in what the will has carried out in the movements of the physical and etheric bodies from morning to evening. The astral body and ego have experienced and co-operated in all this. And now they leave, and everything continues to vibrate, it is all still in there. But while the day's experiences here (see drawing below, points are drawn) are continuing to vibrate, they come up everywhere against the surrounding spiritual world, and a chaotic, disordered interplay arises between the activity of the outer spiritual world and what continues to vibrate in the astral body. There is a disordered chaos—that is a tautology, so let us simply say a chaos arises. And the human being is inside all this and perceives it. What he has brought with him makes an impression on him, goes on vibrating and becomes the dream.

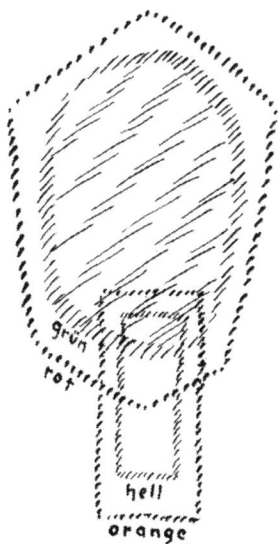

[from top to bottom: green, red, light, orange]

But you will certainly appreciate that in terms of reality this is not of much use. But how is it for the initiate? The initiate is able, when he passes here (Steiner draws on the board) out of his physical and etheric bodies, to suppress all these reminiscences and after-vibrations. So he suppresses what proceeds from the physical and etheric bodies. Besides this, the initiate has been able, through concentration, meditation and the development of empty consciousness, to acquire eyes and ears of soul. He no longer perceives what is happening in himself but what is happening in the spiritual world outside him. Instead of dreams, perceptions of the spiritual world arise. We can therefore say: *dream-consciousness is a chaotic counterpart of spiritual perception.*

When at the first higher stage the initiate has developed these inner astral organs, this astral sight and hearing, he stands perpetually in a kind of conflict, a conflict where he has to suppress these reminiscences and vibrations from the physical and etheric bodies. When he enters into the imaginative world, into the perceptions of the spiritual, he has to fight continually against allowing dreams to assert themselves. There is a constant interplay between what wants to become dreamlike and deceive him, and what represents the truth of the spiritual world.

Every would-be initiate comes to know this conflict. He learns to realize that at the moment he strives to enter the spiritual world with knowledge, the after-pictures of the physical world rise up again and again and interpose themselves as disturbing images before the true pictures of the spiritual world. And only patience and endurance can overcome the intense inner conflict that arises. If we are superficially satisfied with our consciousness being filled with spiritual pictures, we can very easily dream ourselves into a world of illusion instead of passing into the world of spiritual reality. Anyone who is approaching initiation must possess an inner stance that is exceptionally strong and rational. Just think what all this entails! But when it is a question of speaking of the paths into the spiritual world, of spiritual research, attention must be directed to such things.

To approach the spiritual world at all we must be able on the one hand to have a real enthusiasm for entering it. Any kind of inner lethargy, inner indifference, inner languor, is a hindrance. We must have real inner mobility, inner energy. This may, on the other hand, easily lead us into a realm of fantasy, to fantasize up any number of things. We must have a disposition that could, if we were to let ourselves go, lead us into the loftiest heights of imagination on the one hand, and on the other we must combine this inner mobility and activity with a calm sobriety.

The initiate must possess both these qualities. It is not good simply to let oneself go; neither is it good to be led prosaically by the intellect and to try to reason everything out. We must be able to weave both together harmoniously. We must have the disposition on the one hand to become a thorough dreamer, but also always the possibility of *not* becoming one. We must constantly have in the soul, in *status nascendi,* the ability to rise up into all sorts of things of the mobile imagination. But on the other hand we must always have the ability, as soon as the *status* shows itself, to take ourselves in hand with inner firmness. We must have the potential to be an imaginative poet, but at the same time the potential not to need to give way to this. At any moment when we wish to pursue knowledge, we must also have the potential to create a drama, a lyrical poem and plenty more. But we must be able to stop this tendency to drift into the imagination, and be able to hold ourselves firmly to the forces which otherwise have significance only in the most sober life. Then we do not pass into a world of fantasy but into spiritual reality.

This inner constitution of soul is of the very greatest importance in genuine spiritual research. When we direct our attention with understanding to dream consciousness and recognize it to be what throws up chaotic pictures out of the spiritual world, we also realize that, in order to acquire spiritual knowledge, the whole force of the personality must now flow into the soul-power that otherwise only dreams. Only then do we get an idea of what it means to enter into the spiritual world. I have said that dream consciousness does indeed throw up the spiritual. This may appear to contradict the fact that dream consciousness also presents us with pictures derived from corporeal life. But the body is not only bodily, it is permeated everywhere with spirituality. Suppose someone dreams that a tasty meal is before them, smelling superb and promising to taste delicious, and—in the dream of course—they set about eating it although they have in their pocket not one tenth of the money this meal would cost. In the symbol of the meal the real spiritual, astral content of the organs of digestion is presented in a picture. It is always the spirit there in the dream, albeit the spirit that has its seat in the bodily nature. The dream always brings up the spiritual element, but very often it is the spiritual element in the bodily nature. This must be realized and understood.

We must recognize that if we dream of snakes, there we have a symbol of the coils of the digestive organs or of the blood vessels in the head. We must penetrate into these secrets, for we can only form an idea of these subtle, intimate elements that must make their appearance in the soul, when we begin to practise spiritual research through initiation science, that is to say, when we study these things in their most intimate sense.

The ages of life as organs of perception

A third state we pass through in ordinary life is that of *dreamless sleep*. Let us be clear once more how things stand for us in dreamless sleep. The physical and etheric bodies lie in the bed. The astral body and ego-organization are outside the physical and etheric bodies. The vibrations and reminiscences from the physical and etheric bodies have ceased. We are in the spiritual world only in our astral body and ego. But we have no organs. We can perceive nothing. Around us all is darkness. We sleep. This is what existence in sleep is: living in the ego and astral body without being able to perceive the rich, manifold world around us. Think of a blind man. All the colours and forms which you perceive around you with your eyes do not exist for him. He is asleep to colours and forms. We cannot sleep in general, we can only be asleep to something in particular.

Now imagine someone living in their astral body and ego, but without any organs. So far as the spiritual is concerned they sleep. This is our condition in dreamless sleep. The purpose of meditation and concentration is to develop spiritual eyes and ears in the astral body and ego-organization, and then we begin to behold and perceive all the richness and abundance that is there. We perceive spiritually. Precisely with this we perceive spiritually what in ordinary consciousness we pass by in the world asleep. We must arouse this through meditation and concentration. The unorganized elements we otherwise have in us must be organized. Then we gaze into the spiritual world. And then we stand in this spiritual world in the same way as we stand in the physical world with eyes and ears. This is true initiation-knowledge. It is not possible by external means to make someone ready to perceive the spiritual. It is only possible for them to do this themselves by really ordering their own inner being which otherwise remains disordered.

Now at all times in the evolution of humanity there has existed the endeavour to bring certain individuals to initiation. This endeavour has, however, suffered a certain interruption in the age of crude materialism from the fifteenth century to our day. People have forgotten, as it were, what real initiation is. They have wanted to gain without initiation all the knowledge they sought, and so have gradually come to believe that only the physical world is relevant.

But what is this physical world in reality? We do not know it if we only know it as physical world. We only get to know it when we can also really grasp the spirit that it always bears within itself. Humanity must attain to this once more. The significance of the great turning point of our age lies in the fact that the world presents a picture of destruction, of increasing chaos; but in this chaos, in this terrible fury of human passions that casts darkness over everything and would finally bring it all into decadence, there is revealed, to those who have insight, the impulse of the spiritual powers who stand behind it all and are ready to lead humanity into a new spirituality. And the right preparation for anthroposophical spiritual science consists in listening to the voice of the spirit that is sounding into our materialistic existence.

I have said that in all ages there has been a striving to develop the human organization so as to enable it to see into the spiritual world. But conditions were different then. When we go back into very ancient times of human evolution, into the Chaldean epoch for instance, or even just to epochs like that of Brunetto Latini, we find that people were not so firmly united with their physical and etheric bodies as they are today. Today people are thoroughly entrenched in their physical and etheric bodies. And they have to be entrenched, for that is how they are educated. Indeed, how can people be expected to converse with spirits when they have had to learn to read and write before the change of teeth! Angels— spiritual beings—cannot read and write; reading and writing were invented in the course of human evolution as the result of physical conditions. And if we direct our whole being to something invented only in the physical world, it is naturally difficult for us to get out of our physical and etheric bodies.

In a sense our age prides itself on having organized all our culture in such a way that it prevents us, when we separate from our physical and etheric bodies, from experiencing anything. I am not complaining about this culture, and I have no wish to criticize it. It had to come and be how it is. I will talk in due course about what this signifies, but this is how it is.

In olden times the astral body and ego were much more independent of the physical and etheric bodies, also during waking, than they are today. But this natural greater independence was something the initiates also depended on. In very ancient times of human evolution almost everyone could be initiated into the mysteries. Anyone could be chosen from humanity. But this was in very ancient times, in the oldest days of the primal Indian and primal Persian civilizations.

Then came epochs when it was necessary to select individuals for initiation who left their physical and etheric bodies easily, individuals whose astral body and ego had a relatively high degree of independence. The fact that humanity was now dependent on certain conditions was no hindrance in the way of the efforts that could be made to bring someone as far in initiation as was possible. And efforts were indeed made. But beyond a certain point the success was largely dependent on whether the individual could attain to independence in their ego and astral body easily or only with difficulty. It depended on a particular nature in the human being, on disposition. This is because we are placed in the world, and in a certain sense we must necessarily be dependent on the world [for our nature and disposition] as long as we are living between birth and death.

Now you could ask whether people today are still subject in initiation to conditions of this kind? In a certain sense they are. And I am going to tell you of these conditions, because I want to speak very clearly and fully in these lectures of the true and false paths into the spiritual worlds. We should place everything clearly before our souls.

The human being of ancient times was more dependent on natural disposition when he became an initiate. The modern human being can also be brought to initiation and it is right that by means of an adequate training and discipline of soul he can so fashion his astral body and ego that they can gaze into the spiritual world and have spiritual perceptions. But so far as the completeness, the perfection of these perceptions is concerned, he is still today dependent on something. Here we must consider something that is very subtle and intimate, and I ask you not to come to any final judgement of what I shall say today before you have considered the content of the next lectures. I can only develop very gradually the things I have to say to you.

In initiation today we are in a certain sense dependent on our age in life. To take a concrete case, let us suppose that a man is 37 years old when he approaches initiation. He has lived from birth to his thirty-seventh year, and intends to go on living. Suppose that under guidance, as is usual, or by independent reading, he now undertakes meditation, concentration, or some other soul-discipline, and as the result of repeated penetration into a thought-content, acquires first of all the faculty to look back over his earthly life. His earthly life stands before his soul as a single, integrated tableau.

So he is 37 years old. Just as we otherwise look into space and see people sitting here in the first row, then the second row, over there a table, and behind that the wall and so on, just as we see it all there in perspective, so at a certain stage of initiation we see *time*. It is as if the course of time had become spatial. You see [over] there that you are 37 years old; [there] you had certain experiences when you were 36; other experiences [there] when you were 35. And so it goes on to your birth. You can look at it and have it before you as a single tableau.

But now let us suppose that we make this backward review at a certain stage of initiation. If we are 37, we will be able to look back into the period through which we passed from birth until about the seventh year, to the time of the change of teeth. It lies far back, and we look at it. Then we will be able to look into the period between the seventh and fourteenth year, up to the age of puberty. And then we can look back on the period between 14 and 21 and see what is there. We can then look at the rest of life up to our thirty-seventh year.

We can see all this in what we could call a 'space-time perspective'. If we can now add to our gaze in the space-time perspective the consciousness that proceeds from empty waking consciousness, a certain power of vision jerks through us. We become inspired. But the inspirations are of very different kinds. Our experiences from birth to the seventh year inspire us differently, conjure up before our soul something that differs from the experiences of the fourteenth to the twenty-first year and so on. Every such life-period yields a different power.

But we can, of course, grow older than 37. We can reach 63 or 64. Then we have an overview of the later life-periods also. The period between 21 and 42 appears more or less uniform. After that the whole thing becomes differentiated again. There are significant differences in what we see from the forty-second to the forty-ninth year, from the forty-ninth to the fifty-sixth, and again from the fifty-sixth to the sixty-third year. As we look back, the differences are very evident. But this is we ourselves, what we are spiritually in our earthly life. When we are inspired, our childhood from the seventh to the fourteenth year gives us a different inspiration from that of our adolescence, from the fourteenth to the twenty-first year. Again a somewhat different inspiration comes from the experiences of our life between 21 and 42, and after that again come the somewhat more differentiated forces that proceed from the later life-periods.

Let us suppose, then, that we have acquired the capacity to look with picture-consciousness into our own experiences, and have also attained to the inspiration of empty consciousness, so that we have then extinguished the [picture-]consciousness and its forces, and we no longer look at the eyes but *through* the eyes. Suppose that through inspiration we have reached a point where we no longer look at our life-periods with their events, but we see and hear *through* them. We look through the life-periods lying between the seventh and fourteenth year, between the forty-ninth and fifty-sixth year, and so on, just as we once saw and heard in the ordinary world. In the ordinary world we make use of eyes and ears; in the world of inspiration we make use of a force that proceeds from the period between the seventh and fourteenth years, or of a force that proceeds from the period between the forty-second and forty-ninth year. [In the world of inspiration] the life-periods have become differentiated organs of cognition.

So today we are in a certain sense dependent on our age. At the age of 37 we can speak very well out of [the wisdom of] initiation, but we can speak differently out of initiation at the age of 63 because other organs have then unfolded within us. The life-periods are organs.

Now suppose that, not out of books but out of the consciousness of inspiration, we set out to describe personalities like Brunetto Latini or Alanus ab Insulis—I take these more familiar examples because we have been considering them so recently—so suppose I wish to describe them. If we try to describe them when we are 37, we have the following experience. The personalities stand there in the spiritual world before our awakened sleep-consciousness. We can converse with them as we do with physical human beings—I say this, of course, somewhat *cum grano salis*. But the curious thing is that, when they converse in the language of the spiritual life, they can only elucidate for us the wisdom, the inner spirituality, that they have attained at precisely this moment. And then we realize that we can learn very much from them. But we must take it from these spirits on trust and faith. One must hear it from them.

And we do indeed believe it, ladies and gentlemen, for after all it is no trivial matter to stand before a personality like, say, Brunetto Latini in the spiritual world. If the necessary preparation has been made, we do indeed have the possibility of discerning whether we are confronting an illusory dream-image or a spiritual reality. It is then possible to set a value on the communications we receive.

Suppose then we were to converse with Brunetto Latini[13] in the spiritual world, if I can put it so again *cum grano salis*. (You mustn't imagine this as though we were talking in this hall, but we can nevertheless call it a conversation.) So suppose at the age of 37 we had a conversation with Brunetto Latini. He would tell us all sorts of things. But we then get the desire to know many things with greater exactitude, with more accuracy. And lo and behold, Brunetto Latini says to us: 'Yes, but in that case I would have to go back with you from the twentieth century where we now are, back through the nineteenth and eighteenth to my own century. We would have to go back to when I was the teacher of Dante.' And he would say, 'If you wish to take this path with me you must first grow a little older, you must have lived a bit beyond your present life-period. I can tell you everything and you can know it all. You can become a deep initiate, but you cannot come with me. In reality it is through your spiritual will that you cannot really take the path backwards.'

You see, for this we have to be older. We must certainly have passed our forty-second year, and indeed have reached our sixtieth year if we want to go back completely unhindered in the spiritual world with the personality in question.

These things will show you the deeper aspects of our being, and the significance of youth or ripe age. Only when we study these things can we understand why it is that many people die young and many live to riper age, and of this I shall have more to say.

Overlapping starry spheres

We have seen how human soul-life can unfold in perception of the spiritual world as the result of our evolution as a human being. I have shown how our communication with a being living as a discarnate soul in the spiritual world, such as Brunetto Latini, changes according to the conditions of initiation, if the initiate is perceiving with organs yielded by the period of youth or of ripe age. All that can confront us in this way as the outlook for human beings in the earthly world and its evolution, can be expanded if we now ask: how can human insight, human consciousness, grow in another direction? Today I will indicate another such direction in order to speak of it in greater detail in the following lectures.

While we live in the ordinary consciousness of earthly life between birth and death, we have the earth environment around us. If our dreaming were not chaotic, if we perceived in deep dreamless sleep in place of our ordinary consciousness, we would no longer have merely the earth environment around us. We have there other conditions of perception and consciousness, not just the ordinary ones.

Let us now consider the following. Ordinary everyday consciousness is surrounded by the earthly world. I will indicate the immediate
environment of the earth like this (see drawing, page 102, green). We
do not see into the interior of the earth. This is what we have before
us in our ordinary consciousness. Everything else in the cosmos—
sun, moon, and all the other stars—shine into this sphere. We see,
as it were, the cosmic indication of their presence—more strongly
in the case of sun and moon, and more feebly for the other stars.
They send just an indication of their existence into this our physical
world. And physicists would be thoroughly amazed if they could
experience in their way—for they don't want to experience things in
our way—how things really look in the sphere of the moon or the
sun. For things do not look at all as we find them in the textbooks
on astronomy, astrophysics and the like. What we see are only indica-
tions. In ordinary life when people want to know someone standing
in front of them, whom they could talk to, they do not as a rule say:
'My experience of this person is not exact; they must go a long way
off, so far that I can hardly see them; then I will understand them
more precisely, and then I will describe them.'

It is, of course, the result of cosmic necessity, but the physicists
can only describe the stars if they are a long, long way off. But a
transformed and extended consciousness places one in the world
of stars itself. And the first thing we learn is to speak of these star
worlds in a completely differently way from how we speak of them
in ordinary life.

In ordinary life we would say: 'I am here. When it's night I see
the moon there above.' This is correct, of course. We have to slip
into another kind of consciousness to speak differently. It often
takes a long time, but when we do slip into another consciousness,
then we can look at our experiences with that first consciousness
that is able to follow the dead, and can perceive all that we have
lived through from birth to our seventh year, up to the time of the
change of teeth, with a consciousness that has slipped into inspiration and become an inner power of vision—then we see another
world around us. The ordinary world grows dim and indistinct, and
we see another world.

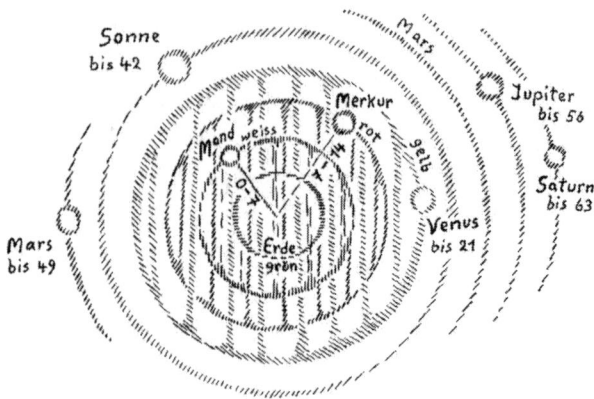

[bis = up to; Mond = moon; Erde = Earth; weiss = white;
grün = green; gelb = yellow; rot = red]

This other world is the moon sphere. (See diagram, white.) And now, when we enter this experience, we no longer say 'I am standing here, and out there is the moon.' We say 'I am within the moon.' Everything within this circle or globe is the moon (diagram), for the orbit of the moon is only the outermost boundary of the moon sphere. We experience ourselves as being within the moon. Now if a child of eight years could be initiated and look back at the first seven years of its life, it could live in the moon sphere in this way. It would be able to gaze into the moon sphere most easily at this point, because it would not be confused by later life. One would naturally not initiate an eight-year-old child, but theoretically it is certainly possible.

So, using the force derived from the first life-period—from birth to the seventh year—we are able to gaze into this moon sphere. Things there are utterly different from how we describe them with ordinary consciousness. I will make a comparison to clarify this for you. When a biologist studies the embryo today, and follows its development from the first stages to later ones, he studies the germ at a certain stage. At a spot lying here at the outer edge a thickening of the substance takes place. There is an inclusion. A kind of germ can be seen. But, although this can be distinctly seen with a microscope, we cannot say that only this is the germ, the embryo, because other things are involved. So it is with the moon, and with the other stars. What one sees there in the sky is only a kind of nucleus, but the whole sphere here (shaded white) belongs to the moon. And the earth is within the moon. And if the germ could turn, the nucleus here would also turn. The moon turns. The whole little body turns. Hence the moon moves here in its orbit.

Hence the ancients, who still knew something of these things, did not speak of the moon but of the *moon sphere*, and in what we now call the moon they saw only a point on the outermost boundary. Every day this point is somewhere else, and in the course of 28 days we see the whole boundary of the moon sphere. The power enabling us to look into the moon sphere, which remains clear when the earth grows dim, is acquired when our inner experiences between birth and the seventh year become inspirative force.

When the experiences of the second life-period—between the change of teeth and puberty—become inspirative force, then we experience the sphere of Mercury (diagram, red.) This is how we experience the second sphere. This here (white) comes from the force of the beginning of life to our seventh year; and this (red) comes from the force of our seventh to fourteenth year.

Here again the earth is within Mercury. The experiences of the Mercury sphere only become visible when we can consciously penetrate back with perception into our earthly experiences between our seventh and fourteenth year. With the inspirative force that proceeds from the period after puberty up to the twenty-first year, we live in the Venus sphere (diagram, yellow). The ancients were by no means ignorant. With their dreamlike knowledge they knew a great deal about these things, and they designated the planetary sphere into which human beings pass after puberty by a name associated with the love-life which begins during this period.

When we consciously look back on our experiences between the twenty-first and forty-second years, we know ourselves to be within the sun sphere (diagram).

The single life-periods, when they are transformed in this way into inner organs, give us the power to extend our consciousness step by step out into the cosmos.

Again it is not the case that we cannot know anything about the sun sphere before our forty-second year. But the Mercury beings can tell us, for they certainly know about it. In that case we learn about it indirectly, through supersensory instruction, so to speak. But in order to have direct experience in the sun sphere in our own consciousness, to be able to enter into it and to experience it like going for a walk in Torquay, we must not only be living in the period between the twenty-first and forty-second years, but we must already have passed our forty-second year and be able to look back, for only in the backward review are the mysteries revealed.

Likewise, when we are able to look back on our life up to our forty-ninth year, the Mars mysteries are revealed. If we can look back on our life up to the fifty-sixth year, the Jupiter mysteries are revealed. And the deeply hidden but tremendously illuminating revelations of the Saturn mysteries—these mysteries which, as we shall see in the following lectures, veil the deepest depths of the cosmos— are revealed when we are able to look back on what has happened between our fifty-sixth and the sixty-third years.

This will show you, ladies and gentlemen, that man is in truth a 'little world,' a microcosm. He is connected with things he himself never becomes aware of with the ordinary consciousness of the earth; but he would not be able inwardly to shape and direct his life if the moon forces were not working within him from birth to his seventh year. Later on he perceives how these forces work. He would not be able to bring about what he experiences between the seventh and fourteenth years if the Mercury mysteries did not live within him. He would not be able to bring about what he experiences between the fourteenth and twenty-first years—the period when, for instance, tremendously creative artistic forces draw into the human being who is karmically disposed to them—if he were not inwardly connected with the Venus sphere.

And he would not be able to develop mature understanding and experience of the world between the twenty-first and forty-second year—the period when he leaves the years of apprenticeship and passes into the journeyman phase—if he were not inwardly united with the sun sphere. In earlier times things were organized along these lines. First, one was an apprentice up to one's twenty-first year, then a journeyman, and only later a master. Everything that needs to take place in our inner being between the age of 21 and 42 is connected with the sun sphere. Everything that happens in our waning years, between the age of 56 and 63, proceeds from the fact that this phase belongs to the Saturn sphere.

Together with the earth we are situated within overlapping spheres. There are seven overlapping spheres; and we grow into this overlapping structure, become connected [sequentially] with each sphere, during the course of our life. Our life evolves from its dispositional potential by virtue of the star spheres drawing us along, so to speak, from birth to death. When we have reached the Saturn sphere we have passed through all that the beings of the planetary spheres can, in grace, do for us; and then, speaking in the occult sense, we are bestowed with life that moves freely in the cosmos, life that looks back on the planetary life from the standpoint of the initiate, and can, in a certain sense, be emancipated from what in the earlier life-periods are still necessities.

In the following lectures I shall speak further on all these matters.

LECTURE 7

18 AUGUST 1924

Star Knowledge

*The spiritual background to the differentiated development
of humanity*

IN the last lecture we saw how man, by reviewing his different life-periods with spiritual sight, and mastering them, comes to inspiration which enables him to raise his consciousness step by step to everything that the world of stars can say to him. The 'world of stars' must, of course, be thought of as an expression, a revelation, of purely spiritual beings and facts.

The essential point in connection with paths into the spiritual world and with research into the spiritual world, is that the corresponding states of consciousness and qualities of soul must be striven for, and that we must not fall into the error of attempting to reach the spiritual world with ordinary everyday consciousness. I would like to clarify this for you today by means of particular examples, or rather, particular cases. I want to show you where the potential for error in spiritual research can lie. Let me therefore say the following as an introduction.

When we really enter into spiritual work that can open up the spiritual world to us, that enables us to behold and, if I may use the expression, to hold converse with the spiritual world, we perceive in humanity's historical evolution and the spiritual background behind it that we are looking for, great differentiations, great differences. For example, there is the epoch that immediately preceded our own. Our epoch which, as I have indicated, we can call the Michael epoch—I will talk about the reasons for this in the coming lectures—begins with the last third of the nineteenth century, around the 1870s. But this epoch was preceded by another that lasted for three or four centuries and, for someone who has researched the spiritual world, has a very different nature. This epoch in turn was preceded by another, again of an entirely different nature. So when we look back with initiation knowledge into the various pasts, we receive quite different impressions from each epoch. I do not want to describe these impressions abstractly, but to place them very concretely before your souls.

In the course of these lectures I have spoken about personalities who lived in various circumstances within the evolution of humanity, of Brunetto Latini for example, the great teacher of Dante. I have spoken of the teachers of the School of Chartres, of Bernardus Sylvestris, of Alanus ab Insulis, of Joachim of Flora, and I could speak of hundreds of others from the ninth to the twelfth centuries, and even to the thirteenth century. And through these personalities we characterized a very specific age.[14]

When we wish to investigate the historical life of humanity along spiritual-scientific lines, and we approach, let us say, the epoch of Dante, of Giotto—the epoch, in other words, that preceded the Renaissance—we have the impression that it is essential that we communicate with human beings in the spiritual world, that is with discarnate human souls; we have to come face to face as it were—naturally only comparatively—with human souls in their life between death and their next birth. In initiation-knowledge we have the definite feeling that we would like to associate spiritually with an individuality like Brunetto Latini in the same way that we would associate with human beings here in the physical world. I tried to give a flavour of this in my description. Therefore when I was speaking of Joachim of Flora and of Brunetto Latini I described this epoch in such a way as to bring home to you the need to make the description as personal as possible. I spoke about 'tapping you on the shoulder' and the like.

It is quite different in the case of the subsequent epoch which lasted until the last third of the nineteenth century. For this epoch there is much less need in initiation knowledge to enter into a personal relationship with the disembodied souls who come into question. We would rather see them in their whole environment; we do not feel the need to approach them directly, but to gain access to them in some way from earthly knowledge, from the understanding of ordinary consciousness.

Forgive me if I narrate something here from direct personal experience. In this case, however, the personal experience is completely objective. The epoch immediately preceding our own was the one in which Goethe lived, and I can speak of this because for many decades I was engaged in a study of Goethe. I was conscious of the need to approach Goethe in the first place by finding a way in to him through his own natural scientific writings and through natural science in general. It was not the case at first, but only comparatively later, that the need arose to meet him also in the spiritual world as a spiritual individuality. But this did not come first. What came first was to find him as 'stellar man', so to speak, after his death, in his whole cosmic context, in cosmic relationship, and not in a personal or individual sense.

By contrast, when it is a question of finding a personality like Brunetto Latini in the spiritual world, or individuals who occupied themselves with the study of nature in the same epoch, one feels a direct need to exchange opinions and views with them in a very personal interplay of soul. This is a very important distinction. It is connected with the fact that these epochs differ completely from each other in their inner, spiritual constitution. Today we are living in an age when individuals, indeed the whole of humanity, must lay hold of spiritual facts directly as spiritual facts; this means spreading externally as human knowledge the initiation science which sees into spiritual life. This epoch which has only just begun must not run its course without those whom we call educated people really understanding the most important spiritual facts that must be attained—not earthly, sense-perceptible facts, but spiritual facts. From now on therefore a spiritual science that shines a light directly into the spiritual world must be energetically represented [in society], otherwise humanity will not be able to achieve its task in the way intended for it. We must enter into a spiritual age more and more.

In the preceding epoch, entirely different forces governed human evolution. And when we speak from the point of view referred to in the last lecture, from the point of view of real, genuine stellar knowledge, we say: in the age we human beings entered in the 70s of the last century [i.e. the nineteenth century], it is above all the spiritual forces coming from the sun that must become predominant in everything, in the physical life of man, in soul life, in science, art and religion. Everything that the sun has to say to the world, what the sun has to do in the world, must assert itself in our epoch more and more.

Now for those who have real knowledge, the sun is not the physical globe of gas described by modern physics, but a sun of spiritual beings. And the most important spiritual beings—who ray out, as it were, the spiritual element from the sun, just as the sun's light sends out physical or etheric rays—the most important beings are grouped around a certain being who, according to ancient Christian-Pagan or also Judeo-Christian terminology, we can call the Michael-being. Michael works from the sun. And everything the sun has to give spiritually to the world may also be said to be what Michael and his hosts have to give.

In the epoch preceding our own it was not the sun's forces that gave the impulses to man's life, knowledge, and action, but the moon's. The moon forces had to give the impulses for the epoch that ended in the 1870s and had lasted from three to four centuries before that.

And here again the leading beings who influenced earthly and human evolution, were grouped around one being who, again according to ancient terminology, can be called Gabriel. We could use another name equally well—the terminology is not the essential point—but since the name already exists, we can keep it. So, following Judeo-Christian custom, we may call this being Gabriel.

In the way I have described, we learn to know the spiritual activity in man that comes from the world of stars. If with initiation-knowledge we learn to know what works in man from birth to the change of teeth, we learn to know everything that is the working from the moon in the cosmos. That is to say, through the backward review, with inspirational knowledge of the first years of childhood, we gain knowledge of the Gabriel epoch where the moon is especially active.

By contrast we must have become more mature, must have entered into our 40s, to be able to look back upon what works in us as human beings between our twentieth and fortieth year or, to speak more precisely, between the twenty-first and forty-second year. Then we perceive the special characteristics of an epoch such as our own. So that in the epoch preceding our own it was little children, infants and very young children who were of the greatest importance so far as the cosmic guidance of the world was concerned. The forces necessary for that age flowed as impulses into early childhood. In our epoch it is the individuals who have reached the ages of 20 or 30 years who must receive the impulses from the sun forces. In our epoch it is particularly the grown-up people who are important in the cosmic guidance of the whole world.

These things are a direct, practical result of the genuine kind of perception I described the day before yesterday. I am not speaking of theories but of results from actual perception.

From this you can also see that for knowledge of the Gabrielic epoch preceding our own Michaelic epoch, it was not particularly necessary for one to meet the discarnate human souls of that epoch in a personal way. One felt like a little child standing before a grown-up, because one had to confront these souls with the inspired perception of the first years of childhood.

Things are quite different when we research the preceding epoch, the epoch of Alanus ab Insulis, Bernardus Sylvestris, Joachim of Flora, John of Auville, Brunetto Latini. This age was governed by the forces we acquire when we look back upon what is working in the life-period between the change of teeth and puberty. These, as we saw in the last lecture, are the Mercury forces. We enter into something extraordinary, something magnificent, when we develop the corresponding organs for perception of the spiritual, taking our start from this life-period. For between the time of the change of teeth and puberty, man is a child with such an eagerness to learn. And we become such a child again now. Hence we want to meet the men of this epoch in an entirely personal way and we do so with initiation-knowledge. We would like to stand face to face with a personality like Brunetto Latini just as a child of 10 or 12 years stands before someone who knows more than he does, someone who can teach and instruct him. In true initiation-science, of course, we are not unconscious of the things of the external, physical world. We are at the same time both a grown adult and a curious child thirsty for knowledge. We stand on an equal footing with Brunetto Latini, and yet with an intense eagerness to learn from him.

This gives the specific colouring for the initiation-knowledge of the age that extends from the fifteenth century back to the ninth century; it is an epoch where the main impulses for the earth and humanity are given by Mercury. And the being around whom everything groups itself, the being of special significance in this age, can also be designated by the ancient name of Raphael. Raphael is Mercury in the age that preceded the Renaissance, the age of Dante, of Giotto. There we feel the need to know in a personal way the beings who appear somewhat obscurely in history, who have not become part of external history.

When we enter the realm of spiritual science we have a curious feeling in connection with this epoch. At first we are inclined to be irritated that so little is to be found in the textbooks about Brunetto Latini, or men like Alanus ab Insulis and so on; we would like to know more about them than we can find externally. But after a while we move on and are very glad, very thankful that outer history is silent. For what history documents externally is nothing but a few shreds.

Just imagine what would be passed down from our time to future ages if what was deemed by the various branches of history to be a valid or invalid source was based on our newspaper articles! We can only be thankful that we are not disturbed by what is in the encyclopedias about these personalities. And with all the means at our disposal in the present age within the Anthroposophical Society, we try to stand before these men in a spiritual sense, to find out all that can be taught about them in the light of spiritual science.

In this connection it is of very great importance to approach personalities who were associated with knowledge of nature in the Raphael epoch. A deeper understanding of nature, a deeper medical understanding can be communicated through many personalities who emerge for spiritual perception out of what I might call the grey spiritual darkness of this age from the ninth to the fifteenth centuries. They can introduce us to how people thought about matter at that time, how they thought about the whole cosmos and man's connection with it. And when we enter into this and get to know many personalities who cannot be named because their name has not come down to posterity—but the personalities exist—when we look with spiritual sight into this age we find many personalities there, such that we say: 'Paracelsus[15] the Greater' (*major*) is there, but is not named, whereas 'Paracelsus the Lesser' (*minor*) lived at a later age, in the Gabriel epoch, and still had reminiscences, echoes of 'Paracelsus the Greater,' although no longer in the pure, magnificent way, the spiritual way, in which they were with 'Paracelsus the Greater'.

Then there is also Jacob Boehme[15]. 'Jacob Boehme the Lesser' also appears in the later Gabriel epoch. Here again we say to ourselves: 'Jacob Boehme discovered magnificent things, came across them in various documents, had real Inspirations himself.' But when the figure of 'Jacob Boehme the Greater' is revealed to us—who did not pass down to posterity, whose name only surfaces sporadically like that of Alanus ab Insulis or Brunetto Latini—then we understand 'Jacob Boehme the Lesser' for the first time. We must therefore say: this pre-Renaissance epoch, at the culmination of which there shine forth the great figures of Dante and Brunetto Latini, and then the teachers of Chartres, with Scotus Erigena[15] there in the midst like, I should like to say, a kind of erratic block—this epoch contains something that can act as a tremendous spiritual stimulus. External medieval history is dark, but behind this darkness there is a mighty light precisely for the age I have just been speaking about.

Moon beings

When we penetrate into this Raphael epoch of the ninth to the fifteenth centuries, we are struck by the prominence of figures such as Dante, Giotto, but also those whose names have not come down to posterity in external history, as well as all the others I have named. These figures make a directly human impression upon us. Raphael himself, who was never incarnated in a physical body, remains as a figure more in the background, and other spiritual beings who are permanently in the spiritual world—at least are permanently there today—also appear less prominently. It is precisely human beings, the dead, who appear in extraordinarily strong relief during this age before the spiritual gaze.

In the following Gabriel epoch, we have the impression that even figures like Goethe, Spencer, Byron, or Voltaire behave or conduct themselves in the spiritual world in a very shadowy way. In contrast to this, beings appear there with great and impressive intensity, beings who do not make a human impression but a superhuman one. They are beings we become aware of through spiritual knowledge, who live constantly in the moon sphere just as we human beings live on earth between birth and death. They are inhabitants of the moon sphere. These impressive figures, who today are the permanent inhabitants of the moon sphere, are the ones we perceive above all else; and the souls of human beings recede more into the background. With regard to these figures we discover that they were once connected with the earth just as human beings are today. But human beings walk about in physical bodies whereas these beings once moved on earth in subtle, more ethereal bodies. And we come to recognize that here we are meeting beings who were once on the earth, who in primordial ages were connected with humanity, and were humanity's supersensory teachers on earth. When their tasks on earth were fulfilled they withdrew to the moon sphere and are no longer bound up with the earth today.

From my *Outline of Occult Science* you know that the moon itself, as a cosmic body, was once united with the earth and then separated from it. During the separation these beings followed the moon. Later they themselves became inhabitants of the moon sphere, having once been inhabitants of the earth sphere. So at the stage of knowledge we have been discussing over these days, where we can follow the dead in the early years of their after-death existence, we enter into a world where, because we still have the earlier knowledge of our ordinary consciousness, we have around us people whom we learn to know today as physical people in everyday waking consciousness. But then we come to recognize, when we enter this other consciousness, that among these people there are always spiritual figures who belong to the moon, just as we belong to the earth, who are present everywhere and have an interest in human affairs although in a somewhat different way from the physical way in which people have.

Among these beings who were once the great teachers of humanity, and who no longer dwell on the earth, but—if we may express it like this, *cum grano salis*—inhabit the moon, among such beings are some who appear in great sublimity, who are the most perfected amongst them, the most considered, those permeated with spiritual greatness. We can learn a great deal from them concerning the mysteries of the cosmos. Their knowledge far surpasses any knowledge that is possible for the human being of the present level of consciousness. But they cannot express this knowledge in abstract thoughts. I would like to put it by saying that they 'poeticize' at us when we approach them, they express everything in poetic form, in artistic pictures; they conjure up before us something which, in its own way, is greater than what Homer wrote, than is contained in the ancient Indian epics that are known to the world. But there is a profound wisdom in what these beings conjure before us.

Now there are also less perfect beings among them. Just as on earth there are individuals who are congenial companions, so to speak, and others who are uncongenial, so among these other beings there are those who have not attained the greatness and perfection of their companions, but who, because they were the pupils or indeed the servants of the others, had nevertheless reached a point where they were able to leave the earth and live and work in the moon sphere. When—if I may put it somewhat trivially—we make the acquaintance of this kind of being, we find that they have a burning interest in earthly affairs, but their interest is of a completely different kind [from their more advanced companions].

Don't immediately start imagining these beings as uncongenial or frightening figures. Although in comparison with their companions they are imperfect, they far surpass any refinement, cleverness, or insight that can be attained by the present-day earthly human being with ordinary consciousness. They have the habits of their companions; different habits, different inclinations from those of an ordinary earth inhabitant today.

Here I want to point out something particular. When we come into contact with such beings we naturally feel the need to talk to them—we can't avoid putting such things somewhat trivially— to discuss one thing or another with them. Suppose that we are having a discussion with these beings about, let's say, human writing, about what has been written by human beings. So let's say that someone has written just their name, and someone else has also written their name. So just the strokes of their name. Now if we discuss with these beings what we actually have here, they say: 'Oh, you humans are interested in the least interesting aspect of all. You are interested in what you say the word means. If you have [the word] *smith* in front of you, you are interested in the fact that it means *smith*. Or if you have the word *hairdresser,* you are only interested in what the word denotes. But the fact that a word denotes *hairdresser* is the least interesting thing about it. It is far more interesting to watch how a person who is writing these things makes their movements, how one person writes in one way, another person in another way, the one quickly, the other slowly, the one skilfully, the other clumsily, the one automatically, the other as though painting.' The particular way in which a person writes, what they are doing when they write—this is what these beings pay special attention to. This interests them.

And in the spiritual world I am speaking about here, they [the lower moon beings] in turn have their spirit-entourage: all kinds of spiritual beings who also do not live on earth and are lower than earthly beings, but others too who are higher. They do not teach them to express earthly things in a sense-related way, but teach them to do writing movements, to do the writing movements that human beings have developed since the time when they themselves [the moon beings] were on the earth. When these beings, who became moon inhabitants, were still on the earth, writing did not yet exist as we understand it now.

Now, in their association with human beings, they always observed with interest how writing came into existence; they were interested in what could already interest them at that time, namely the fact that people made all kinds of deft movements with their fingers; this interested them even then. And the fact that this skill of the fingers was supported by a tube from which something flowed, this came only later. They had little interest in what appeared on the paper, but an extraordinary interest in the movements that were made.

Added to this was something that was in the earth and remained there [after the departure of the moon] but was then less noticed by humanity. In fact, there are a number of such things. Firstly, if we start with what I have just mentioned, there is what emanates from people in their movements. So, *the movements emanated from people*[16] is something that is particularly important in dealings with these beings.

But this is something that does not yet bring us to the true region of these beings since at the time they lived on earth it did not yet exist. By contrast there is a certain contempt for human beings—but in a good sense—when these beings speak of the scant disposition of present-day humanity to understand the evaporation, the emanation of the fluid element from man. They have a particular understanding for this; but present-day humanity doesn't notice it. So, emanations of the fluid element, *skin emanations of the fluid element*, was something that, during that epoch, was very important and essential for these beings. One got to know the human being by something that later went unnoticed: by what he spread out around him by evaporation.

The third thing these beings are especially receptive to, is the expiration of the skin—in other words, the aeriform elements emanated by the human being. For all these emanations of physical nature, but which, as we will soon hear, can definitely take on a semi-spiritual character, for all these human emanations—in the solid element in writing, in the watery element in evaporation through the skin, in the airy element by expiration through the skin (for we are also constantly breathing out through our skin)—these beings are particularly receptive.

Then fourthly [these beings are interested] in *the emanation of warmth*. All these things as they take place on earth have special importance for these moon beings, and they form their judgements of a human being according to the configuration of his movements in writing, and according to the particular nature of his emanations.

Then, fifthly, comes *light emanation*, which certainly also exists. Every human being not only shines in his aura, but also shines, radiates light, in connection with his physical and etheric organism. This light-emanation is so weak that under ordinary conditions it cannot be seen. But it has already been made visible in specially equipped darkrooms by researchers such as Moriz Benedikt[17]. In the darkroom the rays and glow of red, yellow and blue around the human organism can be made visible; they vary at different places round the body. We can learn from the scientist Moriz Benedikt how he made this coloured light-emanation visible in his darkroom in such a way that the left side can be seen to shine with a yellowish-orange light, and the other side with a blue light. It is just a matter of setting up the necessary physical conditions.

Then there is a sixth emanation, the *emanation of chemical forces*. This emanation is actually only present on the earth today in exceptional and rare cases. That is to say, it is indeed always present but comes into consideration in rare cases, is involved only in rare cases, and namely where black magic is practised. So when people become conscious of their chemical emanations, and use them, then black magic arises on earth.

A seventh kind of emanation is the directly spiritual life-emanation. Just as black magic—into which, in our day, the chemical emanations almost invariably degenerate—is reprehensible and evil, so the life-emanations have an equal importance. These moon beings I am speaking about can from their side always reckon and work with the forces in these life-emanations—but in a good sense, for they are no black magicians; only those who practise these things on the earth and fall into evil are black magicians. But the moon beings can only work with these life-emanations at full moon, when the moon is fully illumined by the sun and they can take themselves into the region of sunlight; then, under the influence of the sun's light, they can reckon with the life-emanations.

Now these life-emanations are what must enter into our age as the element of good in contrast to all that is reprehensible; for in connection with all the impulses that are to be given in the Michael age there must gradually come about this control of the life-emanation. People must above all learn to work in a living and not in a dead way with what comes from the spiritual world. The task of the age is to find living ideas, living concepts, living perceptions, living feelings, and not dead theories. This comes directly from the beings who are united with the being we call Michael.

In contrast to this, during the Gabriel age that has run its course, people were more focused on the earth. They would not penetrate to the beings who, under certain conditions, stand very near to man, because these beings were concerned with something rather alien to that age, namely all these occult-emanations that proceed from human beings.

Immediately adjoining the physical world that we have between birth and death, there is a spiritual world, a world in which the dead are to be found in the way I described. But in this world there is a great deal more besides, including the active power of such forces that live in the radiations, the emanations of man. In a certain sense this is a highly dangerous region of the cosmos that we enter. And in our times we must have the soul-spiritual stance and composure I have often mentioned, in order that what comes from these moon beings may be directed in a good and not in an evil way.

For the situation is that all the forces and impulses of the present epoch must hasten towards the application of the vital emanation on the earth. But it is terribly easy to enter into what lies between this life-emanation and all the other emanations that man would so much like to possess—[to enter into] black magic. People would really like to make visible what comes to expression in movements (we still have to speak about this), and make visible what is present in our fluid evaporation, in the light-emanation, and so on. This is all connected in a certain sense with something that is good, and that can only be good because the Michael age is dawning for human beings.

But between all this lies black magic, which must be warded off if the good and true paths to supersensory research, and not the false ones, are to be taken.

(On the board)

1. Movements emanating from man.
2. Skin emanations of the fluid element.
3. Skin emanations of the air element.
4. Warmth emanation.
5. Light emanation.
6. Emanation of chemical forces (black magic).
7. Vital emanation.

The nature of mediums and their emanations

Now when this communication takes place in the spiritual world between human beings on earth and moon beings (and it is constantly taking place in our subconscious) it is possible that the interest developed by certain moon beings for the movements humans carry out when writing or drawing—an interest which manifests spiritually in these moon beings—itself becomes a matter of interest to certain elemental beings of the spiritual world. These elemental beings are at a lower level than the moon beings. They never incarnate on earth but live as spiritual-etheric beings in the world I have spoken about, bordering our own. When these beings in turn take an interest in everything that is happening, then the following can occur. When we observe someone here on earth, we see that their thoughts, which they then communicate through writing, work upon their whole human being. The thoughts are initially present in the ego, but work down from there into the astral body, which carries out movements in accordance with these movements that we make out of the ego when writing. They work on into the etheric body and right down into the physical body. Certain elemental beings perceive these effects working into the physical body, and they get a longing, so to speak, to move in the same way. But they cannot do this because different laws govern their world from those in the world in which writing takes place. Writing only takes place in the physical world of man here on earth.

But the following is possible. There are certain people who when they write, or think, or even feel, are deeply rooted in their etheric body. Everything in their etheric body participates [in this activity] and then impresses itself strongly in the physical body. What then happens with people like this is that they completely suppress what is in their ego, and an imitation of writing or drawing is activated in their astral, etheric and physical bodies. These people are mediums. Such mediums, because their ego is suppressed, can then take up into themselves these fast-learning elemental beings of the spiritual world who have, as it were, learnt the movements of writing from the moon beings. These mediums then come into an activity in which they do not make the movements of writing in accordance with their ego, in accordance with their full consciousness, but in accordance with the elemental being within them. All mediumistic writing, mediumistic drawing and the like, is brought about through the movements produced by the human being in a state of reduced consciousness—all usual mediumistic activity. So here the emanated movements are used.

The second kind of emanation can be used by certain beings who, under the influence of the moon beings, assimilate in particular the artistic element living in human souls. These beings also pass into human beings who have dulled their upper consciousness and who have a certain artistic factor in their etheric and astral bodies which is directed by these into their emanations. It can be highly interesting to see how such a person can be possessed, as it were, by elemental spiritual beings, and how there flows into his emanations something like malleable (*plastisch existierende*) dreams that are in part composites of what the person has himself perceived in life, because this has slipped down into the etheric and astral bodies and appears in the emanations; and are in part communications from the world in which the elemental beings themselves exist that have crept into the human being.

The researcher Schrenck-Notzing[18] got results of this kind. He carried out experiments with people with a mediumistic disposition who, when their consciousness had slipped to a lower level, that is to say, when the ego had been shut out, could be manipulated by these elemental beings through the skin emanations of the fluid element. Schrenck-Notzing published an interesting book. Some people regard it as pure charlatanism, others are delighted with it. We need not be surprised that those who find it delightful accept it all as a wonderful thing. And it *is* a wonderful thing. It is something wonderful when a medium who is part of the experiment sits there, and then a moving shape comes out from a particular area of their body which has something spiritual about it, something not found on earth. But it is often the case that mixed in with the form is a picture recently seen by the medium in an illustrated paper, a picture of Poincaré*, for example, as seen in the newspapers, perhaps in a humorous paper.

It need not surprise us that people are amazed at these things. But we cannot help being surprised at fashionable people, people aware of polite behaviour, even ladies, who while they prefer not to speak about skin exudations, or to mention things that come to light in the human being in this way, nevertheless long to see the medium who materializes these moving shapes out of nothing else than ordinary skin exudations.

The phenomena in Schrenck-Notzing's experiments, ladies and gentleman, are—to put it plainly—perspired. And into what is perspired there flows a plastic entity, stimulated by the elemental beings, that can come to expression in the skin emanations. In the same way, expirations through the skin, in other words the air that comes out, can be stimulated by certain elemental beings. But the air emanation is so bound up with the [medium's own] human form, the person impresses their own human form so strongly into it, that for the most part these beings cannot do much more than produce a phantom of the person themselves. Then we get those manifestations, those phenomena, where the phantom appears out of the human being. We get the appearance of the phantom. Here (see table below) by point 2 we have mediumistic shapes. Here by point 3 we have the appearance of the phantom.

Now it is not so easy to produce warmth- and light-emanations from the human being in a way that reveals something of what is being stimulated in them by elemental beings under the influence of the moon beings. Certain preparations are required.

---

* Jules Henri Poincaré (1854–1912) was a French mathematician, theoretical physicist, engineer and philosopher of science.

As I have said, natural science has managed to make visible in a physics darkroom certain light-emanations which are connected with warmth-emanations. In this regard Moriz Benedikt's experiments are extraordinarily interesting. But it has always been the case, and is still so today, that the only individuals who can work with light- and warmth-emanations are those who make certain preparations beforehand in which not only the usual machinations of the physical world come to expression, but who make certain preparations with particular kinds of smoke, produce special kinds of vapour or particular odours by mixing special substances and so on. By this means there arise all those magical processes that are described so prolifically in the older literature on magic.

The purpose of all these magical preparations is to create conditions in which the forces inherent in human light- and warmth-emanations can be taken advantage of. And you can find highly dubious and highly dangerous instructions regarding these things in the writings of Eliphas Levi[19]—also in those of Encausse[19] who wrote under the name of Papus. You find dubious and decidedly dangerous instructions for such things. But since we must speak here about the objective aspect of these things and their essential nature, they have to be mentioned. All this then leads directly into black magic, which works with the spiritual element hidden in earthly things.

What is this spiritual element ?

I have told you, and you can read it in my *Outline of Occult Science*, that at one time the moon was united with the earth. But there were innumerable forces that the moon did not take away with it, not even all those that belonged to it. Many remained behind in the earth and now permeate the minerals, plants and animals. They are still here, these moon forces. So when we work with the moon forces here in the earth—forces that do not really belong to normal mineral, plant, animal, and human forces—it is possible to enter, in an improper way, directly into the region where we come into contact with the elemental beings who have learnt so much from the moon beings, but have learnt it in a way that does not belong to our world.

So the black magician works, on the one hand, with the moon forces that are still here on the earth. But because he works in this way he comes into contact with elemental beings who, as it were, watch—as one watches a game of halma* or chess—all that takes place in a legitimate way between human beings and the moon beings, and have thus learnt to draw as close to the physical world as possible; they either look into this physical world, or even enter it. The ordinary person, in whom all this remains in the subconscious, has nothing to do with these beings. But the black magician, who works with the moon forces, who possesses the moon forces in his retorts, in his crucibles and smoke, is surrounded by a swarm of these forces.

Even a good person can learn much from black magicians. In the first part of his *Faust,* Goethe gives a picture of the condition of a being surrounded by these swarming forces, a condition that comes dubiously close to black magic. By using these moon forces we come into the region where entities in the service of the moon beings are ready to interact with human beings. Centres of black magic then arise where the magicians work with moon forces, with spirits who have entered directly into the service of the moon forces, but into an evil service.

It is because of the fact that a great many activities of this kind have been going on, more particularly in the course of recent centuries, that a dubious atmosphere has been created in the earth. This dubious atmosphere really exists. It swarms with forces that come from a union of human activities with moon ingredients, moon dynamics—elemental beings who stand in the service of improper Moon forces. This atmosphere exists, and is the region that stands in strong contrast and opposition to all that is to come in our Age of Michael from the sun region, and will concern most especially the vital [or life] emanation in the pure soul-spiritual principle. We will take this further tomorrow.

(Written by Steiner on the board:)

1. Movements emanated by human beings. Mediumship.
2. Skin emanations of the fluid element. Mediumistic shapes.
3. Skin emanations. Manifestation of the Phantom.
4. Warmth emanation.
5. Light emanation.
6. Emanation of chemical forces. Black magic.
7. Vital emanation.

---

* Board game invented in the 1880s.

LECTURE 8

19 AUGUST 1924

Possible Aberrations in Spiritual Research

Ahrimanic elemental beings

W HEN we develop the states of consciousness I have spoken about, we enter with each state into a specific cosmic region. I will describe schematically how our perception relates to these different regions into which we can enter by our efforts to attain the particular states of consciousness I have described. Of course, we have to draw the worlds next to each other even though they actually interpenetrate. I have already shown how the moon world, the moon sphere, permeates our sphere, and how the Mercury sphere too permeates our own. Now, to describe these various worlds, I have to place them next to each other.

[our world – light yellow red]

If we draw this as our world (see drawing, light), then, by developing other states of consciousness, we enter with each state into another world. Let us suppose we develop the state of consciousness we need in order to enter the world where we can follow the dead during the years immediately following their death. I will characterize this world by drawing it immediately next to our own (yellow).

If we were to develop the next level of consciousness, [we would attain] the state of consciousness by which we go further into the life of the dead, [the phase] they enter once they have completed their backward path and which I called the condition of empty but waking consciousness with regard to the physical world. We would enter a further world (red), the world where, for example, we come together very particularly with the Mercury beings, with the happenings and facts of the sphere of Raphael, as I described yesterday. Here we gain knowledge above all of the healing forces inherent in human nature.

With each state of consciousness we enter a specific region of the universe, and as a result of this we learn to know the beings who belong to these regions at any given time. If we want to learn to know human beings in the years after their death, we must go ourselves, with the corresponding consciousness, to the world where the dead wander. We cannot observe them in their real, true form in any other world. If we want to observe the Mercury beings we must enter with our consciousness into their world. From this you will see that as human beings we take the worlds to be separate from each other in a certain sense, and can develop a particular state of consciousness for each world. Indeed this must be done if we want to learn to know the universe in the right way, for only by this means can we prepare ourselves to know every being in its true character. I will show you by a simple example where such knowledge leads—knowledge, in other words, that seeks to develop in the right way the appropriate states of consciousness for specific cosmic regions.

Let us suppose we look at a plant, at its leaves and flowers. We have seen how a plant is actually a reflected image of what gives shape, what is formed, out there in the cosmos. We find what is in the world we have just spoken about reflected on the earth in the plants. How do we get to know the plants? We gain knowledge of plants by raising our consciousness into this world. But something very important is revealed here. What is revealed is that we must make a big, a huge distinction between the different plants that we find in the earthly realm. When we look at a particular plant, at chicory for instance, or any other plant, it also appears different spiritually speaking from many other plants.

For example, let us take the common violet and compare it—as a radical example—with belladonna, deadly nightshade. When we look at the plant world in the way I described, we will see how openly the violet stands before the eye of our soul when we are in the world the violet belongs to, in the world of empty waking consciousness.

When it comes to deadly nightshade, things are different. Deadly nightshade, belladonna, draws in its essence from still other worlds. I can describe it like this: we learn to know an ordinary plant by seeing that it has its physical body and its etheric body, and that the flowers and fruit are surrounded by the general astrality of the cosmos. So we look at the plant: everywhere the physical nature of the plant sprouts out of the earth; everywhere the plant has its etheric body, and above this, like clouds, is astrality. This is how it is with plants like the violet.

It is different with a plant like belladonna. With belladonna the situation is that the plant grows, has its flower here (Steiner draws on the board), and here inside it develops its fruit. But in this case the astrality goes into the fruit. The violet develops its fruit only in the etheric element. The deadly nightshade sucks astrality into its fruit. As a result of this, it becomes poisonous. All plants that suck astrality out of the cosmos and into any of their parts, become poisonous. So the same thing which, when it enters the animal, gives the animal an astral body, forms the animal inwardly into a creature of sentience— this same thing when it enters a plant, makes it poisonous.

This is very interesting, because we can say: our astral body is the bearer of forces which, when they get into the plant, manifest as poison. And this is how we must think of poison. We can only come to an inner understanding of poison when we know that in our astral body we normally have the forces of all the poisons there are, for they belong to our human being.

I only want here to give a specific concept which we will need later on in order to understand the difference between right and erroneous paths of spiritual research.

What do we learn from an example like this? We have the violet and deadly nightshade. When we have developed the corresponding state of consciousness for each world, we see that the violet is a being that remains in its own proper world and draws nothing from a world that is foreign to it. With deadly nightshade we see that it *does* draw something out of a foreign world. Belladonna appropriates to itself something that a plant ought not to have, something that only an animal should have. And this is the case with all poisonous plants. They absorb into themselves something that plants as such should not have, but which belongs properly to the animal kingdom.

Now there are many beings in the cosmos belonging to the most varied cosmic regions. Precisely in the region that we find when we enter directly into the world in which we can follow the dead for ten, twenty, thirty years after their death until they leave that world, there are a number of beings who do indeed exist, but who do not enter visibly into our physical world. I should like to describe them as a particular class of elemental being. So when we follow the dead after they have passed through the gate of death, we come into a world where there are all kinds of elemental beings who have forms, and who really belong to that same world. We can therefore say that since these beings belong to that world, they ought really to make use only of the forces proper to it.

But now among these elemental beings there are those that do not restrict themselves to these forces, but watch human beings, for example when they write, and look at all the activities that are carried out in the human world—that is to say, the world human beings pass through between birth and death. Such beings are constantly watching these things. Now this watching in itself is not a bad thing, because the whole plan underlying what I am now describing is that all the worlds that touch our own—in other words the [first] world we enter immediately after death, [and] the [second] world we enter many decades after death—that none of these worlds contains what we have around us on earth, and what we learn on earth. When we enter these worlds next to our own, there is in them, for instance, no writing, no reading as we would understand it; there are no aeroplanes, no cars as we know them, not even an ordinary horse and carriage as we understand it. None of these things exists in the worlds bordering our own. But we cannot say that here on earth our manufacturing of cars, our writing and reading, our writing of books on earth that are not read by the angels—we cannot say that all these things have no significance for the cosmos in general. It is the case that the beings we have just been speaking about are sent with a task from the world immediately adjacent to our own. They have to keep an eye, as it were, on what humans are doing. So, from other worlds, they are given the special task of concerning themselves with human nature, and preserving what they learn for future times.

We human beings can carry our karma from one life into the other; we can also carry from one life to another everything that happens with our karma through external culture. What we experience as human beings in our cars, we can carry from one earthly life into another—but not the construction of the car. What has arisen purely from earthly forces we cannot ourselves carry from one life to another. Because of this, humanity has established something in the course of civilization which it would lose if other beings did not come to its aid.

The beings I spoke about are detailed to the task of preserving for the future what we are unable to carry from one earthly life into another. This is the significant thing, that among us, in the world adjoining our own, there are beings whose mission it is to carry over what man is unable to carry over from his external civilization, so that he can have it again in the future. For a great deal, a very great deal of what was already discovered in ancient civilizations has been lost to humanity because it has become extremely difficult for many of these beings to fulfil their task.

So the important point I am trying to convey here is that there are beings among us who, in accord with the cosmic plan, have been charged with the mission of carrying over into the future what man himself is unable to take from one earthly life to another. Above all, for example, this includes the abstract contents of our libraries—that is something we humans cannot carry from one life to the next. For this, beings of a special kind are necessary. Even those spiritual beings with whom we are directly connected cannot do it; so we as human beings cannot do it either. These beings must make use of the services of other entities who for long ages were alien to them, and who have passed through a completely different evolution than the spiritual beings directly connected with human beings.

In my books I have called these other beings, who have passed through a wholly different evolution, ahrimanic beings. Their evolution is an altogether different one; but on certain occasions it comes together with our own, for example when we manufacture a motor car. These are beings who, out of their ahrimanic cosmic forces, can understand a piece of modern technology—like the construction of a motor car—and carry the achievements [of one age] of human civilization into future times, and what the human being cannot carry over from one incarnation to the next.

Possession

Having got so far, we are now in a position to describe what a [person who is a] *medium* really is. Here we must of course differentiate between a mediumistic person in the very broadest sense, and one whom we call a medium in the ordinary sense of the word. For fundamentally speaking, ladies and gentlemen, we are all mediums if we use the expression in the widest sense possible. For example, we are beings of soul and spirit before we descend into the earthly world of life between birth and death. What we are in the spiritual world is incorporated into what we are here in the physical world. In the physical world we are a medium for our own spirit. So if we take the word *medium* in the broadest sense possible, we can say that every being is in some way a medium. But this is not what is meant when we speak of a mediumistic person in the usual sense. In our world, which we experience between birth and death, a mediumistic person is someone who has developed certain portions of his brain in such a way that they can be disconnected from his being as a whole.

In a medium there are certain times when precisely those portions of the brain which particularly support, and are the foundation for, our ego-activity, are not available.

When we really say 'I' to ourselves, when we bring our ego fully into our consciousness, this consciousness is always supported by specific portions of the brain. In someone who is a medium, these portions of the brain get shut down. Because of this, certain beings of the kind I have just characterized, get an appetite to creep into these portions of the brain, in place of the human ego. Such a medium then becomes the bearer of those beings whose real task it is to carry civilization over into the future.

When these beings catch hold of a brain that at certain times is not occupied by its ego, they get an enormous appetite to submerse themselves into it. And when a medium is in a trance, as we say, and the brain is shut down, one of these beings that is under ahrimanic influence, and whose real task it is to carry civilization over into the future, slips into the brain. Instead of being the bearer of a human ego, the individual becomes, for this period of time, the bearer of an elemental being that is neglecting its duty in the cosmos. Please take this expression completely literally: a being that is neglecting its duty in the cosmos.

The duty of such a being in the cosmos is to see how people write. They write with forces that are anchored in the same portions of the brain I have just been speaking about. Instead of just watching, which is what they are otherwise supposed to be doing, these beings are on the alert for where they can find a mediumistic brain which can be shut off. Then they creep into it, and bear into the present-day world of humans what their observation has already taught them of the art of writing [for instance]. So that with the help of mediumistic individuals they project into the present what, in accordance with their mission, they ought to carry over into the future. Mediumship rests on the fact that what ought properly to be developed as faculties in the future gets developed already in the present in a chaotic and irregular way. Hence the prophetic qualities of the mediumistic person, and the fascination others have towards them. It is really something that works more perfectly in the present than man does, but it is introduced by beings in the way described.

Just as belladonna is a medium for the astral world, a medium for certain astral forces that it draws into its fruit, so a mediumistic person, through their particular kind of brain, is a medium for these elemental beings who at some point are required to participate in our civilization because humans cannot carry everything from one earthly life over into the next. This is the real mystery of mediumship: being possessed by these particular beings.

Now as you will realize, these beings are on the one hand the real creations of ahrimanic beings. Ahrimanic beings exist in the cosmos as beings with an intelligence that far surpasses that of humanity. As soon as we develop perception of the world immediately adjacent to our own, or are able to approach the ahrimanic beings in this physical world as well, we are astounded by their stupendous, their surpassing intelligence. They are far more intelligent than any human being can be. In intelligence they are truly superhuman. And we learn to respect such beings only when we realize how infinitely intelligent they are.

Something of this intelligence passes over into their creations, the elemental beings who slip into mediumistic brains, so that all manner of important things can come to light in this way through mediums. We can experience many significant things, particularly if we are able, with full and properly developed consciousness, to observe what such mediums produce. When we really understand the nature and constitution of the spiritual world we do not deny that a great deal that is correct can flow through mediums from the spiritual world into the physical. Many things of importance and significance can be experienced through mediums, but this is not the appropriate path. Why not?

We can understand this precisely from those plants that are plant-mediums, mediums for certain astral forces which make them poisonous. And in turn we only learn to understand these things by means of a well developed consciousness. I should like to describe this process in the following way, for when it comes to portraying spiritual worlds, it is better to describe things pictorially rather than to construct abstract concepts.

Let us suppose that we enter with initiation knowledge into the world where the dead are, after their death. We follow them. It is really the case that when we follow the dead in this way, we enter an entirely different world. I have described a part of this, and characterized for you how it makes a far more real impression on us than our world does in which we find ourselves between birth and death. But when we enter this world we notice immediately what other strange creatures there are here apart from the human souls of the dead. Shortly after someone has died, we see, if we follow them, that among the human souls of the dead there are strange demon-like creatures. At the very entrance of this soul land that the dead enter, whom we can accompany with a certain clairvoyant sight, we see demonic figures that have enormously large webbed feet, like ducks, or aquatic animals in general. (Of course, when we speak of large and small it can always only be in comparison with earthly conditions.) These webbed feet are continually changing shape. These beings have a form somewhat comparable to the form of a kangaroo, but half bird-like, half mammalian, and large and powerful. We pass through whole wide regions of such beings when we follow the dead.

Now if we ask ourselves: where are these beings?—we just need to have the right idea about how to consider the 'where' of these beings, where they are.

They are always around us, for we are in the same world in which the dead are. These beings are always around us, only just not in this hall. And this is where a genuine and rigorous path of spiritual research begins.

Suppose the following. You are walking over a meadow in autumn where you find many plants growing of the species *Colchicum autumnale*, the autumn crocus. You walk there and find autumn crocuses everywhere. While you are standing among these autumn crocuses you try to summon up the state of consciousness that can follow the dead, and you see, wherever an autumn crocus is growing, a being of the kind I have described, with the webbed feet and curious kangaroo-like body. Every autumn crocus turns into one of these beings. And if you go to another area, where belladonna, black deadly nightshade is growing beside the path, and put yourself into the state of consciousness we have been speaking about, you meet there quite different beings, terrible, demonic beings who also belong to that world.

So we can say that *Colchicum autumnale* and belladonna are mediums that let the next world into themselves, and with their other nature belong to the world of the dead.

If you bear this in mind, you will say to yourselves : 'All around us there is also what we call another world.' It is just a matter of entering with our consciousness, of not just seeing *Colchicum autumnale* and belladonna with our ordinary everyday consciousness, but with the higher consciousness that sees them in the realm of the dead. Then, with higher consciousness, we see belladonna where it is situated in the realm of the dead.

Now I would like you to consider the following. Let's say that here is a meadow where autumn crocuses are growing. Now, to find a deadly nightshade, you have to go far away, perhaps even up a hill. In the physical world belladonna and *Colchicum autumnale* do not grow near each other. But in the spiritual world next to our own, they exist side by side. Space is organized very differently [there]. What might be far apart in the physical world can be side by side in the spiritual world. The spiritual world has its own unique laws—everything is different there.

Now suppose that you come upon these plants in the world of the dead, if I can express it like that. The dead have by no means the terrible impression of these plants that the human being on the earth has, for they know that the existence of these demoniacal forms is founded on the wise cosmic plan. If you initially follow the dead in soul-land, you will find this soul-land occupied by the demonic forms corresponding to poisonous plants.

If you go farther and approach the regions which the dead leave after ten, twenty, thirty years in order to enter into a higher realm, that is where you begin to find what corresponds to our non-poisonous plants. That is where you first find the violet, for example, and similar plants that are not poisonous. So the plant world has its significance both in the physical and in the next higher world, but we see it there in other forms.

What I described as having its true form in the world of the stars is reflected on earth in the forms of a belladonna, an autumn crocus, or a violet. It is also reflected in the world of the dead. Immediately after death it is reflected in the way I described. Everything in one world also works upon the others. But in order to know these things in their reality, we must enter consciously into their own proper world. The same thing also applies to the beings of these other worlds. We can only know what these beings are, these elemental beings that are actually creatures of their ahrimanic masters, when we enter into the world immediately next to our own.

Now these beings make their appearance through mediums: they take possession of mediums, and in this way temporarily enter our world. So if we get to know these beings only through a medium in our world, then we are getting to know them in a world which should really be foreign to them; we are not acquainting ourselves with them in their true form. So for someone who only learns to know them by their manifestation through mediums, there is no possibility of reaching the truth, because the beings are manifesting in a world foreign to them. Spiritual revelations are definitely going on; but an understanding of them is impossible because we are only gaining knowledge of these beings in a world where they do not belong at all.

The deceptive and highly illusionary quality of everything that comes into the world through mediumistic consciousness is due to the fact that those who contact these beings have no knowledge of their real nature.

Now because they enter the world in this way, these beings have a very particular destiny. You see, we learn many other things when we get to know the world in the way I have described. When we enter the world of the dead and pass through the demoniacal forest of *Colchicum autumnale*, of *Digitalis purpurea* (foxglove) of *Datura stramonium* (thorn-apple) and so on, when we pass through this whole region, we realize that violets will undergo a metamorphosis; in the future they will have quite other forms. They have a significance for the future of the cosmos. *Colchicum autumnale* by its own nature partakes of death, for which it is destined. Poisonous plants are dying plants, plants that are dying out, that will not pass over into future forms. In future times there will be other poisonous entities. But the entities that are poisonous today will die out in our epoch. The epoch, of course, lasts a long time, but they carry the impulse of death in themselves. And this extends over all vegetation. When we look at vegetation with this kind of vision, we see aspects that are arising, developing, with impulses towards the future, and aspects that are dying off, uniting themselves with death.

And so it is with the beings who take possession of mediums. They separate themselves off from their companions whose task it is to bear the present over into far futures. Through the medium they penetrate into the world of the present, but here they unite themselves also with the destiny of the earthly, and lose their mission for the future.

But as a result of this they also rob man, from a higher perspective (*in einem hohen Sinne*), of his future mission. This is what we are confronted with directly when we come to understand the nature of mediumship. What mediumship really implies is: the future must die, the present is everything. Hence we are really astonished when, with a genuine insight into the facts and essence of the cosmos, we go to a spiritualistic seance, and see how the circle sitting there and participating in some kind of spiritualistic phenomena, is actually surrounded by what appears to us in the form of poisonous plants. Every spiritualistic seance is really hemmed in by a garden of poisonous plants which are not how they are in the world of the dead, but which grow up around the spiritualistic circle, and demoniacal beings can be seen rising out of their flowers and fruits.

That is what we experience at a spiritualistic seance if we are able to look into this other world. We pass through a kind of cosmic hedge that surrounds it, a hedge of poisonous plants that move in themselves, are as though alive, having something animal-like about them. Only by their forms do we recognize that they are poisonous plants.

From this we can clearly see how what is working in this mediumistic form, how what is supposed to flow onwards in the course of human evolution and become fruitful in the future, is banished to the present where it does not belong, and even becomes harmful for humanity. Such is the inner mystery of mediumship which we will explore during these lectures.

The inner mystery of mediumship

Now we can indicate very exactly where in the mediumistic make-up the pertinent point, so to speak, of the human constitution lies. Here I shall have to give you a seemingly abstract explanation, but it will help us to take a look into the nature of mediumship.

You see, the human brain as it lies in the cranium, has an average weight of about 1,500 grammes, or a little more. That is actually a considerable weight, and if this human brain were to press with its own weight on the delicate veins in the head below it, they would immediately be crushed. We human beings go about the world for a longer or shorter time as the case may be, but the weight of our brain does not press upon the system of veins below it. We can understand this directly we look at it in the right way.

Let us show the human being constituted like this (Steiner draws on the board). I will draw it very diagrammatically. You can see how the spinal canal goes upwards and spreads out into the brain (red). With the exception of a few portions that are semi-solid, the spinal canal is filled with fluid, and the brain floats in this fluid (lilac). And now think of the Archimedes principle; you will have learnt about it in your physics classes. This law was established by the ancient sage Archimedes, and it is said that he discovered it through his genius while he was in the bath. He made the first experiment while his whole body was lying in the bath. He lifted first one leg and then the other out of the water, and noticed that according to whether his legs were in the water or out of it, they had a different weight. They felt heavy when they were out of the water, and immediately lost their weight when they were in it. This was a different experience for an Archimedes than it would be for an ordinary person. An ordinary person just plays around. But Archimedes made a great, a stupendous discovery. 'Eureka!'—I have found it! For he discovered that every body floating in water, or in some fluid medium, loses in this fluid as much of its weight as is equivalent to the weight of the fluid displaced.

[lilac, red]

Let's imagine a vessel full of water. I place a solid body into the water. If I weigh the body as it is suspended in the water I can show that the body gets lighter in the water, weighs less than when it is out of the water. Now if we imagine a body of water of the same size, it also has a certain weight. This weight must be subtracted from the weight of the body when it is in the water. The body loses in the water as much of its weight as is equivalent to the weight of the body of water of the same volume. This is Archimedes' principle.

This Archimedes principle stands us in good stead in our human constitution, for the brain floats in cerebral fluid and loses as much of its weight as is equivalent to the weight of the cerebral fluid of an equal volume as the brain. So that the brain we carry about with us is not 1,500 grammes in weight, but it loses the equivalent weight of a fluid brain; it loses 1,480 grammes, which leaves only around 20 grammes. In reality we do not carry about a brain of 1,500 grammes, but only of 20 grammes. The rest of the weight is lost, for the brain floats in cerebral fluid in conformity with the Archimedes principle. So we have here in our organism something that is lighter than its actual weight. In us the brain weighs only 20 grammes. But we must pay attention to these 20 grammes that still have some weight. For it is only these 20 grammes that are able to receive our ego. Everything else of us is situated elsewhere.

Now the whole body is filled with all manner of solid constituents which also float in fluid, for example the blood-corpuscles. They all lose something of their weight; but the weight that remains also has the ego in it, so that the ego is spread out in the blood, but with less weight than the weight of the blood. We need to observe very carefully everything that still has any weight within us as we go about the world. Indeed, ladies and gentlemen, you must all take tremendous care of what is here (see drawing: brain) within you and still has weight in the original and literal sense. For it is there that the ego may rightly be. It may not rightly be anywhere else; everywhere else there must be astral body, etheric body, and so on.

A medium is simply a person in whom this weight constituent, this 20 grammes of the brain, no longer contains the ego. The ego is driven out of gravity, out of weight. And then the beings I have spoken about can immediately enter.

You will notice something peculiar in what I have been presenting. The materialistic mode of thinking wants to localize everything. It asks: 'Yes, but where exactly is the part of the human being that the elemental being occupies when it takes possession of the medium?' We can't talk about these things in this way; only the materialistic intellect talks like this. This is how someone speaks who thinks mechanically and mathematically. But life doesn't take its course mathematically and mechanically, but dynamically. Hence we mustn't say that the medium is possessed here or there, localizing the thing in terms of mathematics or geometry; but we must say: 'The medium is possessed in those parts of his constitution that remain heavy in him, in those parts that are pulled towards the earth.' That is where the ahrimanic beings can get in. And not only there, but elsewhere as well. You see, what I have presented very exactly here is only the very basics of the matter. There are more subtle aspects.

How do we see on the physical plane? We have our eyes (see diagram). The optic nerve runs backwards from the eye towards the brain. It spreads out in the eye and runs backwards to the brain. The optic nerve is the basis of colour perception. Now the materialists start thinking about how the optic nerve carries colour to the brain and deposits it there. The materialists imagine it all like the unloading of a ship or a train. Something is loaded externally into the optic nerve, is transported by the nerves, is then unloaded somewhere, and then passes into the soul—well, not quite as crudely as that, but it comes to the same thing. What actually happens is utterly different!

The truth is that the optic nerve is not there to carry colour perception backwards into the brain, but, at a specific point, to extinguish it. Colour is only there externally at the periphery. The farther inwards we go, we find that the function of the optic nerve is to extinguish colour so that the brain is as colourless as possible, so that only very weak, fading colours reach the brain. And not only colours are extinguished, but every relationship with the external world is extinguished in the brain as well. Hearing, sight, are in the senses. As they approach the brain, the visual, auditory and warmth nerves extinguish everything they have received from the periphery to a faint shadow. The faint shadow has the same ratio to perception as the 20 grammes has to the 1,500. For the 20 grammes is also only a shadow of the weight of the brain.

We are left there with so little. We look at the huge, gigantic rosy dawn that is in our senses, and have only a faint shadow of it in our brain. But we must pay attention again to these faint shadows, for it is only there that our ego can enter.

The moment the ego is shut out, when someone becomes mediumistic, an elemental being of the kind I have been describing immediately creeps into these faint shadows, or into the faint sounds that come from hearing, and so on. Everywhere where the ego belongs, where the external sense-perception is extinguished, this being creeps in and possesses the medium. Then it creeps into the ramifications of the nerves, right into the will-system; that is to say, right into the nerves that pass into the will-system. And then it happens that the medium starts to become active, because the part of him that should be held only by the ego, has been taken over [by the being]. The remnants of weight in the brain, the remnants of colour-perception, of auditory perception and so on, all these faint shadow elements that fill us like a phantom—for this 20 grammes of weight, these faint shadows of colours that go into our interior are phantom-like—it is into this that the elemental being submerses itself. And then the person lying there becomes completely still, his body becomes lethargic, and everything becomes active in him which should really be filled by the ego in the faint phantom-like shadows [gap in text], and which otherwise *are* filled by it.

So look at a medium. A human being can only be a medium by allowing everything in which a normal person functions, to sink down into lethargy, into absolute inertia, allowing the phantom I have described to become active. And you can observe this, for example, in the way a medium writes. They would naturally not be able to write if everything inside them were not lighter just as in the brain; for all the weight is floating in fluid; in feeling and sensation it becomes lighter, and the medium then writes in the lightness in which the ego otherwise guides the pen. It is in this human phantom that the elemental being guides the pen of the medium.

You see, it is true to say that when a medium is sitting there or manifesting in some other way, there is a projection from another world. Just as ahrimanic beings of another world can project themselves into the movements made by a medium, so they can also project themselves into all the emanations I described yesterday. Powerful emanations of the fluid nature are always present in the regions of the human organism where glands are situated. So these elemental beings penetrate into the fluid-emanations, and likewise into the breath-emanations and light-emanations. Only when we come to the chemical-emanations is there a conscious interaction between the one who is making use of these chemical-emanations and the beings who enter into them. And this is where black magic begins: in the conscious working with these beings who get into us in the way I described.

Mediums and, as a rule, those who experiment with them, are unconscious of the real processes that are going on, whereas the black magician is usually fully conscious that he is invoking these beings of the elemental world into the chemical-emanations of a human being, most often into his own. So the black magician is actually always surrounded by a host of servants consisting of these elemental beings, and he makes it possible for them to use the occult-chemical impulses here in this physical sensory world, either through his own emanations or through fumigation procedures that he carries out in his laboratory.

This brings us to the realization that just as belladonna grows into a world in which it doesn't belong and thereby becomes poisonous, so the spiritual world grows by means of mediumship into the world we inhabit between birth and death. And fundamentally speaking, this danger of the spiritual world growing [into our world] in a similar way to our description of belladonna, is always present every time the level of consciousness, that is to say the presence of the ego (*Ich-Erfüllung*) is suppressed, when a human being is in a dazed, unconscious-like condition, or really unconscious.

Every time human consciousness is lowered not by normal sleep but by something else, there is the danger that a window will be opened for the world I have just described. And the extent to which the opening of such windows through reduced levels of human consciousness plays a highly significant role in human life, we will hear about in the following lectures tomorrow.

LECTURE 9

Abnormal Ways into the Spiritual World and How to Transform Them

The use of scientific thinking for the path of knowledge

OUR studies in these lectures began with a look into an ordinary state in present-day life: into dream-life. It was then possible to move on to a discussion of other states of consciousness in the human soul which are able to penetrate into worlds other than the one we live in between birth and death. This brought us to mediumistic consciousness, to the consciousness, we can say, that leads us into a somnambulist state, for a mediumistic condition is always somnambulistic. Now both modes of experience—dreaming and somnambulism—are indeed inner conditions of the soul which are also to be found in their appropriate form in normal life. It is only when they are intensified that they lead into either correct or false waters.

So let's turn once more today to dream life. We have seen that someone with ordinary consciousness experiences dreams when he passes from the state of waking to sleeping, and that there is a vibration in his astral body that is an echo of what goes on in his etheric and physical bodies during the waking state. Then come the chaotic, albeit wonderful dream experiences that only an initiate is able to interpret properly, because in their usual chaotic condition they are confusing for anyone who does not penetrate more deeply into the nature of the spiritual world.

But we have also seen how, through exercises in meditation and concentration, this web of dream-life becomes permeated by a genuine higher consciousness. So we must picture the human being transported into the wonderful chaotic world of dreams, but at the same time this dream-life suffused with conscious awareness, so that we are as prudent there, and as much in reality, as we are in ordinary life. Then we look into another world, into the world I described where we can accompany the dead in their after-death existence. And we feel ourselves as though split up and spread out in a world far more real than the one we are presently in.

The question now is: which world have we actually entered? I have already spoken about this, but will touch on the subject once more today from another point of view.

As I said, there were once great teachers who lived among human beings on earth. They lived not in a physical body but in a subtle etheric body, and were also able to embody themselves in air. They taught humans through Inspiration, and were the founders of the primordial culture of the earth. When we look back into ancient times with the appropriate condition of consciousness, we find these great primordial spiritual teachers of humanity moving among people. These great teachers withdrew to the moon, and today are only to be found in the moon-sphere. There they have taken into their service all manner of beings who have never been on earth. The great teachers live among these elemental beings, and work upon the human being who has passed through the portal of death, making him aware of what, in accordance with his karma, he needs to do (*wie er sich seinem Karma gemäß zu verhalten hat*). We also have to do with these beings at the first stage when we wish to enter the spiritual world. Just as we can only live earthly life with people, in society with others, together socially with others, so likewise we can only live in higher consciousness in the company of other beings. And it is with these moon beings, who were once the primordial teachers of humanity upon earth, and with the beings who have entered their service, that we research the spiritual world immediately bordering our own.

It is also always here that we find clues regarding the earlier incarnations of individuals, for going back into earlier ages in order to seek out personalities who lived earlier, and with whom we are karmically connected or not. As an example I told you how, by further progress in this state of consciousness, one gradually enters into relationship with earthly beings who are not incarnated on the earth today, such as Brunetto Latini, Dante, Alanus ab Insulis, and so forth.

This state of consciousness is therefore an illumination, an enlightening of the dream-state. The dream-state in ordinary life is the rudiment, so to speak, of this state. Now what is the difference between someone who has ordinary consciousness and an initiate? It is quite easy to get an idea of this difference.

When we are asleep in the ordinary sense, our physical and etheric bodies lie in bed. With our astral body and ego we are outside our physical and etheric. In a dream it is only the ego that has experiences. Although the events experienced in the dream are in the astral body that is outside the physical and etheric bodies, nevertheless it is only the ego that, for normal consciousness, can have experiences in a dream. In the case of the initiate however, the ego and above all the astral body both experience. So the difference between an initiate and an ordinary dreamer is that the dreamer only experiences with his ego when he is outside his physical and etheric bodies, whereas the initiate experiences with the astral body as well.

Now in the ancient mysteries this way of perceiving for research into supersensory worlds was already highly developed. It continued to be developed in a rudimentary, decadent form during the Middle Ages, and also in later epochs, until in modern times it has more or less been lost. Isolated individuals, either by spiritual means or through tradition, have always received information from the ancient teachers in the mysteries as to how ordinary dream-life can be illuminated with consciousness; it has always been possible for individuals to penetrate into the worlds that are entered in this way.

There is always a danger for us when we try to penetrate into these worlds. For example, when in these worlds the initiate dives down with imaginative consciousness into what is otherwise filled out by our dreams, he always immediately has the feeling that he is losing the world, that with his consciousness he is losing himself, so to speak, in a void. He always has the feeling that solid ground, that weight and gravity start to elude him. He feels himself becoming inwardly light, feels how without himself willing it he is being carried out into spiritual expanses of the cosmos, how he could easily lose control over himself because all weight, all heaviness is lost to him.

The exercises described in my book, *Knowledge of the Higher Worlds and its Attainment* are given for the purpose of preventing this. Someone who devotes themselves to the practice of these exercises in the right way, will find that they become a winged being in their soul, that they can then make use of these soul wings, as it were, when gravity and weight are no longer there. But precisely this is the precarious state when, as an initiate, we lose, as it were, our physical feet and our etheric feet, and do not yet have the wings of the astral body and ego. You understand what I mean when I express it pictorially like this. But this is what it is like. By growing carefully into this world that we enter through the exercises, all danger is naturally removed, no danger can present itself. We can gradually grow into this world just as, with our physical and etheric bodies, we grow into the ordinary physical world.

But this is the state primordial humanity was in more or less naturally. We have to attain it through exercises. Primordial humanity didn't need to; primordial humanity had a disposition quite naturally whereby it was always in a condition that was not like our waking, but was spiritual sight such as I described for the Chaldaeans, and a condition that was not like our dreaming, but a perceiving through Imagination. When a human being met another, he did not only see the other's bodily contours but dreamt the aura around him. But this was the real aura, not just a subjectively dreamt-up one.

As well as the gift for perceiving the aura around an earthly human being in physical life, people also possessed the other faculty—for both are connected—of seeing the aura of a spiritual being not incarnated in a physical body. And then he dreamt the form of this spiritual being.

Please note the difference here. When in ancient times one man met another, an earthly man, he saw the earthly man and, in a real dream, 'imagined' the aura around him. When a man met a spirit being, an angel or elemental being, he saw the aura spiritually first, and in a dream process added the form to it.

This was also how primal painters painted—only we no longer know this. The ancient painters saw the spiritual beings and then 'dreamt' the forms to go with them. They painted the beings of the hierarchy of the Angeloi with a fair resemblance to human beings; they painted the Archangeloi with diffused bodies but with clearly defined wings and head; and for the Archai they painted only the head, a winged head, because this was the form they 'dreamt.' All these things were natural, so to speak, for the people of ancient times, just as it is natural for us today to see people's eyes or their noses. Because these things have been gradually lost to humanity, they must be acquired again today through exercises and training. But because this was natural for primal humanity, and could always be relatively easily regained through exercises, this region has in all times been the subject of much investigation. The world governed, so to speak, by the moon-beings was always keenly researched, and the initiates of the ancient mysteries, who were the real researchers into this region, speak a great deal about this world, of their meetings with the dead, of their researches into the moon-sphere, and of how the world appears from the perspective of the moon-sphere. Copernicus based his Copernican system only on the earth-sphere. The ancient Ptolemaic system is not wrong, but is seen from the perspective of the moon-sphere, and there it is correct.

Now there is a particular characteristic we always find in such investigators, and that is that they do not go further than the moon-sphere. You see, you all know that what we call the Anthroposophical Society existed to begin with within the Theosophical Society. The Theosophical Society, which is a similar society, has given a great deal of this nature over time, and has a rich literature. If you read this literature, ladies and gentlemen, you will find—whether rightly or wrongly is not the point for the moment—that it describes the world I have just been speaking about, the world investigated with the moon-beings, the world of the moon-sphere. And it was something of significance for me, I should like to say, something connected with certain difficulties, when it was proposed that I become active in the Theosophical Society. For amongst all the people in the Theosophical Society I only found research and literature that related to this moon-sphere. This certainly includes much that is incorrect, but also much that is exceptionally significant, great, stupendous—especially in the writings of H. P. Blavatsky[20]. But everything that is to be found in Blavatsky's writings is as it is because she herself stood within the sphere I have just described, and because she was connected with initiates who modestly remained within this moon-sphere. Now it is fair to say that I have got to know many of these initiates and seen how minds of this nature penetrate into the moon-sphere, and how they become disinterested in going any further.

So when I wrote my book, *Occult Science*—I wrote it between 1906 and 1909—I described the earth in its former embodiment as Moon, in its former embodiment as Sun, in its former embodiment as Saturn. You find in this book that I did not stop at the Moon embodiment, but went right back to Saturn, whereas all the initiates who spoke of these things stopped between Moon and Sun, actually only went back to the moon-sphere. They lost interest, at times even became agitated if it was suggested to them that they go back further. They said it was impossible, that you come to a boundary where there is an impenetrable veil.

It was, of course, extremely important and interesting to find the reason for this. You see, the reason is that initiates like this—when you got to know them well you soon noticed it—had an aversion, an antipathy towards acquainting themselves with the type of thoughts and thinking that are related to modern science. One even found that when one approached these initiates with concepts such as live in Darwinism, Haeckelism and so on, they became completely indignant, regarded these as so much childishness and stupidity on the part of modern humanity, and wouldn't look at them. If you approached them with Goethean ideas, at first they were not indignant, but later they felt that Goethe did express himself in the same way as modern scientific researchers, and they threw the whole thing out.

In short, when it came to these ideas one could get nowhere with these initiates. And only once I had impressed modern scientific ideas into my soul, between 1906 and 1909, in order to bring them into the region where otherwise Imaginations are to be found, was it possible for me to penetrate through to Sun and Saturn. I did not use these scientific ideas in order to understand things in the way Haeckel or Huxley understood them, but used them as an inner activity to get beyond the boundary that initiates had been subject to at a time when the new scientific mode of thinking was not yet developed, and one therefore could only reach higher consciousness by impregnating the dream world with Imaginations.

So in writing my *Outline of Occult Science,* the attempt was made to take the wholly conscious world of ideas that is otherwise only related to external objects of nature, and apply it inwardly in order to impregnate the imaginative world with it. It then became possible to penetrate into this whole sequence of Saturn, Sun, and Moon. One then came to the idea of researching on earth what the ancient initiates had also researched.

I am relating how this understanding developed so that you can see how these things take their course. You could say that this is a personal matter. But in this case the personal element is actually completely objective. And if people have found fault with my *Outline of Occult Science,* it is to say that it is written like a textbook on mathematics, that I didn't try to introduce any subjective element but described the whole course I just mentioned [of Saturn, Sun, Moon, etc.] with mathematical coolness. But that is how it is. It came about by taking the mode of thinking that has existed since Copernicus, Galileo and so on, and was so greatly deepened by Goethe, and transferring it into the same state of soul that one otherwise has in Imagination. It thus became possible to carry this region, which had always been accessible to initiates, farther towards its beginning, farther in time to the point of Saturn.

You will perhaps see from this example that the important thing in these matters is not to proceed vaguely, but with clarity and sound sense, precisely to apply sound sense where otherwise lack of it easily begins. So here we have an example where dream-life that usually only takes hold of the ego, also takes hold of the astral body.

To the question: what is the difference between modern natural science and what I have given in *An Outline of Occult Science?*—I should like to reply: the difference is that the modern scientific thinker can only have recourse to the ego, and immediately starts to dream when he leaves the ego; and that I was able to tell the astral body what sort of ideas the science researchers have. As a result of this, the astral body was able to penetrate into the worlds I had to describe. This is a path that can be described to you very precisely and, as an example, can perhaps show you more precisely than anything else how the right paths differ from the wrong.

Overcoming the caricature of the scientific method for research into mediumism and somnambulism

Now the polar opposite condition to the dream-state is the state of somnambulism or mediumship. The dreamer lives wholly in his ego and astral body; even though he has no conscious perceptions in the astral body, he nevertheless lives within it. The dreamer lives completely in his ego and astral body, outside his physical and etheric bodies. So he is sunk down, submerged in his own being and, because his own being is connected with other worlds, is in those worlds due to his own being [and also, to a certain extent, in his physical organism]. The dreamer thus dives down into his own being, and thereby into the cosmos. The exact opposite is the case with mediums and somnambulists. A person is only in a mediumistic or a somnambulist state when they are also outside their physical and etheric bodies with their ego and astral body, but in this case the ego and astral body, as discussed yesterday, are permeated by a foreign being.

So with a medium or somnambulist we have their physical being, but the ego and astral body are outside the physical and etheric bodies. The ego is suppressed, put in a state of servitude, and so is the astral body because another being is occupying it, as I described yesterday. As a result of this, a medium cannot work back in the right way on their physical and etheric bodies. For even when we are in dreamless sleep for example, we still work back on the physical and etheric bodies. When we are awake, we permeate the physical and etheric bodies in a certain sense from inside; when we are asleep we protect them from outside. With a somnambulist this no longer happens. Mediums or somnambulists cannot look after their physical and etheric bodies, which become a deserted area, so to speak. This is the characteristic feature of mediums or somnambulists, that their physical and etheric bodies are a deserted region.

When we look at the human being that has the normal soul-constitution for someone of the present day, we see that it is only the forces of minerals and plants that have an influence on his physical and etheric bodies—nothing else, just the forces of minerals and plants. If the forces of the mineral, of the mineral earth, did not work upon our physical body, we would not be able to walk, we would not be able to move, because these are the physical forces that we use. We are permitted to enter into these forces; that is the normal condition. But they must not come into the etheric body.

It is the same thing with plants. They may still work in a certain sense on the etheric body, but not too strongly. But neither the forces that bring about sentience in animals, nor the forces of another human being, should influence the human physical body, or especially the etheric body. Because the physical and etheric bodies of mediums and somnambulists are deserted, animal and earthly-human forces are able to influence them. They are influenced by suggestion.

Just as a thought sinks down out of dreaming, so now the human will sinks down out of the human being and into his surroundings. And we can suggest to the somnambulist or the medium that he should walk. We can give him a potato and suggest to him that it is a tasty pear, and so on. By suggestion we gain direct access to the medium's or somnambulist's physical body, and via that to their etheric. Somnambulists and mediums carry in their etheric body the physical surroundings they should only carry, as is the case with a normal person, in their physical body. A normal person is given up in a dreaming way to the inner spirit world. The somnambulist or medium is given up to the external natural world.

Now being mediumistic or somnambulist is a normal condition in the circumstances where it *is* normal: for the fact that we can walk, that we can hold things, that we are able to do anything at all in space, is a magical-somnambulistic process in everyone. It is just that it must not rise up into the etheric body; it must remain in the physical body. But it is always possible for what is normal to cross over into something abnormal. You see, the dreamer is completely within his own being; the medium or somnambulist is completely out of himself. The physical and etheric bodies of mediums and somnambulists are like automata, as it were, that we can influence because they are not taken care of by their own ego and astral body. Just as a connection is produced in the dreamer with the inner spirit world, so in the somnambulist and medium a connection is produced with the outer world of nature, with the world of shape and formation, with everything that is perceptible, spatial, and temporal.

When we sink into the dream-world, we are submersed into an element of formlessness, of eternal change. When we penetrate into the world where the somnambulist or medium exercises their will under the influence of suggestion—in other words, the physical and etheric bodies penetrate into this world—we find everything there defined, with clear contours. Everything that is done due to an external influence is carried out with extraordinary precision. This is the exact opposite of the dreamer's world; with the medium it is a realized dreaming, as it were, produced externally by nature, where dreaming takes place in activity instead of in inner experience only. This antithesis is significant and of the greatest interest when we look at it from an initiate standpoint. As I told you, the initiate has his difficulties when he sinks down into the world of dreams in order to permeate it with Imagination, for he has the feeling that he is losing gravity and weight: he loses everything of the external world that gives him solid ground. When the initiate begins to get used to this world—and he must do this now *consciously*, he must develop a consciousness that enables him to go out into this world just as the somnambulist goes out into it unconsciously—he has the feeling that at any moment he could lose consciousness. This possibility of losing consciousness is a situation he faces constantly, and it is therefore always necessary for him to keep a firm inner grip on himself so that consciousness is not lost.

I should like to say that when we proceed in that world, we must, as initiates, move there as sensibly as reasonably sensible, respectable people do in our world. There should be nothing about the initiate that causes others to notice that while he is going about among people, animals and stones, he is living with full consciousness in a spiritual world. For if he should think for only a moment that he had no feet but was flying through this world, he would very, very easily fall prey to all kinds of affectations which people around him would find dubious. They would say 'What kind of madman is this!' This could happen if he did not keep a tight hold of himself in order to maintain full consciousness as he passes through the spiritual world that is present everywhere, just as the physical sense-world is everywhere.

An area [of study] is opening up here that has not become a domain of the Theosophical Society but is an area with which eminent natural-scientific researchers are concerning themselves: namely, the area they term psychical research, and so on. It is an area in which people who are scientifically trained, but unable to accomplish much in science, make statistical records of these kinds of things, do experiments with mediums in order to find out about the spiritual world. In all kinds of societies and from all kinds of points of view an area [of study] is created where people now try to investigate from outside what is going on when a person moves their limbs or behaves not with their usual consciousness but with a reduced or completely extinguished consciousness, when other beings have taken possession of their soul. Records are then made of what people do in this state.

The suggestion has even been made by certain people who are enthusiastic about this kind of research that I myself, with what I have to say to the world, should put myself at their disposal in their laboratories so that they can investigate from outside what is going on in this inner world. This is about as sensible as someone saying: 'I don't understand anything about mathematics, so I can't say whether the assertions of a mathematician are true or false, but he should come to me in my psychical laboratory and I will do experiments on him to find out whether he is a great mathematician or not.'

This is approximately how it is. I am speaking here of an area at the present time where, using a caricature of the scientific method, people also want to research the world of the somnambulist and the medium. But they do it from the outside, and do not actually want to look at the inner aspect of it. For if they did look at the inner side, they would see that in mediumship and somnambulism they are faced with an external phenomenon, an automaton of the physical and etheric bodies; that they are therefore not researching what they want to research—the actual spiritual or mental element—for what they have before them has been deserted by this. But people simply do not want to look into these more subtle attributes of the spiritual world. They mostly just want to have the spiritual before them as an external perception and not as an inner experience. They want to have the spiritual before them as outwardly visible, sense-perceptible activity.

This kind of thing may also crop up in another way. It appears in such things as occurred later in the Theosophical Society—specifically during the time when I was going through the inner process I described—where people were looking for the spiritual figure of Christ in a physical personality.[21] People wanted to have something purely spiritual in the outer physical world.

Art as a bridge between matter and spirit

But we must let the physical world be physical, and look for the spiritual where it actually exists, which is of course also in the physical world but really in the spheres that permeate the physical world and are spiritual. But these are a different region. And man, in his healthy state, feels himself called upon to build a bridge between the one region and the other, between the regions of inner experience and external perception, between the world in which, abnormally, the dreamer is to be found, and the world in which, abnormally, the medium or the somnambulist lives. When the two worlds are brought together and mutually fructified, the result is art. For in art what is externally perceptible to the senses is permeated with spirit, with the impulses of the spiritual world, and what is perceptible in the inner world of soul is represented in an outer embodiment.

So while the Theosophical Society was engaged in presenting an external physical being as a spiritual one[21], we in the Anthroposophical Society were impelled to let the occult stream flow over into art. The Mystery Plays came into being. Eurythmy came into being.

The art of speech-formation was developed. All that came about here in the anthroposophical movement came from the impulse to build a bridge from the spiritual into the physical, so that consciousness can flow from the world the dreamer enters chaotically, and over into the world the somnambulist or medium enters chaotically. In art, the two worlds are consciously integrated.

One day people will understand this. They will come to see what it means for instance that, through these endeavours, speech-formation as practised by Marie Steiner is to be brought back again to the level it once had when human beings were still instinctively spiritual. In those days, rhythm and measure in speech had more value than the external, abstract meaning of a word. This must be mastered once again. And in eurythmy, mastery is brought back again with respect to the human being in movement, who unfolds before us as a being of soul and spirit. That is what you see in eurythmy.

So in art we have had in the first place to build this bridge from the world in which the dreamer roams, to the world in which the somnambulist, the medium, stumbles and blunders about. In our present materialistic age the dreamer stands there and muses in solitude, knowing nothing of the structures and material forms which express and reveal the spiritual. The somnambulists on the other hand—irrespective of whether they are revered as mediums, or, as Bolshevists, create pure theory about the State and, like mediums, realize all manner of things in the outer world—somnambulists wander through the modern world, and have no inkling of the spiritual.

The essential thing is to rediscover the bridge from spirit into matter, from matter to spirit. The first thing to be done in the arts is to build this bridge, to stop groping and stumbling about in the external world, and gain understanding of it through spiritual movements that are not the usual ones.

So you see, the true, inner beginning of eurythmy is an initiate impulse, and everything we practise as the art of speech-formation also derives from this impulse. And when the forthcoming course on dramatic art is held at Dornach, an effort will be made to bring the art of acting back to a point where the spiritual will be present on stage. For a long time people have only been thinking about how to put the actor on stage in a way that has as much resemblance to ordinary life as possible. The discussions on this in the 1890s were just comic. The question was discussed (and finally decided in favour of naturalism) whether Schiller's characters should speak their heroic sentences on stage with their hands in their pockets, because this happened to be the fashion!

You see, there is good reason to find the path to proper research into the spiritual world. And the path through the realm of art is by no means an entirely incorrect one.

It was of great significance to push forward from the ancient initiation knowledge, which was absorbed in the mysteries of the moon and everything this involved, to what can only be penetrated when the attainments (I mean here the soul attainments) of natural science are impregnated into the level of soul that is capable of occult understanding. But whereas this is of tremendous significance [on the one hand], it is no less significant on the other hand that the unclear, dilettante experiments that are done to try to get behind what it is, in the medium or somnambulist whose mind has left them, that moves in the guise of the mind (*in den Formen des Geistigen*) under spiritual influence—it was no less significant that this became a specific area of research. For these two paths must actually be regarded as one: the breakthrough from within via the dream world that has now lost its chaotic quality, and the conscious comprehension of the outer world which natural science understands only through its mineral attributes that are to be investigated dilettantishly using so-called psychical research. It is important, particularly since we are living in a scientific age, to take this path of spiritual research as well, to conduct thorough spiritual research in the other region, the region that is the polar opposite of dreaming.

When we have a somnambulist or medium before us, something happens through them that we are not used to in ordinary life. A somnambulist does not write like an ordinary person, does not move like an ordinary person, does not talk like an ordinary person, does not experience taste like an ordinary person, because their astral body and ego are outside their physical and etheric bodies, and we are dealing with a physical body and etheric body that are abandoned and are now under the influence of the cosmos, are given up to the influence of the cosmos. So what we are dealing with here are manifestations of the physical and etheric bodies that are not the usual natural phenomena, but derive from the spiritual world. For, in principle, it is one and the same whether we stand before a medium and suggest something to him, or if the medium is open to some kind of stellar influence which he absorbs into his etheric body, or a climatic influence, or the influence of a metal, and so on.

In a medium we have before us an organization that is open to the spiritual in a magical way. This is what we must bear in mind. We cannot study these phenomena without already being acquainted with the spiritual, which is what the societies for external psychical research would like to do, who want to conduct experiments around this in an external way. We need to be able to look at the spiritual connections. In the foreground we have what is happening through the medium or somnambulist or any other person, but in the background we need to see what is happening spiritually.

But these effects we see in mediums and somnambulists are all related to other mediumistic phenomena. When we have a medium sitting here who, in a specific state, performs certain actions under a human or cosmic influence—which means that a physical and etheric body perform these actions—this is exactly the same, only in a transient and temporary way, as what from a different cause is active in poisonous plants, which make us ill. We could say that it is only the transient mask of the illness that shows itself in the somnambulist or mediumistic condition. And from a certain point of view, which we will discuss further in the following lectures, we can see in the phenomena of somnambulism and mediumship (or we might not see it, but it is possible) what is really happening in a human being who is ill: that in an abnormal way their ego and astral body have withdrawn from an organ or from the whole organism, and the person has become exposed to particular spiritual influences.

You see, in ancient times people knew of this connection, and because of this the mysteries were always associated with healing. And because people were not as inquisitive then as they are today, they did not consider it necessary to concern themselves with mediums and somnambulists, the effects around whom they understood in the way they understood conditions of illness. They occupied themselves with these things more from a medical standpoint. And this was a standpoint we need to attain once more.

And the other approach, which enters the spiritual directly through natural phenomena—this other approach, which is taken dilettant-ishly, must be taken in the appropriate way. What is in the world and comes to expression particularly in pathological conditions in human beings and animals must again be pursued in the right way. Only by this will people reach a stage where they are able to investigate what the Society for Psychical Research would like to investigate.

This path too has been entered upon in the Anthroposophical Society. It was made possible by researching pathological phenomena in such a way that, through them, access to the spiritual world opens up. This has been possible because, in the co-operation between Dr Ita Wegman and myself, we have tried to follow in the right way the path that has eluded physical research. It was also possible because Dr Ita Wegman has not only the knowledge acquired by the modern doctor, but also the intuitive and therapeutic impulses that lead directly from the clinical picture of the disease into the spiritual world, and come to a remedy there.

Here, then, lies the path for research into the region I have been speaking about. An attempt has been made through this work to develop a true initiated medical science, which in itself is an initiated natural science. In this way the right path can be shown to the world, in contrast to the wrong ones. And the first volume of a book writ-ten by Dr Ita Wegman and myself[22] which will shortly be published, will indicate how this path needs to be taken.

As you see, the simplest way to show the differences between the appropriate and the mistaken paths is by examples, and that is why it seemed appropriate to present them here. I said previously that a way must be opened up into art which will bring the sphere of the spiritual and the sphere of what is formed in matter closer together. I must add to this that, under the conditions of modern civilization, it is directly apparent that the right path to art will only be found when the right path in natural phenomena is followed. For where the arts are concerned, humanity is so far removed today from building the bridge I spoke about, that people will perhaps only realize and understand the life and weaving of the spirit, also in the arts, when they can be convinced of the working of the spiritual element in the intensive way one sees it in the genesis of pathology, and see how the spirit lives and reveals itself in matter. This will be shown in the co-operative work of Dr Ita Wegman and myself. When people are able to see this in the realm of nature, then perhaps enthusiasm, a full enthusiasm, can awaken for the necessity of placing these things before the world in art itself.

Tomorrow I shall speak further on these things.

LECTURE 10

21 AUGUST 1924

Influences of the Extraterrestrial Cosmos on Human Consciousness

Influences exerted by sun and moon

Y ESTERDAY I showed how the abnormal, pathological paths into the spiritual world—on the one hand the path of an inner mysticism, a deeper penetration into the dream world, and on the other hand that path which, using a caricature, we could say, of the scientific method, examines in an external way the phenomena associated with somnambulists and mediums—how both these paths must be taken up and continued in a fruitful way if real initiation knowledge is to come about. Today we will go more deeply into this realm by considering the cosmic influences under which human consciousness stands, and indeed human consciousness together with our whole human being.

It is easy to see that among all the influences working on us, over and above those of the earth, the influences of the sun and moon are predominant. People do not usually give this much attention, but it is even scientifically quite evident today that nothing on earth would exist were it not for the sun forces coming from the extraterrestrial cosmos.

The sun's influences conjure up the entire plant world; they are essential to all animal life, but also to everything in the human being of a physical and etheric nature. Solar activity can be found everywhere—if people are only willing to look—and is certainly also significant for the higher human members-of-being.

Less attention is paid to lunar influences. A good deal of superstition is connected with these, and what could be known scientifically about them gets distorted in many ways because of these notions, so that those who wish to work scientifically, and feel themselves to be above superstition, reject the significant aspects of lunar influences, regarding them as unscientific. Here and there not only poets, who know how the magic of the moon can stimulate their imagination; not only lovers, who like to arrange their trysts by moonlight; but even researchers have an inkling that there are lunar influences on the earth, albeit of a very different kind.

One can come across some very curious things in this connection. In the middle of the nineteenth century there lived in Germany two professors. One was called Schleiden,[23] and the other Gustav Theodor Fechner.[23] Fechner liked to study, from a precise scientific standpoint, the more mysterious workings of nature in human beings and in nature at large. He collected data and drew up a statistical record of how the amount of rainfall in a particular district was connected with full moon and new moon. The results, according to him, showed greater rainfall for that particular area during certain phases of the moon than during others. He presented this view, and was not embarrassed to uphold this kind of science against the accepted science of the day. But his university colleague, Professor Schleiden the eminent botanist, had a different opinion. He ridiculed this idea of Fechner's and said that lunar influences of this kind were out of the question.

The curious thing was this: both these professors were married and lived in what was at that time a comparatively small university town (although it is now one of the larger towns in Germany) where patriarchal conditions prevailed. Circumstances at that time were such that the wives used to collect the rain-water because they thought it particularly good for doing the laundry. Now, there was a Frau Professor Fechner and a Frau Professor Schleiden, and it so happened that it was not only the two professors who discussed this question but their wives got to hear about it too. And what should happen but Professor Fechner said to his wife: 'Professor Schleiden doesn't believe the phases of the moon have any effect on rainfall.

I want you to say that you will take the rain-water that falls during [full and new moon], and that Frau Professor Schleiden can have the rainwater that falls during the other phases. Since Professor Schleiden doesn't believe the phases of the moon have anything to do with it at all, there can be no possible objection.' But just look what happened: Frau Professor Schleiden didn't want to hand over to Frau Professor Fechner those moon phases which her husband didn't believe had greater rainfall! There was a regular university families' squabble about it. But it had a scientific background. If we look at these influences with the methods of spiritual science, we find that it is indeed possible to speak of strong solar and lunar influences, not merely superstitiously but truly scientifically.

But, with that said, we have really exhausted all that exists in the ordinary consciousness of the modern person on the subject. The present-day human being lives, as it were, under the influence of earth, sun and moon. The present-day human being is also essentially dependent on earth, sun and moon. For as indicated, the externally visible aspect of the stars is not what is most important, nor the externally visible aspect of the sun or moon. We said explicitly that the moon-sphere holds within it beings who were once the great primordial teachers of humanity. The sun-sphere likewise contains a vast multitude of spiritual beings. Every star is a colony of beings in the same way that the earth is the cosmic colony of humanity.

But as we said: during the period between birth and death, the human being lives today almost exclusively under the influence of earth, sun and moon. So now we need to look more closely at how we live in our conscious and bodily condition—that is to say, in our spiritual, psychological and physical condition—under the influence of sun and moon.

Let's take the most extreme states of consciousness, between which lies the dream state: let's take waking day-consciousness and consciousness-empty (if I can coin this contradiction) sleep-consciousness or dreamless sleep. When we examine the condition of the human being during sleep—where physical and etheric bodies are separated from astral body and ego—we find that, between falling asleep and waking up, in the astral body and ego which are withdrawn from the physical and etheric, we inwardly preserve the influences of the sun with great care.

Between waking and sleeping we gaze upon the sun externally. Its effect is visible even when the sky is completely overcast, for what we see of the things around us is the reflected rays of the sun. The whole time we are awake we are under the influence of the sun that is shining externally on everything. The moment we pass over in sleep into the other condition, the sun begins to gleam, perceptibly for the spiritual eye, in our ego and astral body. Between falling asleep and waking we have the sun within us. As you know, there are certain minerals which, when exposed to rays of light and then placed in a dark space, retain the light and radiate it back into the darkness. With spiritual perception it is the same in the human ego and astral body. During waking they are in a certain sense drowned out by the external sunlight. They begin to glimmer and glow between sleeping and waking because they now bear the sunlight within them.

So we can say: in waking we are under the influence of external solar activity; in sleep we are under the influence of the solar activity we now carry within ourselves until we awaken. We have sun within us when we sleep, and only leave behind the physical and etheric bodies during the night. During sleep, with the preserved sunlight we now have in ourselves, we shine down spiritually from outside on our physical and etheric bodies. If we did not do this, if we did not shine the stored-up sunlight onto our skin, and indeed right into the interior of our sense-organs, we would dry up prematurely, become withered and fade. We generate the freshness, the growth-forces and the vitality of our organism by radiating the preserved sunlight from outside onto our skin and into our senses. And it is actually the case during sleep that, by being outside our physical and etheric bodies with our astral body and ego, we first shine the sunlight on our skin, but secondly we pour it through the eyes and ears back into the nerves. This is the phenomenon of human sleep: the sun shines from the human ego and astral body onto the skin and right into the human being through the doors of the senses (See drawing, 'Sleeping', p. 163, red).

And then, no matter whether it is new moon or full moon—for the influences are always there although they change with the phases of the moon—it comes about that the moon-forces approach us from outside and spread themselves out over the physical and etheric bodies. So (drawing)—I should really draw the whole human being— in the physical and etheric bodies during sleep we have solar effects coming from the ego and astral body, and lunar effects working from outside on the physical and etheric bodies. This characterizes the sleeping state in its relation to the cosmos. We are related through our inner being to the sun, and are related externally to the moon (for the astral body and ego do indeed constitute our inner being even when they are outside). (See drawing, 'Sleeping'.)

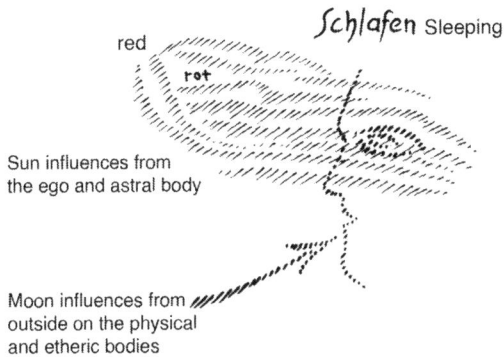

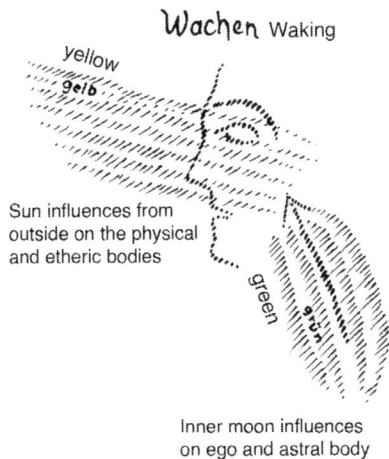

Schlafen Sleeping

red
rot

Sun influences from
the ego and astral body

Moon influences from
outside on the physical
and etheric bodies

Wachen Waking

yellow
gelb

Sun influences from
outside on the physical
and etheric bodies

green

Inner moon influences
on ego and astral body

During waking it is the other way round. When we wake up we carry the lunar activity internally, deep inside us; and the solar activity comes to us from outside. So we can say: while we are awake the sun's influences coming from outside go directly to our physical and etheric bodies; and the ego and astral body in our inner being come under the influences of the preserved moon forces. If we draw this diagrammatically for waking, we have the solar influences on our physical and etheric bodies—in other words, solar influences from *outside* (yellow)—and lunar influences *internally* on our ego and astral body (green). (See drawing, 'Waking'.)

So, while we are awake and solar activity shines externally onto our physical and etheric bodies, within us we carry preserved lunar effects. The sun lives in our ego and astral body during sleep, and the moon during waking. The sun lives in the physical and etheric bodies during waking, and the moon during sleep. And even if someone becomes a night reveller and, instead of sleeping during the night, prepares for himself the next morning's headache, these influences are still present; for even though the external constellation may go unnoticed, these things are such that, through sluggishness, through the inertia in the cosmos, they still take their course for the human being.

Even if he sleeps by day and wakes by night, the human being still bears the lunar influences within his ego and astral body during nocturnal waking, and the sun influences still work upon him, only now they come in the form of street-lighting or, if he is lying in the fields, in the form of pale starlight, and so on. But it is everywhere the sun-forces which man stores up during sleep, and the moon-forces which he bears in his inner being during waking-life. The reverse is the case with the physical and etheric bodies. It is thanks to this constellation that the human being has his ordinary consciousness between birth and death.

We shall now consider how things change with the ascent into other forms of consciousness. For the initiate's relationship to sun and moon changes somewhat, and changes more and more; and it is this change in the relationship to the cosmos that constitutes the path into the spiritual world.

A living grasp of the moon-sphere as starting point for a path of initiation

I do not need to describe how we stand in the world and encounter sun and moon with our ordinary consciousness; this is clear to everyone when they think about the conditions by day, and how we live by day and night. The moment the human being begins to strengthen his inner soul forces for the otherwise chaotic dream-consciousness, the moment he is able to make this otherwise dreaming consciousness into an instrument for the apprehension of reality, in that moment he does indeed become aware of how the stored-up moon is there in his ego during the waking state. The moment, through initiation knowledge, we really transform dream into reality, we feel ourselves permeated, as it were, by a second man, but we know that the forces of the moon-sphere live within this second being.

So, at the early stages of initiation consciousness we are able to say: 'The moon forces are living within me; they always have the tendency to develop a second man within me whom I then carry in my first being as though within a protective envelope.' And this is where a struggle now begins, when the moon starts to become inwardly active not in waking day-consciousness, but in sleep consciousness, and in such a way that this second man is released by the inner moon forces and asserts itself in the dulled sleeping state. Then this second man, which is in the first, wants to move about in the moonlight, taking the other with it; and there arises the somnambulistic condition we see in sleepwalkers.

Picture to yourselves how, when there is moonshine outside, this second being can be awakened, and it then brings into activity certain magical effects—in other words, unusual effects that diverge from those of nature. The person wanders about. Picture this sleepwalker to yourselves. While his consciousness is dulled he does all sorts of things he wouldn't do in his normal consciousness. In the ordinary run of things he would be quietly lying in bed. That is where he ought to be, but instead of this he wanders about outside, climbs on roofs, and so on. He is looking for the region that ought properly to lie outside his physical body.

You see, where this becomes a *conscious* inner experience—that is, where it becomes normal—is in the initial stages of initiation consciousness; only here we do not approach the actual moon influences from outside, but let the moon-forces that are carried in our inner being develop consciousness of this second man. And we must now hold all our forces together to prevent this second being from breaking loose. With the first man we would remain calm. But this second being could break loose, wander mindlessly (*wesenlos*) into error, and take entirely the wrong path. We must keep hold of him.

Inner resolution and composure are absolutely essential for the attainment of initiation-consciousness in order that this second being, which would like to break loose, is kept within us. It must be held in check by the ordinary matter-of-fact consciousness we have in our physical body. But we have to fight continually to prevent this second being, which has developed as a result of this strengthened inner moon-nature, from breaking loose from us. And this second being is very strongly attracted to all the activity of metabolism and movement in us, to everything that proceeds from the stomach and other organs. Its attraction towards all this is very, very strong, and it makes great demands on these forces.

You see, this is what we find, this is an initial experience in the early stages of initiation-consciousness, that this is one of the two paths we have to take: the path of the development and realization of the dream-world. Now if we ponder on this—which we need to do, as I mentioned earlier—we realize that although it might be day externally, internally we carry the night in us. And in the middle of the day there awakens something like an inner night.

When this initiation-consciousness arises, the day is still day for our external eyes, still day for taking hold of things externally, but everywhere in space during this day, moonlight begins to weave and live, which beams and rays out all around. The spiritual begins to shine. We realize that through our own soul we bring night into day. When this happens in full consciousness, in the same way as anything else that is done during the day by a person of good sense, when this person of good sense is able to conjure nocturnal lunar influences into the day, then he is on the right path. But if he brings anything into himself without full consciousness, in such a way that, out of his own inner forces, night arises during the day, then he wanders onto the wrong path that ultimately leads to mediumship.

The essential thing here is *full consciousness*, the inner control of the facts as one meets them, not the phenomena in themselves, not the fact in itself, but the way in which one lives into them. If the ordinary sleepwalker could develop complete 'good sense' (*Besonnenheit*) at the moment he was climbing on the roof, he would be an initiate. He does not do this, and if you shout to him to wake him up, he falls off. If he did not fall but developed full waking consciousness and could remain in this condition, he would be an initiate. The task of initiation science is to develop, not merely in a healthy but in a 'super-healthy' way, what develops pathologically in the sleepwalker. You will realize from this how there is but a hair's breadth between the right and the wrong in the spiritual world. In the physical world it is easy to distinguish wrong from right because we have our basic logic and our basic practical experience. As soon as we break through into the spiritual world it is exceedingly difficult to make this distinction, and we are wholly dependent on inner control, on inner good sense.

And further, when we have awakened night in day, the moonlight gradually loses its character of external radiance. It no longer shines so externally; it only produces a generalized feeling of life. But something else appears. *Mercury* now shines in this spiritual heaven of night with a wonderful, glimmering light. The star Mercury really rises in this night conjured into the day; not however, as we see Mercury through a telescope, but we become conscious that this is something living. We cannot yet distinguish the living spirit-beings that inhabit Mercury, but we become aware in a general way, from how Mercury approaches us, that this is a spiritual world.

When in the spirit the moonlight becomes a general elixir of life in which we feel ourselves, the spiritual star of Mercury gradually rises in this night that has been conjured into the day. Out of the sparkling twilight and twilit sparkling in which Mercury appears, there arises the being whom we then call the divine being Mercury. We need him. We need him unquestionably, for otherwise confusion will set in. This is the being whom we must first find in the spiritual world, a being who, as we are clearly aware, belongs to the beings of Mercury. By becoming acquainted with this being, we are able to master at will the 'second man' that has been activated within us. We no longer need to give ourselves up to ill-defined paths like a sleepwalker, but can be led by the hand of this messenger of the gods, Mercury, along the clearly-defined paths into the spiritual world.

So the essential point is this: if we wish to find the appropriate paths into the spiritual world, we must first undergo certain specific experiences that can guide and lead us. The ordinary mystic sinks down into his inner being. This gives rise to a stew of feeling in which everything is mixed up together: God and universe and angel and devil, are all stirred together in the usual mystic. At most they may result in generalized dreams where it is impossible to distinguish whether they come from the sexual sphere or the head sphere. As a rule the experiences bubble and mix, or get stirred together in a kind of stew. This is the obscure, nebulous mysticism that does not illumine the dream but throws it into still greater chaos, which is then comprehensible only to the initiate.

Such experiences, which are so wonderful, so magnificently poetic, as described by Catherine of Siena and others like her, can only be understood by an initiate, for only an initiate knows what is actually going on. Hence we can say that if you work on your initiation with a full consciousness that is as clear and translucent as the consciousness you use when you do arithmetic or geometry, if you go into these things with complete good sense, you will find the right path. Only by knowing that you conjure the inner light of the moon into the external day do you find the real spiritual world. Just as nobody can deny that the moon rises, that Mercury rises in the outer world of space, and that this is something real and not merely dreamt up, so too, when we enter this world with full consciousness, we meet spirit-beings there in the same way as we meet human beings in the physical world.

Erroneous paths are always taken when people try to seek the spirit without becoming aware of what there is in the spiritual world. When people only remain on the earth and do experiments on mediums without really penetrating into the spiritual world, only wanting to experiment with the external phenomena produced by mediums, and not really meeting the spiritual—then people are on the wrong path. Everything that does not awaken consciousness in the spiritual world, but just wanders on asleep, only wanting to study effects, as is the case with external occultism, is on a wrong path. Everything that, on entering the spiritual world, immediately meets this world as a reality, a spiritual reality, is on the right path.

And you see that the inner, living understanding of the moon-sphere is the starting point of the one path of initiation. And we can say: in waking life the human moon works within; but now in the initiate, with respect to sun and moon, the corresponding thing occurs during waking life which ordinarily occurs in sleep. We become aware of the moon influences as though they were external. We conjure the night into the day. And instead of the heavens being immediately sown with stars, which is what we ordinarily see when we look out into the night, the first thing that happens is that the star of Mercury rises spiritually. And if we have reached the point where, following the path described in *Knowledge of the Higher Worlds*, we are able to develop genuine imaginations, then we encounter, in this moon-sphere during waking life, the world of imaginations as reality.

But when we enter into the sphere of Mercury's activity, these imaginations lead to their beings. We do not now experience mere visions with nothing real behind them, but have visions that are imaginations, and these imaginations lead to the beings they correspond to. So, if you have not advanced far enough on the path of initiation, you can have a vision of an archangelos, an archangel, but it remains just a vision. Only at a further stage does the vision really lead to the archangel, and you then behold the vision of the archangel who is within it. At an earlier stage, with just moonlight, the archangel was not necessarily there, but now it is. And so you become conscious of Mercury's influences when your visionary world flows into a sphere where there is true perception of the spiritual. It needs to be repeated again and again that all this can only be attained in the right way with the fullest good sense (*bei vollster Besonnenheit*).

When we advance in our meditations, strengthen further our inner being and make it more and more active, we reach a stage where the activity of Venus is added to that of Mercury. And lo and behold, when the Venus activity appears, when Venus rises in this inner night that has been conjured into the day, the visions of the beings that have appeared in the imagination-pictures, in the real visions, are lost, and we stand before the spiritual world with empty consciousness. We know the spiritual beings are there. We have reached the Venus-sphere. The spiritual beings are there. We wait until the sun-sphere comes towards us. The whole process is a preparation for experiencing the sun a second time. All this is done during day-waking when we are in the external solar influences. We advance along the path I described, through moon, Mercury, Venus, and then the visions disappear. We press on further. The whole path has been from earth to moon, to Mercury, to Venus, and to the sun. We enter into the inner being of the sun, and behold the sun a second time, spiritually. The sun is not yet steady, it is unclear, but we know that we are beholding it spiritually. We are gazing into the inner being of the sun.

If I may use a rather rough comparison, it is as though we were to say to ourselves: I see something there in the distance. I draw closer to it. At first I think it is something made artificially. I get closer, touch it, and it grabs my hand with its teeth. Now I know that it is not artificial but a real dog. I become aware that this was an inner being. This crude comparison may help you to realize that this is something with reality. We pass from the earth, through the influences of the moon, Mercury, and Venus, and come to the point where we behold the sun, and we realize: the sun is a living spirit being, and there are beings inhabiting it.

This is the initial path that can be developed, and it shows clearly with every step how, as the initiate progresses, he must retain complete sound sense and will then keep to the right path. It also shows that if someone, by going out of himself in some way, is completely unaware that he is entering the cosmos, and the cosmos becomes spiritual before his spiritual gaze—he is on a wrong path. As you see, we must learn to distinguish inwardly between right and erroneous paths in spiritual perception.

Comprehending the human organism in Imaginations

Yesterday I pointed out how, as a result of a necessity of the age, the most varied psychical and occult societies, working with methods that are a caricature of those of natural science, are making attempts to research the spiritual world by means of external phenomena. Please do not misunderstand me. I have no wish to come forward as a critic of these methods, for I know only too well how intense the longing can be to penetrate into the nature of the spiritual world by observing external phenomena using the methods of natural science. I merely wish to show how these paths lead into error, and how by contrast the right paths are followed. Because we are living in a scientific age today, and must continue to do so, it is completely understandable that there are people who want to research the spiritual world in the same direct way they research natural science, and who regard other, purely spiritual, paths as unreliable. This leads them to say: on the one side there is the normal world, where people go about carrying out their aims based on external social life; they go about thinking and acting in accordance with this external social life. And there is nothing unusual in this because we are used to it. In this context natural science conducts its experiments, looking at external phenomena, at heat, electricity, magnetism, and so on.

But there are also facts in life that are not normal. There are people who do automatic writing, perform all kinds of things under hypnosis, instigated through suggestion. People suppose that an unknown world is revealed in this way in the ordinary world. They want to explain these external signs and abnormal phenomena. They want to explain how it comes about that if a person in New York thinks or experiences something strongly, a second person, who is emotionally close to the first but living in Europe, can receive the news inwardly; this second person knows what otherwise would be transmitted externally by wireless telegraphy. Phenomena like this, and they can be cited in the hundreds and thousands, are investigated by statistical, external, scientific methods.

This path cannot lead to any goal because, if we do not have a spiritual orientation, which is required to give us direction and which must itself be in the spiritual world, then all these phenomena, wonderful though they may be, are just aggregations in the external world, one thing juxtaposed against the other. We can never gain knowledge or understanding of them; we can only record them, look on them as so many wonders, and formulate hypotheses about the spiritual world—hypotheses, however, that have no meaning because the phenomena themselves, in the external world in which they are placed, do not tell this external world what they [really] are. We can spend as much time as we like with mediums, with external scientific facts, and the spiritual world is indeed revealed in phenomena; but it does not tell us what it is in reality.

You see, this is where the research comes in that I mentioned yesterday when I said that Dr Wegman and I are now endeavouring to present [our findings] very precisely. I have just spoken of the other line of research which seeks to illumine the inner life of dreams, but not by avoiding the spiritual world. The same applies to the research [of Dr Wegman and myself]. This is conducted directly with aims that reveal themselves in the spiritual world, taking the phenomena as they present themselves [in the light of the spirit]. But these phenomena do not lie in the scattered, miraculous events we meet in the ways just described, in the outer world. They lie in the realm which is seen by one who is thoroughly trained in anatomy, physiology, and medicine, and who is able to ascend from the external comprehension of a human organ—lung, or liver, or any other organ—to an imaginative penetration of the organ; when he gradually becomes able to place the human organization before his soul in Imaginations.

You see, this is possible when we are able to study the organs of the human being, which in the normal run of things do not function like the external phenomena of nature but rather function normally like the abnormal phenomena—when we are able to study these organs, and when we start from a scientific, anatomical understanding of the human being and rise from there to a spiritual perception and penetration of the human organism. In the method I described before, we take our start from the human being as a whole. In the path I am now describing we take our start from the individual human organs which we comprehend by means of a spiritual anatomy, and perceive directly. This is the path that can lead to accurate results as opposed to the erroneous path which, using a caricature of the scientific method, comprehends external phenomena by drawing up statistics. From this you can understand that, in order for these things to be presented properly, there first had to be someone who could work in this way, but who also had the regular medical qualifications.

Now it is important that when a human organ is comprehended spiritually in this way by someone who has this kind of perception of anatomy, that this goal does not live in that person's thoughts as something vague or uncertain. And now it is not an inner man that opens up in the sense I described earlier, but an outer man, a cosmic man opens up, who still appears somewhat nebulously, but nonetheless a mighty, gigantic human being, not now perceived as an earthly totality, but through an inner, spiritual perception of his organs. Because these organs manifest themselves in the spirit, it is no longer merely earthly man who stands there, but man who encompasses the cosmos. Then we see that just as in the earlier stages we conjured the night world, the moon world into the world of day, so now into this being—who is not the whole man with his defined contours, but man consisting of his individual organs—we conjure the impulses of the Saturn-sphere.

In the same way that the moon-sphere was conjured into the ordinary consciousness of the day, the Saturn-sphere is now conjured into the scientific consciousness, and we become aware that the forces of Saturn work in a specific way in each organ. They work, for example, most strongly in the liver, comparatively very feebly in the lungs, and least of all in the head. We become conscious of the goal in the realization that we have to look everywhere for Saturn. Just as in the earlier stages we advanced through meditation, we now penetrate—by living into this search for Saturn, for the inner spiritual structure in every organ—into the Jupiter-sphere where we come to understand that every organ is the earthly image or reflection of a divine-spiritual being. In his organs the human being bears the inner reflection of divine-spiritual beings. The whole cosmos which was initially a great human being in the Saturn-sphere, the whole human being becomes clear as a gigantic cosmic being, appearing as the sum-total, the inner-organic collaborative work of generations of gods.

Again, it is necessary that this path be trodden with complete sound sense. The forces able to sustain and control all these things must be active along this path. You need to realize that all these workings and influences are there initially *in statu nascendi*, they are there but pass away again almost immediately. It is easy to realize that they exist, but it is impossible to describe them, to hold them fast, to mould them into thought-pictures, if we succumb to the danger that is here. The danger is that everything I have described appears and immediately passes away again from our consciousness, so that we do not get to the point of really perceiving it.

It does not occur to those who pursue modern psychical research to really address the spiritual. They want to carry out all these things experimentally by summoning people as subject A, B, and C into their laboratories. The spiritual realities however do not allow themselves to be brought like this into the world that can be known by man, above all when the intention is to lay hold of them by these methods, and then describe them in scientific terms.

The medical book I spoke about yesterday can only represent the first and most elementary beginnings of what will become a developed science only many years from now when we are no longer living. But to the extent that these things exist in the spiritual world today, to the extent, for example, that they are indeed usual to the beings who live not on earth but in the sun—to that extent they can be brought into earthly consciousness in the way I described. But we must not imagine that laboratory experiments can be made in this connection, nor that we can make progress by means of the abstract anatomy in our textbooks. What is important here is that all this flows through a living human being. Why is this so?

It is because these things can only be held fast when they are grasped, understood, and controlled by the forces that arise when people strive together, when they are encompassed, so to speak, by the forces we carry in ourselves from earlier incarnations on earth. When this happens, what we can call the Mars-sphere enters into the world of the Saturn- and Jupiter-sphere. From then onwards these things begin to speak; from then onwards these things are revealed through Inspiration. And then we come back to the sun with inspirative consciousness.

This is the other path that is required by natural science today, and it is a path which the initiates I was speaking of yesterday would like to avoid. They feel ill at ease when they come across this path, but for all that, it is a path which must be taken.

For the path through the moon-sphere, as you will realize from yesterday's lecture, is the one that was traversed so wonderfully by the ancient initiates. We also learn many wonderful things connected with this moon-path from H. P. Blavatsky's *Secret Doctrine*. We just need to be able to distinguish between what is correct and what is incorrect, then there are magnificent truths in this *Secret Doctrine*. But what H. P. Blavatsky was able to experience in a wonderful way was the path that leads through the moon's astral light; and she was wonderfully guided in her interpretations by a Mercury messenger. When we follow her writings we can see everywhere how she directs Imagination to the right place. The wonderful thing about Blavatsky is that when she is working on an Imagination, this Imagination is there, guided by the Mercury messenger. He it was who guided her to a hidden library. An idea arose in her, and the Mercury messenger led her to a book carefully preserved by the Vatican. Blavatsky read in the book, and we find many things in her writings that she would not otherwise have been able to discover, for the reason that they have been carefully guarded by the Vatican for centuries! This path is the one that has been trodden many, many times, and which we must carefully distinguish from everything that is done with sure inner composure, as I mentioned.

The other path takes the course I described, reckoning with the methods of modern natural science, which H. P. Blavatsky hated like the night; that is, she hated the night, but ordinary people are scared of ghosts. This is the path that must be taken in the way I characterized, where we must be aware that it gets its support and strength from the development of karmic forces in people, not so much to [help us] find memories, but in order to hold them fast [once we have them] so that they can be described. The science of the present day must be deepened in a human sense, in the way I characterized yesterday with regard to my colleague [Dr Wegman] in this area. So you see that an example is the best way to demonstrate how the right and the wrong paths arise. This cannot be done using definitions, but by actual examples.

In order to bring this course to a certain conclusion, tomorrow I will add as much as can be said of these matters in the short time available.

LECTURE 11

22 AUGUST 1924

To What Extent is Spiritual Research Accepted?

Two possible routes in research

NATURALLY a very great deal might still be said in continuation of everything I have touched on in these lectures; but today we will endeavour to round off by bringing before our souls a kind of summary of the lectures.

The content of these lectures lies before us, above all, in the form of a question, and this question is: What is the situation regarding the understanding of anthroposophy, of spiritual research in the form in which it is to be brought before the world in anthroposophy? What is the position regarding insight into everything that is given out through anthroposophy, as opposed to the fact that by no means everyone of the present day can take up the exercises and practices that will bring them quickly to the point of perceiving for themselves in the corresponding worlds what they hear in anthroposophy, and so testing it fully for themselves? This is a deep question for all those who have a certain urge, a certain longing, for anthroposophy. But this question is always seen in the wrong light, and can be most especially so when we speak about what is right, as I have done in these lectures. People may say: 'Yes, but of what use to me are all these descriptions of the spiritual world if I can't look into the spiritual world myself?' Because of this, I should like to weave this question into my concluding discussion today.

It is simply not the case that one cannot attain insight or understanding of the things given by anthroposophy until one can research the spiritual world oneself. We need to make a distinction, especially at the present time, between *research* into the facts of the various worlds, and the *comprehension* of the facts resulting from research. You will be able to grasp this distinction when you recollect that man, as he stands before us today, actually belongs to different worlds, and that all his experiences come to him out of these different worlds. Man as he is today attains through ordinary life his usual consciousness of everyday existence and his ordinary knowledge, which was our starting point in these lectures. This consciousness, during day-waking, gives him a certain overview of a section of the world, of all those things in the world revealed to him by his senses, and which can be interpreted and grasped by the intellect, which he has acquired during the course of human evolution.

In dreaming, as I described, man reaches with his understanding very indistinctly into a world immediately bordering this one but hidden from it. And, during dreamless sleep, he reaches with his soul while on earth into that world the human being lives through between death and a new birth, a sleep in which, for the soul, it is dark and black, and where he leads a life he usually has no memory of.

This consciousness with its threefold state—waking, dreaming, and deep sleep—is what man is familiar with. But he does not live only in the worlds that are accessible to him through this three-fold consciousness: man is a being that lives in a whole series of worlds. His physical body lives in a different world from his etheric body, his etheric body in a different world again from his astral body, and all these together in different worlds from the ego. And these states of consciousness—bright waking consciousness, dream consciousness, sleeping 'non-consciousness' we could almost say, but we must say a dull consciousness—these are the states of consciousness that the ego has as it is at present. And this ego, as it is today, when it looks inwards, also has three states. It has three states when it looks *outwards* from itself—waking day-consciousness, dream-consciousness, and sleep-consciousness. And if it looks *inwards*, it has bright thinking; it has the more opaque feeling-consciousness that resembles dream-life far more closely than people usually believe; and it

has the dim, dull will-consciousness that is very similar to sleep-consciousness. How our will comes about is utterly unknown to ordinary
consciousness—as unknown as [deep] sleep. When someone wills
something, they have a thought; this is clear and bright. They then
develop something somewhat darker around this thought: a feeling.
Then the thought, permeated with feeling, sinks into the limbs. What
takes place there is not experienced by ordinary consciousness. For
the kind of research I spoke about yesterday and the day before,
what happens with the will looks like this: When a thought wills
something in the head and then flows down through feeling into the
whole body, and a person wills it through their whole body, a process
resembling a kind of delicate, subtle and intimate combustion takes
place. Someone who attains initiate consciousness can experience
this will that is influenced by warmth. But for ordinary consciousness it remains completely underground. That is just one example of
how something that remains underground for ordinary consciousness can be raised up by initiation consciousness.

When the things in the book I mentioned yesterday come more
and more into the world and are understood, it will be possible, for
example, to understand that when someone wills something, and
their willing is observed with initiation consciousness, it is like looking at the outer process of a candle burning, or any kind of light that
gives off heat. Just as we get a clear picture by looking externally, so
we can see the thought striking into the will in such a way that we
say: the thought unfolds feeling, and warmth, a flame, is given off
by the feeling and moves downwards—in the human being it moves
from above downwards—and this flame *wills*. The process unfolds
step by step.

We can show this ordinary consciousness schematically like this:

Looking inwards:	*Looking outwards:*
Clear thinking	Waking day-consciousness
Feeling life	Dream-consciousness
Will-consciousness	Deep sleep-consciousness

Looking outwards is the day-consciousness, and looking inwards
is clear thinking; outwards is dream-consciousness, and inwards is

unclear but warm feeling life; outwards is sleep-consciousness, and inwards is completely obscure will-consciousness.

But in order to do research into the spiritual world—that is to say, to find facts that can be revealed from out of the spiritual world— we are obliged to carry our consciousness into whichever world it is we wish to penetrate with our cognition, and then, if the results of this research are communicated accurately, what is communicated as ideas through words goes into the consciousness of others. You will perhaps see that there are two sides to this. In the first place we do research, for example, into the world of human organs, as I discussed yesterday, and investigate there the relevant facts using the forces that come to us when we live into the spiritual world. That is where we find the pertinent facts. For our cognition, they lay themselves before our soul; we have access to them there. [Certain] individuals have these facts before them, which are then communicated and presented by these individuals to the world. When the facts are presented to the world by an individual, they can be grasped by ordinary consciousness as long as they are met with sufficient open-mindedness. Hence, in the course of human evolution, things have always been arranged so that a few individuals worked at researching facts regarding the spiritual world, and when they had done the research, they communicated [the results] to others.

Now there is just one obstacle to accepting such findings, and this is that people as a general rule grow up in a social environment and an educational system that teaches habits of feeling and sentiment that make them able to believe only in the external world of facts, in the world of the senses and what the intellect tells them about it. This habit is so strong that it always inclines people to say: Take this university; people graduated at this university, and now they teach there. They also do research into certain facts, or confirm the facts of the sensory world that other people have researched. People believe this! They don't research these things themselves, but they believe them. It is precisely in connection with modern science that people are boundlessly credulous. They believe things which, for someone who has insight, are not only highly problematic but certainly completely untrue. All this is only due to a centuries-old form of education.

We can safely say that the people of earlier centuries did not have this education. They were more inclined—because they still had something of a perception into the spiritual world, a familiarity with the spiritual world that came out of their feeling and will—to believe those who researched into spiritual facts. People today are simply not used to this and have become accustomed to a way of seeing which—in a more theoretical way on the continent and a more practical way in England and America—has become fully established.

On the continent there are extensive theories on this, while in England and America there is more of a feeling for these things that cannot easily be inwardly overcome. The reason is that people have become accustomed to what has arisen in the course of centuries: namely, a natural science whose reference point is the external senses; and accustomed to absorbing astronomy, for example, or botany, zoology, medicine, in the form prepared for them in the recognized schools or centres of learning. This is the habit of centuries, and people cling to it terribly strongly. And when a chemist researches something in his laboratory that people do not have the faintest idea about, and which is then reported, they say it is true, that these are true findings. 'This is not belief,' they say, 'These are scientific findings.' But of course, it *is* pure belief! Nevertheless people call it scientific fact.

By none of the methods used to research the sense-world so as to discover its laws by means of the intellect, by none of these methods do we find out anything about the spiritual world. But there are very few people who can do without the spiritual world altogether, and they persuade themselves into it, are not honest with themselves. People have a fundamental need to know something also about the spiritual world. They do not yet listen today to those who can tell them something in a modern way about the spiritual world, but they listen to historical tradition, to what is in books, in the sacred texts of the East, and what is in the Bible. They listen to these because they cannot help but have a connection somehow to the spiritual world. And despite the fact that everything in the Bible or in the sacred scriptures of the East was also only researched by individual initiates, they say: Yes, but that was a different way of perceiving things.

It is not the same as understanding the external sense-world, as the understanding of science. It is based on faith; you have to believe it. And then people make a firm distinction between knowledge [or science] and faith. And they connect science with the sensory world, and faith with the spiritual world.

Among theologians of the Protestant church on the continent—not among the Roman Catholic theologians, for they have retained the old traditions and do not make the same distinction as the Protestant theologians or the scientists—there are on the continent entire theses on the point where knowledge ends and faith begins. Here in England theories are not so popular so there are fewer of them. Instead there is the custom of living properly, on the one hand, by listening to what science has to say and accepting it, and, on the other hand, of living properly in piety (I will not say 'pietistically'), in faith; and keeping the two things strictly apart.

Not only do lay people manage to do this but scholars do it too, and thus it has been for a long time. Newton[24] discovered, on the one hand, the theory of gravity: that is, a worldview of space which by its very nature excludes any perception of the spiritual. If the world were really as Newton conceived it, it could not contain spirit. It is just that people do not have the courage to admit this to themselves. A divine-spiritual governance and weaving can no more be imagined in the Newtonian world than a human being can be imagined in a spinning-wheel, that a spinning-wheel could become a human being. But one lacks the inner courage to admit it.

But it is not only those who accept such a thing who manage, on the one hand, to devote themselves to a worldview of space and time that excludes the spirit, but also those who do research themselves. Newton is an excellent example of this: on the one hand he establishes a worldview that excludes anything spiritual, yet on the other, completely separating his soul from this [worldview], he interprets the Apocalypse.

The bridges are broken between science or understanding of the external sense-world and knowledge and understanding of the spiritual world. Even in the places where theories are popular, strict attempts are made today to prove this. And where theories are unpopular, efforts are made to ensure that this eats into the habits of thought and feeling, so that there is no getting away from it.

On the other hand the human intellect, human understanding, the power of ideation, the capacity for ideas, is so advanced today that, if these capacities are thoroughly taken in hand and pondered over, what arises from initiation science can be fully comprehended by the intellect, just not researched by it.

So what is needed here? Our views must change. Initially what can be researched of the spiritual world should be researched by the individuals who, in their present life, can call on the help of forces they have from previous incarnations and which enable them to draw on what is needed to do the research. Further, the results of this research need to be received and understood by a number of people, by more and more people, in a form by which they can become comprehensible: in the form of ideas. And then precisely, through the results of spiritual research having been absorbed with sound understanding, a foundation is created for these other people to see into the spiritual world as well. For I have often remarked that the healthiest way initially to enter the spiritual world is to interest oneself in reading about it, to absorb what is reported out of the spiritual world.

If we absorb such thoughts as these, they become inwardly quickened, and we reach not only understanding but also clairvoyant vision, if our karma permits it. And precisely on this point we need to be clear in our view of karma. People today tend not to think about karma. When someone has so-called abnormalities, people talk about needing to research these in the laboratory, much as one would research sulphur in a laboratory. [They think] we ought to do experiments on someone with abnormal understanding in the way one would conduct experiments with sulphur. But sulphur, of course, doesn't have any karma. Only the 'sulphur' that comes out of people's mouths has karma! Normal mineral sulphur doesn't have karma; only human beings have karma. And never can it be presumed that it is in someone's karma to be experimented on in a laboratory, which would actually have to be the case for the research to produce fruitful results.

This is why we should have a spiritual science in the first place. We should investigate the karmic conditions that allow us to learn something about the spiritual world from an individual. I talk about this clearly at the end of the later editions of my book, *Theosophy*. But the modern world is not suited to accepting these things—not through lack of capacity but through habit. Yet this is infinitely important. Above all it is important to understand clearly that you do not have to penetrate immediately on paths of research into the spiritual world, but, as long as you do not use unhealthy faculties here on the physical plane, like experimenting with karma which is not karmically determined, or with mediums whose behaviour you do not understand; as long as you rely on the consciousness that is right for this world, which I described as everyday consciousness; as long as you rely properly on this everyday consciousness—then you will arrive at a complete understanding of what is said out of initiation-knowledge.

If people believe they cannot have such an understanding without first being able to penetrate [into the spiritual world] themselves, they are labouring under a great error. This then is yet another of the false paths taken by people today, to say to themselves: What is the spiritual world to me if I can't see into it myself? This is one of the greatest, the most dangerous, and most obvious errors of all. And this error is one which a movement such as is embodied in the Anthroposophical Society must be fully conscious of.

Birth, death, and evil

That human beings belong, in our existence here in the physical world, to various worlds, is evident to an open-minded consciousness by the fact that what we experience in life, the way in which things present themselves within the totality of human experience, particularly with regards to the really important moments in life, comes up against the incomprehension of everyday consciousness, because things seem disjointed whereas in certain cases they are closely connected.

So in this summary I should like to focus on our coming into the physical world, and to our passing out of it; I should like to speak about birth and death. These two most incisive events of human earthly life appear to ordinary consciousness to be two unrelated occurrences. Everything that precedes birth, everything that is connected with the human being entering earthly existence, is put at the beginning of earthly life. Death is put at the end of it. They seem to be separate. For someone who does research in the region of spiritual life, they move closer and closer together. For when we take the path that I characterized as the one on which we penetrate into the moon mysteries, whereby we conjure the night into the day, as I described, we see that in all the processes involved in being born, the physical and etheric bodies increasingly bud and burgeon; we see how they emerge from the tiny ovum, gradually shape themselves into the human form, how during earthly life they continue to show, we could say, life in the ascent, until around the age of 35 they begin to decline, to show life in descent. We can also see this externally. But someone on the moon path I described yesterday, sees how, at the same time as a sprouting and budding life begins and continues to unfold for the physical and etheric aspects, another life, which in anthroposophy we summarize as the astral body and ego, actually dies, is subject to death.

When we enter the mystical life I spoke about in concrete detail yesterday, we see not only a coming to birth of the physical and etheric, but also a dying process in the astral and ego. We see death weaving itself into life, the process of dying away wedded to that of bursting into life. And further, when with initiation consciousness we observe the human being, we see, from the age of 35 onwards when the body declines, the beginning of a burgeoning life in the astral body and ego. It is just that these are disturbed by what is dying around them in the physical and etheric bodies. But a real burgeoning of life takes place. And so by means of this path of spiritual research we can learn to recognize death in life, life in death. It is by this means that we can prepare ourselves to follow the progress of what we see dying at the time of birth, follow it back into its pre-earthly life where it shows itself in all its full significance and greatness. And again, by seeing the astral body and ego becoming gradually fresher within the dying earth life, but taken into captivity by the etheric and physical principles, we can prepare ourselves to follow what goes out through the portal of death from the physical and etheric, and follow it into the spiritual world. Death and birth draw close to each other, whereas in ordinary consciousness they exist as disjointed facts.

But everything that is discovered by research into the spiritual world can be grasped by ordinary consciousness in the way I described in the first part of today's lecture. We just need to break the habit of what this ordinary consciousness wants nowadays. You see, I once knew someone who said: A stone falls to the ground. If I pick up a chair and let it go, it also falls to the ground. Everything falls to the ground. People maintain that the earth is not resting on anything, so it must also fall. So he said. But this person did not take into account that everything on earth has to fall because the earth is there, but that the earth itself floats freely in space, and that the stars in their totality mutually support and hold each other.

People who maintain that everything has to be proved by the external senses according to the methods of modern science are like someone who says that if the earth is not supported by a great pillar it will fall down. But anthroposophical truths, like the stars, mutually support each other. People need to realize this. Once they have realized it with their ordinary understanding, they will begin to grasp anthroposophy in the form of ideas, even such things as the drawing together of birth and death.

But let's take this further. Take a person who is well versed in what can be learnt in modern science, but who can enter into [anthroposophy] with a lively receptivity, and now doesn't learn to know the whole human being but his organs, as discussed yesterday. You see, through this understanding of the organs that is grasped on the path of initiation, it is not birth and death that present themselves to the soul but something quite different. Birth and death even lose their usual meaning for this organ-understanding, for only the whole human being can die; individual organs cannot die. The lung, for example, doesn't die. Even ordinary science has a bit of an inkling today that when a person has died, the individual organs can still be alive in a certain sense in themselves. The individual organs don't die, irrespective of whether the person is buried or cremated; each organ according to its nature seeks its own path into the cosmos, even when a person is buried and covered with earth. The organs seek a path through water, air, and warmth, out into the cosmos. In reality the organs don't die, but dissipate. Only the whole human being dies.

To speak of death in a person only makes sense in relation to the whole human being. With regard to animals we can speak of the organs dying. A difference between humans and animals is that in humans the organs disperse. They only dissolve quickly in the same way that when you cook an unripe apple [it goes through a ripening process through the cooking] that is quicker than [the process] a ripe apple [has gone through]. Burial is the slow process, cremation the fast process. The organs can be followed in their individual progress out towards infinity. But out there in the cosmos they do not recede into the infinite, but something comes back to us which I described yesterday: the great Cosmic Human Being.

So, when we follow the organs with initiate-consciousness, we see what really happens with the organs at death: this streaming out of them into the regions of the cosmos to which each is related. The heart goes somewhere else from the lung, the liver somewhere else from the lungs and heart. They disperse themselves in the cosmos. We can see this when, on the path of initiation, we develop a consciousness of the organs. Then the human being appears, the human being as he is incorporated into the cosmos. And in the perception of this human being, truly embedded and integrated in the cosmos, something can present itself that lies behind, for example, successive incarnations.

We need this vision that arises not from the human being as a whole but from a spiritual perception of the organs, in order to recognize previous earth lives as they come back to our perception in this earth life. It was because of this that the people on the lunar path—mystics, theosophists, and so on—who gave themselves up to the spiritual world, saw all kinds of things, human souls as they were in previous lives, gods, spirits, but could not actually discern, could not make out, what they were. They could not say decisively: this is Alanus ab Insulis, that is Dante, and that is Brunetto Latini. There were certainly beings there; and sometimes given grotesque names. Previous incarnations were there. But they could not discern whether these were their own incarnations or someone else's, or what they were. So the spiritual world enters into this night world that is conjured into the day, but then dissolves under the influence of the Venus-impulse, and is now there as spiritual world in its totality, but doesn't have the clear definition (*Bestimmtheit*) it should have. You see, it begins to become possible in this world to see how the human being is placed in the whole world, how he exists as a cosmic being.

On the other hand, there is an extraordinarily tragic piece of knowledge connected with this. For if the human being were just the whole human being as he appears in his skin here on earth, he would be such a good, such a tame, such a noble being! As little as one can research death with the ordinary consciousness—we can *understand* it in the sense I mentioned, but not research it—just as little can one research with ordinary consciousness why human beings with their ingenuous faces—and they do have such ingenuous faces—why with their ingenuous faces they can become evil. We do not become evil as whole human beings. Our skin is extraordinarily good. The potential for evil is in the organs.

And because of this we also learn to recognize, in connection with the relationship of the organs with specific regions of the cosmos, from which regions possession by evil comes; because, fundamentally, this is the situation with even the slightest evil. So, out of an understanding of the whole human being, the first thing to emerge is birth and death. Out of an understanding of the organization of the human being's relationship with the cosmos in both sickness and health, the second thing to emerge is evil.

And thus the Being who passed through the Mystery of Golgotha can only appear to the human soul when, out of our human organology, we have the possibility of seeing the cosmic man. For Christ came as cosmic man from the sun; until then he was not yet earthly man. He drew towards us as cosmic man. How can one recognize a cosmic man if one hasn't first prepared oneself to comprehend cosmic man in any way at all? A full Christology can arise precisely from this comprehending of the cosmic man. So you see how the right paths into the spiritual world lead to an understanding of birth and death, to an understanding of the relationship of the human organs to the cosmos, to an understanding of evil, and lead to an understanding of the Cosmic Man: Christ.

When this is presented in a way where each aspect supports the other, it can be understood. And then understanding is the best way of entering into the spiritual world oneself—understanding, and meditating on what one has understood. The other rules for meditation are then additional supports. But this is the right path into the spiritual world for every person of the present day. By contrast, all experimentation on other paths, using ordinary consciousness to research non-ordinary consciousness, all experiments with shutdown consciousness such as with mediumism, somnambulism, hypnosis and so on, all experiments with such cosmic processes that one cannot get near with a consciousness that works like a caricature of modern science—all these are wrong paths because they do not lead into the real spiritual world.

The revelation of heaven in earthly form through art

When, as a result of the research I have indicated, a person becomes aware in their feeling—and this is quite possible—that, through a deeper understanding of the organs, the cosmic man comes back to them, and Christ can be understood in this return, as it were; when that which can emerge for occult research and perception and be absorbed into initiate consciousness arises in a person in their feelings, then in the consciousness I indicated the heavenly element is revealed in the earthly through feeling. And this happens through art. In art there is a semi-subconscious element in the soul that holds on firmly to what approaches us out of the spiritual world on this return path, on the return path I have characterized. Because of this, throughout the ages there have been people who, being predestined for it by their karma, have held the spiritual in earthly matter in art.

Our naturalistic art has deviated from this. But every great achievement in the development of art in humanity represents something spiritual in sensory form, or, we could also say, raises the sensory level into the sphere of the spirit. We value the painter Raphael so much because, to a greater degree than anyone else, he was able to depict in the sense-world something that raises itself up to spirituality.

Now there was a general stream in human development that tended towards the plastic, visual arts. Today we need to find new life in the visual arts, although the immediate elemental impulse in the visual arts was at its height in past times. For many centuries another impulse has gradually been developing: the impulse of musicality. For this reason even the visual arts have been gradually assuming a more or less musical form. The musical element is, in an artistic sense, humanity's future, including all the musicality in the arts of speech and the performing arts. The Goetheanum Building at Dornach was conceived musically (*im Musikalischen gehalten*); and that is why its architecture, sculpture, and painting have thus far been so little understood. Also He who is to arise is difficult to understand because the musical element must be introduced in full accord with human evolution into the plastic, painting and sculptural principles.

What I have indicated as being of the highest significance for human evolution, the approach of the figure of Christ—the living, spiritually-living figure of the Christ—was, in a sense, wonderfully achieved by the painting of the Renaissance and what preceded it, but will have to be found in the future through music. You see, the urge towards this has been there for a while. It was there in Richard Wagner. It brought him finally to his *Parsifal*. But *Parsifal*, with regard to the magical drawing-in of the Christ impulse into the physical sense-world where He wishes to be the most Christian, is only a symbolic hint, so to speak, hovering there: the dove appears, and such like. There is a symbolic communion. The element of musicality doesn't manage to attain what is the essential point of the Christ impulse in the cosmos and earth. But the musical principle is able to present this Christ impulse to the world in musical sound, in sculpted notes, in musical tone imbued through and through with soul and spirit. If music is inspired by anthroposophical spiritual science, it will find the way to do this, for it will solve—purely artistically, in feeling—[the problem of] how what lives as the Christ impulse in the cosmos and earth can be as though brought to life in a symphony of musical sound.

For this we need to be able to reach a point of mysticism by an inner deepening and intensification of our musical experience and feeling of the interval of the major third. If we experience this as something that is musically held (*beschlossen*) deep in our inner being, and then experience the sphere of the major fifth as having a protectively enveloping quality, so that as we grow into the inner structure of the fifth we grow out to the boundary of what is human and what is cosmic, where the cosmos resounds into the realm of humanity and the human yearns outwards towards the cosmos—indeed, rushes yearningly towards it—then, through the mystery of the interplay between the major third and the fifth, we can experience in the musical element something of what in the innermost human being wants to go out into the cosmos.

And if we can also succeed in hearing how cosmic life wells up in the sounding of the dissonances of the interval of the seventh, and how the dissonances of the seventh express a cosmic experience in man as he finds himself on the path towards the various spiritual realms; and if we then succeed in letting the discords of the seventh fade away, so that precisely in their fading they gather something definite into themselves, they at last assume, in their fading away, what appears in the musical experience like a firmament of music.

And then—having already felt a finely drawn indication of a minor-key experience within the major—if we find in this fading away of the seventh's dissonances and their formation into a totality which becomes almost harmonious, almost consonant, because it is fading away; if we can find our way back into the sphere of the minor fifth, and from there to the permeation of the sphere of the fifth with the sphere of the minor third, then on this path we would have created the musical experience of incarnation, and specifically the Incarnation of Christ.

For we will be able to find in this feeling-of-our-way out into the sphere of the seventh (which only appears dissonant from a cosmic perspective) and which we shape into a firmament behind which stands the octave, distantly but as through drawing closer—if we have grasped all this in our feeling, then we return as indicated, and find that it is possible in the germinal form of the minor third concord, to represent the Incarnation as something musical; then, when we go back to the realm of the major third, the Hallelujah of Christ sounds forth from this musical structure in purely musical form, purely in the configuration of musical notes. Then the human being will conjure forth in this structure of musical sound something directly supersensory and available to our musical sensitivity.

The Christ-Impulse can be found in music. And the dissolution of the symphonic principle into something that is no longer entirely musical, as in Beethoven, can be led back once more to the truly cosmic power that is in the musical element. Bruckner[25] tried to do this, but out of a certain narrowness or, we could say, limited by tradition. You can see how he came to a standstill in his Unfinished Symphony; how marvellous it is on the one hand, and how on the other it seems to reach out through the true element of music, yet without being able altogether to attain it. For it cannot be reached except in the way I have described, when we advance in the realm of pure music and find in it its essence, its very being, which can conjure up a whole world of tones.

Unless humanity sinks into decadence, it is quite certain that anthroposophical inspiration will be able to bring about what I have indicated [with regard to music]. It might even reach a point one day—it all depends on humanity—that precisely in the element of musicality the Christ impulse will appear in true form even as an external revelation.

I wanted to bring these things before your souls because you can see from them that anthroposophy seeks to flow into every area of life; and this can happen if life for its part finds the appropriate path to anthroposophical experience and research. And it might even happen that everything that is to be found in the sphere of anthroposophy will some day resound like an echo out of the musical element, as though the echo were a solution to the Christological enigma.

With these words, then, I bring to a conclusion what I have only been able to hint at in the course of these lectures, and indicate the intention behind them. I should just like to add that it has been my desire to awaken in your souls some recognition of anthroposophical truths, so that these truths can really become seeds in every soul, seeds that can come to life and lead to more and more life in our civilization.

May this cycle of lectures be a small contribution to these far-reaching intentions of anthroposophical will.

NOTES

[1] *'Know thyself'*—inscription on the Temple of Apollo at Delphi, attributed to one of the 'seven Greek sages'.

[2] *Charles Darwin*, 1809-1882. British natural scientist
Thomas Huxley, 1825-1895, British natural scientist
Herbert Spencer, 1820-1903, British philosopher
Giordano Bruno, 1548-1600, philosopher
Nicolaus Copernicus, 1473-1543, astronomer
Galileo Galilei, 1564-1642, astronomer and natural scientist

[3] *Raphael* (Raffaello Santi), 1483-1520, Italian painter
Michaelangelo Buonarroti, 1475-1565, Italian sculptor, architect

[4] *an intercalary month*: The ancient Chaldeans had a solar year of 360 days, and intercalated an extra month after every six years.

[5] *Knowledge of the Higher Worlds* (1904/5) GA 10; *Occult Science – An Outline* (1910) GA 13

[6] *my Mystery Dramas*: 'Four Mystery Plays' translated by H Collinson, London 1920. There are now new editions and translations.

[7] *elementary exercises are given there*: Apart from the work indicated here, see also *Practical Training in Thinking* (GA 108) and *Guidance in Esoteric Training* (GA 42/245).

[8] *school of Chartres*: See also *Karmic Relationships* Vol. III 'Karmic Relationships of the Anthroposophical Movement' (GA 237)
Bernardus Sylvestris (Bernard of Tours), died c. 1150.
Bernard of Chartres, died between 1124 and 1130.
Alanus ab Insulis, around 1114—1203, aka Doctor universalis.
Joachim of Flora, died 1202, Cistercian abbot at Floris, Calabria
John of Auville. In one of his notebooks Steiner notes the work by John of Auville, *Architrenius* (1184)

[9] *Dante Alighieri*, 1265-1321.
Brunetto Latini, born between 1210 and 1230, died 1294, Italian statesman, scholar and poet. Wrote *Li livres don Tresor* in French, and encyclopaedia giving a summary of all the knowledge of his time. *Tesoretto*, in Italian verse, is an extract from the encyclopaedia in allegorical guise. See also lecture from

29 December 1918 in 'How can humanity find Christ again?—the Threefold Shadow Existence of our Time and the New Christ Light,' GA 187.

10 *Plato*, 427-347 bc.

Socrates, c. 470-399 bc.

Heraclitus, c. 500 bc, pre-Socratic philosopher from Ephesus.

11 *asafoetida:* Dried latex of the rhizome of an oriental steppe plant, used medicinally.

12 *Dr Wegman's Clinic in Arlesheim:* Dr Ita Wegman, Dutch medical doctor (1876-1943). Founded the Klinisch-Therapeutische Institut in Arlesheim, Switzerland.

13 *Brunetto Latini:* See note 9.

14 *we characterized a very specific age:* There is an entry in one of Steiner's notebooks for this lecture: 'Morning, 18 August, Torquay: 1879-1510 Gabriel/ 1510-1190 Samael/ 1190-850 Raphael/ 850-500 Zachariel/ 500-150 Anael/ 150 bc-200 ad Oriphiel.'

See also *Karmic Relationships*, Vol. III, lecture on 8 August 1924. The teaching on the planetary intelligences derives from Johannes Trithemius of Spondheim (1462-1516): *De septem intelligentiis libellus.*

15 *Paracelsus*, 1493-1541.

Jacob Boehme, 1575-1624.

John Scotus Erigena, c. 810 to 877, translator of the writings of Dionysius the Areopagite, writer of *De divina praedestinatione*, and *De divisione naturae*. In 1225 the Vatican ordered the burning of all his writings.

16 *the movements emanated from people:* These and the following words were written on the board

17 *Moriz Benedikt*, 1835-1920, criminal anthropologist. See *Ruten- und Pendellehre* (Study of dowsing and pendulum), Vienna and Leipzig 1917.

18 *Albert Freiherr von Schrenck-Notzing*, 1862-1929, doctor and psychologist. *Materialisationsphänomene zur mediumistischen Teleplastie* (Materialization phenomena in mediumistic teleplasty), 1914; *Physikalische Phänomene des Mediumismus* (Physical phenomena in mediumism), 1920.

19 Eliphas Levi (Abbé Alphonse Louis Constant), 1810-1875, writer of occult theology. *Dogme et Rituel de la Haute Magie*, 1854-56; *La clef des Grands Mysteres*, 1861. *Dr Encausse:* wrote under the pseudonym of 'Papus'. *Traite methodique de Science occulte*, 1893.

20 *Helena Petrovna Blavatsky*, 1831-1891, *Isis Unveiled*, 1877, and *The Secret Doctrine*, 1887-97.

21 *looking for the spiritual figure of Christ in a physical personality:* Under the name of Alcyone, J Krishnamurti was proclaimed by Annie Besant and her followers to be the reborn Christ. The order, 'Star of the East', was founded for this purpose.

22 *the first volume of a book*: Dr R Steiner and Dr I Wegman, *Grundlegendes für eine Erweiterung der Heilkunst nach geisteswissenschaftlichen Erkenntnissen* (published in English as *Extending Practical Medicine*) (1966), GA 27.

23 *Matthias Jakob Schleiden*, 1804-1881, professor of botany and anthropology. *Gustav Theodor Fechner*, 1801-1887, physicist and philosopher. Regarding the argument between these two, see the chapter on 'Einfluss des Mondes auf die Witterung' (Lunar influences on the weather) in Fechners work *Professor Schleiden und der Mond* (Professor Schleiden and the Moon), Leipzig 1856.

24 *Isaac Newton*, 1642-1727, English nature philosopher. See his work *Philosophiae naturalis principia mathematica*, London 1687.

25 *Anton Bruckner*, 1824-1896. His last symphony, No. 9 in D minor, is unfinished.

Rudolf Steiner's Collected Works

The German Edition of Rudolf Steiner's Collected Works (the *Gesamtausgabe* [GA] published by Rudolf Steiner Verlag, Dornach, Switzerland) presently runs to 354 titles, organized either by type of work (written or spoken), chronology, audience (public or other), or subject (education, art, etc.). For ease of comparison, the Collected Works in English [CW] follows the German organization exactly. A complete listing of the CWs follows with literal translations of the German titles. Other than in the case of the books published in his lifetime, titles were rarely given by Rudolf Steiner himself, and were often provided by the editors of the German editions. The titles in English are not necessarily the same as the German; and, indeed, over the past seventy-five years have frequently been different, with the same book sometimes appearing under different titles.

For ease of identification and to avoid confusion, we suggest that readers looking for a title should do so by CW number. Because the work of creating the Collected Works of Rudolf Steiner is an ongoing process, with new titles being published every year, we have not indicated in this listing which books are presently available. To find out what titles in the Collected Works are currently in print, please check our website at www.rudolfsteinerpress.com (or www.steinerbooks.org for US readers).

Written Work

CW 1 Goethe: Natural-Scientific Writings, Introduction, with Footnotes and Explanations in the text by Rudolf Steiner

CW 2 Outlines of an Epistemology of the Goethean World View, with Special Consideration of Schiller

CW 3 Truth and Science

CW 4 The Philosophy of Freedom

CW 4a Documents to 'The Philosophy of Freedom'

CW 5 Friedrich Nietzsche, A Fighter against His Time

CW 6   Goethe's Worldview

CW 6a   Now in CW 30

CW 7   Mysticism at the Dawn of Modern Spiritual Life and Its Relationship with Modern Worldviews

CW 8   Christianity as Mystical Fact and the Mysteries of Antiquity

CW 9   Theosophy: An Introduction into Supersensible World Knowledge and Human Purpose

CW 10   How Does One Attain Knowledge of Higher Worlds?

CW 11   From the Akasha-Chronicle

CW 12   Levels of Higher Knowledge

CW 13   Occult Science in Outline

CW 14   Four Mystery Dramas

CW 15   The Spiritual Guidance of the Individual and Humanity

CW 16   A Way to Human Self-Knowledge: Eight Meditations

CW 17   The Threshold of the Spiritual World. Aphoristic Comments

CW 18   The Riddles of Philosophy in Their History, Presented as an Outline

CW 19   Contained in CW 24

CW 20   The Riddles of the Human Being: Articulated and Unarticulated in the Thinking, Views and Opinions of a Series of German and Austrian Personalities

CW 21   The Riddles of the Soul

CW 22   Goethe's Spiritual Nature and its Revelation in 'Faust' and through the 'Fairy Tale of the Snake and the Lily'

CW 23   The Central Points of the Social Question in the Necessities of Life in the Present and the Future

CW 24   Essays Concerning the Threefold Division of the Social Organism and the Period 1915-1921

CW 25   Cosmology, Religion and Philosophy

CW 26   Anthroposophical Leading Thoughts

CW 27   Fundamentals for Expansion of the Art of Healing according to Spiritual-Scientific Insights

CW 28   The Course of My Life

CW 29   Collected Essays on Dramaturgy, 1889-1900

CW 30   Methodical Foundations of Anthroposophy: Collected Essays on Philosophy, Natural Science, Aesthetics and Psychology, 1884-1901

CW 31   Collected Essays on Culture and Current Events, 1887-1901

CW 32   Collected Essays on Literature, 1884-1902

CW 33   Biographies and Biographical Sketches, 1894-1905

CW 34   Lucifer-Gnosis: Foundational Essays on Anthroposophy and Reports from the Periodicals 'Lucifer' and 'Lucifer-Gnosis,' 1903-1908

CW 35   Philosophy and Anthroposophy: Collected Essays, 1904-1923

CW 36   The Goetheanum-Idea in the Middle of the Cultural Crisis of the Present: Collected Essays from the Periodical 'Das Goetheanum,' 1921-1925

Public Lectures

Lectures to the Members of the Anthroposophical Society

SIGNIFICANT EVENTS IN THE LIFE OF
RUDOLF STEINER

1829:   June 23: birth of Johann Steiner (1829–1910)—Rudolf Steiner's father—in Geras, Lower Austria.

1834:   May 8: birth of Franciska Blie (1834–1918)—Rudolf Steiner's mother—in Horn, Lower Austria. 'My father and mother were both children of the glorious Lower Austrian forest district north of the Danube.'

1860:   May 16: marriage of Johann Steiner and Franciska Blie.

1861:   February 25: birth of *Rudolf Joseph Lorenz Steiner* in Kraljevec, Croatia, near the border with Hungary, where Johann Steiner works as a telegrapher for the South Austria Railroad. Rudolf Steiner is baptized two days later, February 27, the date usually given as his birthday.

1862:   Summer: the family moves to Modling, Lower Austria.

1863:   The family moves to Pottschach, Lower Austria, near the Styrian border, where Johann Steiner becomes station master. 'The view stretched to the mountains . . . majestic peaks in the distance and the sweet charm of nature in the immediate surroundings.'

1864:   November 15: birth of Rudolf Steiner's sister, Leopoldine (d. November 1, 1927). She will become a seamstress and live with her parents for the rest of her life.

1866:   July 28: birth of Rudolf Steiner's deaf-mute brother, Gustav (d. May 1, 1941).

1867:   Rudolf Steiner enters the village school. Following a disagreement between his father and the schoolmaster, whose wife falsely accused the boy of causing a commotion, Rudolf Steiner is taken out of school and taught at home.

1868:   A critical experience. Unknown to the family, an aunt dies in a distant town. Sitting in the station waiting room, Rudolf Steiner sees her 'form,' which speaks to him, asking for help. 'Beginning with this experience, a new soul life began in the boy, one in which not only the outer trees and mountains spoke to him, but also the worlds that lay behind them. From this moment on, the boy began to live with the spirits of nature . . .'

1869:   The family moves to the peaceful, rural village of Neudorfl, near Wiener Neustadt in present-day Austria. Rudolf Steiner attends the village school. Because of the 'unorthodoxy' of his writing and spelling, he has to do 'extra lessons.'

1870:   Through a book lent to him by his tutor, he discovers geometry: 'To grasp something purely in the spirit brought me inner happiness. I know that I first learned happiness through geometry.' The same tutor allows him to draw, while other students still struggle with their reading and writing. 'An artistic element' thus enters his education.

1871:   Though his parents are not religious, Rudolf Steiner becomes a 'church child,' a favourite of the priest, who was 'an exceptional character.' 'Up to the age of ten or eleven, among those I came to know, he was far and away the most significant.' Among other things, he introduces Steiner to Copernican, heliocentric cosmology. As an altar boy, Rudolf Steiner serves at masses, funerals, and Corpus Christi processions. At year's end, after an incident in which he escapes a thrashing, his father forbids him to go to church.

1872:   Rudolf Steiner transfers to grammar school in Wiener-Neustadt, a five-mile walk from home, which must be done in all weathers.

1873–75:   Through his teachers and on his own, Rudolf Steiner has many wonderful experiences with science and mathematics. Outside school, he teaches himself analytic geometry, trigonometry, differential equations, and calculus.

1876:   Rudolf Steiner begins tutoring other students. He learns bookbinding from his father. He also teaches himself stenography.

1877:   Rudolf Steiner discovers Kant's *Critique of Pure Reason,* which he reads and rereads. He also discovers and reads von Rotteck's *World History.*

1878:   He studies extensively in contemporary psychology and philosophy.

1879:   Rudolf Steiner graduates from high school with honours. His father is transferred to Inzersdorf, near Vienna. He uses his first visit to Vienna 'to purchase a great number of philosophy books'—Kant, Fichte, Schelling, and Hegel, as well as numerous histories of philosophy. His aim: to find a path from the 'I' to nature.

October
1879–1883:   Rudolf Steiner attends the Technical College in Vienna—to study mathematics, chemistry, physics, mineralogy, botany, zoology,

biology, geology, and mechanics—with a scholarship. He also attends lectures in history and literature, while avidly reading philosophy on his own. His two favourite professors are Karl Julius Schroer (German language and literature) and Edmund Reitlinger (physics). He also audits lectures by Robert Zimmermann on aesthetics and Franz Brentano on philosophy. During this year he begins his friendship with Moritz Zitter (1861–1921), who will help support him financially when he is in Berlin.

1880: Rudolf Steiner attends lectures on Schiller and Goethe by Karl Julius Schroer, who becomes his mentor. Also 'through a remarkable combination of circumstances,' he meets Felix Koguzki, a 'herb gatherer' and healer, who could 'see deeply into the secrets of nature.' Rudolf Steiner will meet and study with this 'emissary of the Master' throughout his time in Vienna.

1881: January: '... I didn't sleep a wink. I was busy with philosophical problems until about 12:30 a.m. Then, finally, I threw myself down on my couch. All my striving during the previous year had been to research whether the following statement by Schelling was true or not: *Within everyone dwells a secret, marvelous capacity to draw back from the stream of time—out of the self clothed in all that comes to us from outside—into our innermost being and there, in the immutable form of the Eternal, to look into ourselves.* I believe, and I am still quite certain of it, that I discovered this capacity in myself; I had long had an inkling of it. Now the whole of idealist philosophy stood before me in modified form. What's a sleepless night compared to that!'

Rudolf Steiner begins communicating with leading thinkers of the day, who send him books in return, which he reads eagerly.

July: 'I am not one of those who dives into the day like an animal in human form. I pursue a quite specific goal, an idealistic aim—knowledge of the truth! This cannot be done offhandedly. It requires the greatest striving in the world, free of all egotism, and equally of all resignation.'

August: Steiner puts down on paper for the first time thoughts for a 'Philosophy of Freedom.' 'The striving for the absolute: this human yearning is freedom.' He also seeks to outline a 'peasant philosophy,' describing what the worldview of a 'peasant'—one who lives close to the earth and the old ways—really is.

1881–1882: Felix Koguzki, the herb gatherer, reveals himself to be the envoy of another, higher initiatory personality, who instructs Rudolf Steiner to penetrate Fichte's philosophy and to master modern scientific thinking as a preparation for right entry into the spirit. This 'Master' also teaches him the double (evolutionary and involutionary) nature of time.

1882:   Through the offices of Karl Julius Schroer, Rudolf Steiner is asked by Joseph Kurschner to edit Goethe's scientific works for the *Deutschen National-Literatur* edition. He writes 'A Possible Critique of Atomistic Concepts' and sends it to Friedrich Theodor Vischer.

1883:   Rudolf Steiner completes his college studies and begins work on the Goethe project.

1884:   First volume of Goethe's *Scientific Writings* (CW 1) appears (March). He lectures on Goethe and Lessing, and Goethe's approach to science. In July, he enters the household of Ladislaus and Pauline Specht as tutor to the four Specht boys. He will live there until 1890. At this time, he meets Josef Breuer (1842–1925), the co-author with Sigmund Freud of *Studies in Hysteria*, who is the Specht family doctor.

1885:   While continuing to edit Goethe's writings, Rudolf Steiner reads deeply in contemporary philosophy (Eduard von Hartmann, Johannes Volkelt, and Richard Wahle, among others).

1886:   May: Rudolf Steiner sends Kürschner the manuscript of *Outlines of Goethe's Theory of Knowledge* (CW 2), which appears in October, and which he sends out widely. He also meets the poet Marie Eugenie Delle Grazie and writes 'Nature and Our Ideals' for her. He attends her salon, where he meets many priests, theologians, and philosophers, who will become his friends. Meanwhile, the director of the Goethe Archive in Weimar requests his collaboration with the *Sophien* edition of Goethe's works, particularly the writings on colour.

1887:   At the beginning of the year, Rudolf Steiner is very sick. As the year progresses and his health improves, he becomes increasingly 'a man of letters,' lecturing, writing essays, and taking part in Austrian cultural life. In August–September, the second volume of Goethe's *Scientific Writings* appears.

1888:   January–July: Rudolf Steiner assumes editorship of the 'German Weekly' *(Deutsche Wochenschrift)*. He begins lecturing more intensively, giving, for example, a lecture titled 'Goethe as Father of a New Aesthetics.' He meets and becomes soul friends with Friedrich Eckstein (1861–1939), a vegetarian, philosopher of symbolism, alchemist, and musician, who will introduce him to various spiritual currents (including Theosophy) and with whom he will meditate and interpret esoteric and alchemical texts.

1889:   Rudolf Steiner first reads Nietzsche *(Beyond Good and Evil)*. He encounters Theosophy again and learns of Madame Blavatsky in the theosophical circle around Marie Lang (1858–1934). Here he also meets well-known figures of Austrian life, as well as esoteric figures like the occultist Franz Hartmann and Karl Leinigen-Billigen (translator of C.G. Harrison's *The Transcendental Universe*). During this period, Steiner first reads A.P. Sinnett's *Esoteric Buddhism* and Mabel Collins's *Light on the Path*. He also begins travelling, visiting Budapest, Weimar, and Berlin (where he meets philosopher Eduard von Hartmann).

1890:   Rudolf Steiner finishes Volume 3 of Goethe's scientific writings. He begins his doctoral dissertation, which will become *Truth and Science* (CW 3). He also meets the poet and feminist Rosa Mayreder (1858–1938), with whom he can exchange his most intimate thoughts. In September, Rudolf Steiner moves to Weimar to work in the Goethe-Schiller Archive.

1891:   Volume 3 of the Kürschner edition of Goethe appears. Meanwhile, Rudolf Steiner edits Goethe's studies in mineralogy and scientific writings for the *Sophien* edition. He meets Ludwig Laistner of the Cotta Publishing Company, who asks for a book on the basic question of metaphysics. From this will result, ultimately, *The Philosophy of Freedom* (CW 4), which will be published not by Cotta but by Emil Felber. In October, Rudolf Steiner takes the oral exam for a doctorate in philosophy, mathematics, and mechanics at Rostock University, receiving his doctorate on the twenty-sixth. In November, he gives his first lecture on Goethe's 'Fairy Tale' in Vienna.

1892:   Rudolf Steiner continues work at the Goethe-Schiller Archive and on his *Philosophy of Freedom*. *Truth and Science,* his doctoral dissertation, is published. Steiner undertakes to write introductions to books on Schopenhauer and Jean Paul for Cotta. At year's end, he finds lodging with Anna Eunike, nee Schulz (1853–1911), a widow with four daughters and a son. He also develops a friendship with Otto Erich Hartleben (1864–1905) with whom he shares literary interests.

1893:   Rudolf Steiner begins his habit of producing many reviews and articles. In March, he gives a lecture titled 'Hypnotism, with Reference to Spiritism.' In September, volume 4 of the Kürschner edition is completed. In November, *The Philosophy of Freedom* appears. This year, too, he meets John Henry Mackay (1864–1933), the anarchist, and Max Stirner, a scholar and biographer.

1894:   Rudolf Steiner meets Elisabeth Fürster Nietzsche, the philosopher's sister, and begins to read Nietzsche in earnest, beginning with the as yet unpublished *Antichrist*. He also meets Ernst Haeckel (1834–1919). In the fall, he begins to write *Nietzsche, A Fighter against His Time* (CW 5).

1895:   May, *Nietzsche, A Fighter against His Time* appears.

1896:   January 22: Rudolf Steiner sees Friedrich Nietzsche for the first and only time. Moves between the Nietzsche and the Goethe-Schiller

Archives, where he completes his work before year's end. He falls out with Elisabeth Förster Nietzsche, thus ending his association with the Nietzsche Archive.

1897: Rudolf Steiner finishes the manuscript of *Goethe's Worldview* (CW 6). He moves to Berlin with Anna Eunike and begins editorship of the *Magazin für Literatur*. From now on, Steiner will write countless reviews, literary and philosophical articles, and so on. He begins lecturing at the 'Free Literary Society.' In September, he attends the Zionist Congress in Basel. He sides with Dreyfus in the Dreyfus affair.

1898: Rudolf Steiner is very active as an editor in the political, artistic, and theatrical life of Berlin. He becomes friendly with John Henry Mackay and poet Ludwig Jacobowski (1868–1900). He joins Jacobowski's circle of writers, artists, and scientists—'The Coming Ones' (Die *Kommenden)*—and contributes lectures to the group until 1903. He also lectures at the 'League for College Pedagogy.' He writes an article for Goethe's sesquicentennial, 'Goethe's Secret Revelation,' on the 'Fairy Tale of the Green Snake and the Beautiful Lily.'

1898–99: 'This was a trying time for my soul as I looked at Christianity. . . . I was able to progress only by contemplating, by means of spiritual perception, the evolution of Christianity. . . . Conscious knowledge of real Christianity began to dawn in me around the turn of the century. This seed continued to develop. My soul trial occurred shortly before the beginning of the twentieth century. It was decisive for my soul's development that I stood spiritually before the Mystery of Golgotha in a deep and solemn celebration of knowledge.'

1899: Rudolf Steiner begins teaching and giving lectures and lecture cycles at the Workers' College, founded by Wilhelm Liebknecht (1826–1900). He will continue to do so until 1904. Writes: *Literature and Spiritual Life in the Nineteenth Century; Individualism in Philosophy; Haeckel and His Opponents; Poetry in the Present;* and begins what will become (fifteen years later) *The Riddles of Philosophy* (CW 18). He also meets many artists and writers, including Kothe Kollwitz, Stefan Zweig, and Rainer Maria Rilke. On October 31, he marries Anna Eunike.

1900: 'I thought that the turn of the century must bring humanity a new light. It seemed to me that the separation of human thinking and willing from the spirit had peaked. A turn or reversal of direction in human evolution seemed to me a necessity.' Rudolf Steiner finishes *World and Life Views in the Nineteenth Century* (the second part of what will become *The Riddles of Philosophy)* and dedicates it to

Ernst Haeckel. It is published in March. He continues lecturing at *Die Kommenden,* whose leadership he assumes after the death of Jacobowski. Also, he gives the Gutenberg Jubilee lecture before 7,000 typesetters and printers. In September, Rudolf Steiner is invited by Count and Countess Brockdorff to lecture in the Theosophical Library. His first lecture is on Nietzsche. His second lecture is titled 'Goethe's Secret Revelation.' October 6, he begins a lecture cycle on the mystics that will become *Mystics after Modernism* (CW 7). November–December: 'Marie von Sivers appears in the audience. . . .' Also in November, Steiner gives his first lecture at the Giordano Bruno Bund (where he will continue to lecture until May, 1905). He speaks on Bruno and modern Rome, focusing on the importance of the philosophy of Thomas Aquinas as monism.

1901: In continual financial straits, Rudolf Steiner's early friends Moritz Zitter and Rosa Mayreder help support him. In October, he begins the lecture cycle *Christianity as Mystical Fact* (CW 8) at the Theosophical Library. In November, he gives his first 'theosophical lecture' on Goethe's 'Fairy Tale' in Hamburg at the invitation of Wilhelm Hubbe-Schleiden. He also attends a gathering to celebrate the founding of the Theosophical Society at Count and Countess Brockdorff's. He gives a lecture cycle, 'From Buddha to Christ,' for the circle of the *Kommenden.* November 17, Marie von Sivers asks Rudolf Steiner if Theosophy needs a Western–Christian spiritual movement (to complement Theosophy's Eastern emphasis). 'The question was posed. Now, following spiritual laws, I could begin to give an answer. . . .' In December, Rudolf Steiner writes his first article for a theosophical publication. At year's end, the Brockdorffs and possibly Wilhelm Hubbe-Schleiden ask Rudolf Steiner to join the Theosophical Society and undertake the leadership of the German section. Rudolf Steiner agrees, on the condition that Marie von Sivers (then in Italy) work with him.

1902: Beginning in January, Rudolf Steiner attends the opening of the Workers' School in Spandau with Rosa Luxemburg (1870–1919). January 17, Rudolf Steiner joins the Theosophical Society. In April, he is asked to become general secretary of the German Section of the theosophical society, and works on preparations for its founding. In July, he visits London for a theosophical congress. He meets Bertram Keightly, G.R.S. Mead, A.P. Sinnett, and Annie Besant, among others. In September, *Christianity as Mystical Fact* appears. In October, Rudolf Steiner gives his first public lecture on Theosophy ('Monism and Theosophy') to about three hundred people at the Giordano Bruno Bund. On October 19–21, the

German Section of the Theosophical Society has its first meeting; Rudolf Steiner is the general secretary, and Annie Besant attends. Steiner lectures on practical karma studies. On October 23, Annie Besant inducts Rudolf Steiner into the Esoteric School of the Theosophical Society. On October 25, Steiner begins a weekly series of lectures: 'The Field of Theosophy.' During this year, Rudolf Steiner also first meets Ita Wegman (1876–1943), who will become his close collaborator in his final years.

1903: Rudolf Steiner holds about 300 lectures and seminars. In May, the first issue of the periodical *Luzifer* appears. In June, Rudolf Steiner visits London for the first meeting of the Federation of the European Sections of the Theosophical Society, where he meets Colonel Olcott. He begins to write *Theosophy* (CW 9).

1904: Rudolf Steiner continues lecturing at the Workers' College and elsewhere (about 90 lectures), while lecturing intensively all over Germany among theosophists (about 140 lectures). In February, he meets Carl Unger (1878–1929), who will become a member of the board of the Anthroposophical Society (1913). In March, he meets Michael Bauer (1871–1929), a Christian mystic, who will also be on the board. In May, *Theosophy* appears, with the dedication: 'To the spirit of Giordano Bruno.' Rudolf Steiner and Marie von Sivers visit London for meetings with Annie Besant. June: Rudolf Steiner and Marie von Sivers attend the meeting of the Federation of European Sections of the Theosophical Society in Amsterdam. In July, Steiner begins the articles in *Luzifer-Gnosis* that will become *How to Know Higher Worlds* (CW 10) and *Cosmic Memory* (CW 11). In September, Annie Besant visits Germany. In December, Steiner lectures on Freemasonry. He mentions the High Grade Masonry derived from John Yarker and represented by Theodore Reuss and Karl Kellner as a blank slate 'into which a good image could be placed.'

1905: This year, Steiner ends his non-theosophical lecturing activity. Supported by Marie von Sivers, his theosophical lecturing—both in public and in the Theosophical Society—increases significantly: 'The German Theosophical Movement is of exceptional importance.' Steiner recommends reading, among others, Fichte, Jacob Boehme, and Angelus Silesius. He begins to introduce Christian themes into Theosophy. He also begins to work with doctors (Felix Peipers and Ludwig Noll). In July, he is in London for the Federation of European Sections, where he attends a lecture by Annie Besant: 'I have seldom seen Mrs. Besant speak in so inward and heartfelt a manner...' Through Mrs. Besant I have found the way to H.P. Blavatsky.' September to October, he gives a course of thirty-one lectures for a small group of esoteric students. In October, the annual meeting of the German Section of the Theosophical Society, which still remains very small, takes place. Rudolf Steiner reports membership has risen from 121 to 377 members. In November, seeking to establish esoteric 'continuity,' Rudolf Steiner and Marie von Sivers participate in a 'Memphis-Misraim' Masonic ceremony. They pay forty-five marks for membership. 'Yesterday, you saw how little remains of former esoteric institutions.' 'We are dealing only with a "framework" . . for the present, nothing lies behind it. The occult powers have completely withdrawn.'

1906: Expansion of theosophical work. Rudolf Steiner gives about 245 lectures, only 44 of which take place in Berlin. Cycles are given in Paris, Leipzig, Stuttgart, and Munich. Esoteric work also intensifies. Rudolf Steiner begins writing *An Outline of Esoteric Science* (CW 13). In January, Rudolf Steiner receives permission (a patent) from the Great Orient of the Scottish A & A Thirty-Three Degree Rite of the Order of the Ancient Freemasons of the Memphis-Misraim Rite to direct a chapter under the name 'Mystica Aeterna.' This will become the 'Cognitive-Ritual Section' (also called 'Misraim Service') of the Esoteric School. (See: *Freemasonry and Ritual Work: The Misraim Service,* CW 265.) During this time, Steiner also meets Albert Schweitzer. In May, he is in Paris, where he visits Edouard Schure. Many Russians attend his lectures (including Konstantin Balmont, Dimitri Mereszkovski, Zinaida Hippius, and Maximilian Woloshin). He attends the General Meeting of the European Federation of the Theosophical Society, at which Col. Olcott is present for the last time. He spends the year's end in Venice and Rome, where he writes and works on his translation of H.P. Blavatsky's *Key to Theosophy.*

1907: Further expansion of the German Theosophical Movement according to the Rosicrucian directive to 'introduce spirit into the world'—in education, in social questions, in art, and in science. In February, Col. Olcott dies in Adyar. Before he dies, Olcott indicates that 'the Masters' wish Annie Besant to succeed him: much politicking ensues. Rudolf Steiner supports Besant's candidacy. April–May: preparations for the Congress of the Federation of European Sections of the Theosophical Society—the great, watershed Whitsun 'Munich Congress,' attended by Annie Besant and others. Steiner decides to separate Eastern and Western (Christian–Rosicrucian) esoteric schools. He takes his esoteric school out of the Theosophical Society (Besant and Rudolf Steiner are 'in harmony' on this). Steiner makes his first lecture tours to Austria and Hungary. That summer, he is in Italy. In September, he visits Edouard Schuré, who will write the introduction to the French edition of *Christianity as Mystical Fact* in Barr, Alsace. Rudolf Steiner writes the autobiographical statement known as the 'Barr Document.' In *Luzifer-Gnosis*, 'The Education of the Child' appears.

1908:   The movement grows (membership: 1,150). Lecturing expands. Steiner makes his first extended lecture tour to Holland and Scandinavia, as well as visits to Naples and Sicily. Themes: St. John's Gospel, the Apocalypse, Egypt, science, philosophy, and logic. *Luzifer-Gnosis* ceases publication. In Berlin, Marie von Sivers (with Johanna Mücke (1864–1949) forms the *Philosophisch-Theosophisch* (after 1915 *Philosophisch-Anthroposophisch) Verlag* to publish Steiner's work. Steiner gives lecture cycles titled *The Gospel of St. John* (CW 103) and *The Apocalypse* (104).

1909:   *An Outline of Esoteric Science* appears. Lecturing and travel continues. Rudolf Steiner's spiritual research expands to include the polarity of Lucifer and Ahriman; the work of great individualities in history; the Maitreya Buddha and the Bodhisattvas; spiritual economy (CW 109); the work of the spiritual hierarchies in heaven and on earth (CW 110). He also deepens and intensifies his research into the Gospels, giving lectures on the Gospel of St. Luke (CW 114) with the first mention of two Jesus children. Meets and becomes friends with Christian Morgenstern (1871–1914). In April, he lays the foundation stone for the Malsch model—the building that will lead to the first Goetheanum. In May, the International Congress of the Federation of European Sections of the Theosophical Society takes place in Budapest. Rudolf Steiner receives the Subba Row medal for *How to Know Higher Worlds*. During this time, Charles W. Leadbeater discovers Jiddu Krishnamurti (1895–1986) and proclaims him the future 'world teacher,' the bearer of the Maitreya Buddha and the 'reappearing Christ.' In October, Steiner delivers seminal lectures on 'anthroposophy,' which he will try, unsuccessfully, to rework over the next years into the unfinished work, *Anthroposophy (A Fragment)* (CW 45).

1910:   New themes: *The Reappearance of Christ in the Etheric* (CW 118); *The Fifth Gospel; The Mission of Folk Souls* (CW 121); *Occult History* (CW 126); the evolving development of etheric cognitive capacities. Rudolf Steiner continues his Gospel research with *The Gospel of St. Matthew* (CW 123). In January, his father dies. In April, he takes a month-long trip to Italy, including Rome, Monte Cassino, and Sicily. He also visits Scandinavia again. July–August, he writes the first mystery drama, *The Portal of Initiation* (CW 14). In November, he gives 'psychosophy' lectures. In December, he submits 'On the

Psychological Foundations and Epistemological Framework of Theosophy' to the International Philosophical Congress in Bologna.

1911: The crisis in the Theosophical Society deepens. In January, 'The Order of the Rising Sun,' which will soon become 'The Order of the Star in the East,' is founded for the coming world teacher, Krishnamurti. At the same time, Marie von Sivers, Rudolf Steiner's co-worker, falls ill. Fewer lectures are given, but important new ground is broken. In Prague, in March, Steiner meets Franz Kafka (1883–1924) and Hugo Bergmann (1883–1975). In April, he delivers his paper to the Philosophical Congress. He writes the second mystery drama, *The Soul's Probation* (CW 14). Also, while Marie von Sivers is convalescing, Rudolf Steiner begins work on *Calendar 1912/1913*, which will contain the 'Calendar of the Soul' meditations. On March 19, Anna (Eunike) Steiner dies. In September, Rudolf Steiner visits Einsiedeln, birthplace of Paracelsus. In December, Friedrich Rittelmeyer, future founder of the Christian Community, meets Rudolf Steiner. The *Johannes-Bauverein*, the 'building committee,' which would lead to the first Goetheanum (first planned for Munich), is also founded, and a preliminary committee for the founding of an independent association is created that, in the following year, will become the Anthroposophical Society. Important lecture cycles include *Occult Physiology* (CW 128); *Wonders of the World* (CW 129); *From Jesus to Christ* (CW 131). Other themes: esoteric Christianity; Christian Rosenkreutz; the spiritual guidance of humanity; the sense world and the world of the spirit.

1912: Despite the ongoing, now increasing crisis in the Theosophical Society, much is accomplished: *Calendar 1912/1913* is published; eurythmy is created; both the third mystery drama, *The Guardian of the Threshold* (CW 14) and *A Way of Self-Knowledge* (CW 16) are written. New (or renewed) themes included life between death and rebirth and karma and reincarnation. Other lecture cycles: *Spiritual Beings in the Heavenly Bodies and in the Kingdoms of Nature* (CW 136); *The Human Being in the Light of Occultism, Theosophy, and Philosophy* (CW 137); *The Gospel of St. Mark* (CW 139); and *The Bhagavad Gita and the Epistles of Paul* (CW 142). On May 8, Rudolf Steiner celebrates White Lotus Day, H.P. Blavatsky's death day, which he had faithfully observed for the past decade, for the last time. In August, Rudolf Steiner suggests the 'independent association' be called the 'Anthroposophical Society.' In September, the first eurythmy course takes place. In October, Rudolf Steiner declines recognition of a Theosophical Society lodge dedicated to the Star of the East and decides to expel all Theosophical Society members belonging to the order.

Also, with Marie von Sivers, he first visits Dornach, near Basel, Switzerland, and they stand on the hill where the Goetheanum will be built. In November, a Theosophical Society lodge is opened by direct mandate from Adyar (Annie Besant). In December, a meeting of the German section occurs at which it is decided that belonging to the Order of the Star of the East is incompatible with membership in the Theosophical Society. December 28: informal founding of the Anthroposophical Society in Berlin.

1913:   Expulsion of the German section from the Theosophical Society. February 2–3: Foundation meeting of the Anthroposophical Society. Board members include: Marie von Sivers, Michael Bauer, and Carl Unger. September 20: Laying of the foundation stone for the *Johannes Bau* (Goetheanum) in Dornach. Building begins immediately. The third mystery drama, *The Soul's Awakening* (CW 14), is completed. Also: *The Threshold of the Spiritual World* (CW 147). Lecture cycles include: *The Bhagavad Gita and the Epistles of Paul* and *The Esoteric Meaning of the Bhagavad Gita* (CW 146), which the Russian philosopher Nikolai Berdyaev attends; *The Mysteries of the East and of Christianity* (CW 144); *The Effects of Esoteric Development* (CW 145); and *The Fifth Gospel* (CW 148). In May, Rudolf Steiner is in London and Paris, where anthroposophical work continues.

1914:   Building continues on the *Johannes Bau* (Goetheanum) in Dornach, with artists and co-workers from seventeen nations. The general assembly of the Anthroposophical Society takes place. In May, Rudolf Steiner visits Paris, as well as Chartres Cathedral. June 28: assassination in Sarajevo ('Now the catastrophe has happened!'). August 1: War is declared. Rudolf Steiner returns to Germany from Dornach—he will travel back and forth. He writes the last chapter of *The Riddles of Philosophy*. Lecture cycles include: *Human and Cosmic Thought* (CW 151); *Inner Being of Humanity between Death and a New Birth* (CW 153); *Occult Reading and Occult Hearing* (CW 156). December 24: marriage of Rudolf Steiner and Marie von Sivers.

1915:   Building continues. Life after death becomes a major theme, also art. Writes: *Thoughts during a Time of War* (CW 24). Lectures include: *The Secret of Death* (CW 159); *The Uniting of Humanity through the Christ Impulse* (CW 165).

1916:   Rudolf Steiner begins work with Edith Maryon (1872–1924) on the sculpture 'The Representative of Humanity' ('The Group'—Christ, Lucifer, and Ahriman). He also works with the alchemist Alexander von Bernus on the quarterly *Das Reich*. He writes *The Riddle of Humanity* (CW 20). Lectures include: *Necessity and Freedom in World History and Human Action* (CW 166); *Past and Present in the*

Human Spirit (CW 167); *The Karma of Vocation* (CW 172); *The Karma of Untruthfulness* (CW 173).

1917: Russian Revolution. The U.S. enters the war. Building continues. Rudolf Steiner delineates the idea of the 'threefold nature of the human being' (in a public lecture March 15) and the 'threefold nature of the social organism' (hammered out in May–June with the help of Otto von Lerchenfeld and Ludwig Polzer-Hoditz in the form of two documents titled *Memoranda,* which were distributed in high places). August–September: Rudolf Steiner writes *The Riddles of the Soul* (CW 20). Also: commentary on 'The Chymical Wedding of Christian Rosenkreutz' for Alexander Bernus (Das *Reich*). Lectures include: *The Karma of Materialism* (CW 176); *The Spiritual Background of the Outer World: The Fall of the Spirits of Darkness* (CW 177).

1918: March 18: peace treaty of Brest-Litovsk—'Now everything will truly enter chaos! What is needed is cultural renewal.' June: Rudolf Steiner visits Karlstein (Grail) Castle outside Prague. Lecture cycle: *From Symptom to Reality in Modern History* (CW 185). In mid-November, Emil Molt, of the Waldorf-Astoria Cigarette Company, has the idea of founding a school for his workers' children.

1919: Focus on the threefold social organism: tireless travel, countless lectures, meetings, and publications. At the same time, a new public stage of Anthroposophy emerges as cultural renewal begins. The coming years will see initiatives in pedagogy, medicine, pharmacology, and agriculture. January 27: threefold meeting: 'We must first of all, with the money we have, found free schools that can bring people what they need.' February: first public eurythmy performance in Zurich. Also: 'Appeal to the German People' (CW 24), circulated March 6 as a newspaper insert. In April, *Towards Social Renewal* (CW 23) appears—'perhaps the most widely read of all books on politics appearing since the war.' Rudolf Steiner is asked to undertake the 'direction and leadership' of the school founded by the Waldorf-Astoria Company. Rudolf Steiner begins to talk about the 'renewal' of education. May 30: a building is selected and purchased for the future Waldorf School. August–September, Rudolf Steiner gives a lecture course for Waldorf teachers, *The Foundations of Human Experience (Study of Man)* (CW 293). September 7: Opening of the first Waldorf School. December (into January): first science course, the *Light Course* (CW 320).

1920: The Waldorf School flourishes. New threefold initiatives. Founding of limited companies *Der Kommende Tag* and *Futurum A.G.* to infuse spiritual values into the economic realm. Rudolf Steiner also focuses on the sciences. Lectures: *Introducing Anthroposophical*

Medicine (CW 312); *The Warmth Course* (CW 321); *The Boundaries of Natural Science* (CW 322); *The Redemption of Thinking* (CW 74). February: Johannes Werner Klein—later a co-founder of the Christian Community—asks Rudolf Steiner about the possibility of a 'religious renewal,' a 'Johannine church.' In March, Rudolf Steiner gives the first course for doctors and medical students. In April, a divinity student asks Rudolf Steiner a second time about the possibility of religious renewal. September 27–October 16: anthroposophical 'university course.' December: lectures titled *The Search for the New Isis* (CW 202).

1921:   Rudolf Steiner continues his intensive work on cultural renewal, including the uphill battle for the threefold social order. 'University' arts, scientific, theological, and medical courses include: *The Astronomy Course* (CW 323); *Observation, Mathematics, and Scientific Experiment* (CW 324); the *Second Medical Course* (CW 313); *Colour*. In June and September–October, Rudolf Steiner also gives the first two 'priests' courses' (CW 342 and 343). The 'youth movement' gains momentum. Magazines are founded: *Die Drei* (January), and—under the editorship of Albert Steffen (1884–1963)—the weekly, *Das Goetheanum* (August). In February–March, Rudolf Steiner takes his first trip outside Germany since the war (Holland). On April 7, Steiner receives a letter regarding 'religious renewal,' and May 22–23, he agrees to address the question in a practical way. In June, the Klinical-Therapeutic Institute opens in Arlesheim under the direction of Dr. Ita Wegman. In August, the Chemical-Pharmaceutical Laboratory opens in Arlesheim (Oskar Schmiedel and Ita Wegman are directors). The Clinical Therapeutic Institute is inaugurated in Stuttgart (Dr. Ludwig Noll is director); also the Research Laboratory in Dornach (Ehrenfried Pfeiffer and Gunther Wachsmuth are directors). In November–December, Rudolf Steiner visits Norway.

1922:   The first half of the year involves very active public lecturing (thousands attend); in the second half, Rudolf Steiner begins to withdraw and turn toward the Society—'The Society is asleep.' It is 'too weak' to do what is asked of it. The businesses—*Der Kommende Tag* and *Futurum A.G.*—fail. In January, with the help of an agent, Steiner undertakes a twelve-city German lecture tour, accompanied by eurythmy performances. In two weeks he speaks to more than 2,000 people. In April, he gives a 'university course' in The Hague. He also visits England. In June, he is in Vienna for the East–West Congress. In August–September, he is back in England for the Oxford Conference on Education. Returning to Dornach, he gives the lectures *Philosophy, Cosmology, and Religion*

(CW 215), and gives the third priests' course (CW 344). On September 16, The Christian Community is founded. In October–November, Steiner is in Holland and England. He also speaks to the youth: *The Youth Course* (CW 217). In December, Steiner gives lectures titled *The Origins of Natural Science* (CW 326), and *Humanity and the World of Stars: The Spiritual Communion of Humanity* (CW 219). December 31: Fire at the Goetheanum, which is destroyed.

1923: Despite the fire, Rudolf Steiner continues his work unabated. A very hard year. Internal dispersion, dissension, and apathy abound. There is conflict—between old and new visions—within the Society. A wake-up call is needed, and Rudolf Steiner responds with renewed lecturing vitality. His focus: the spiritual context of human life; initiation science; the course of the year; and community building. As a foundation for an artistic school, he creates a series of pastel sketches. Lecture cycles: *The Anthroposophical Movement; Initiation Science* (CW 227) (in Wales at the Penmaenmawr Summer School); *The Four Seasons and the Archangels* (CW 229); *Harmony of the Creative Word* (CW 230); *The Supersensible Human* (CW 231), given in Holland for the founding of the Dutch society. On November 10, in response to the failed Hitler-Ludendorff putsch in Munich, Steiner closes his Berlin residence and moves the *Philosophisch-Anthroposophisch Verlag* (Press) to Dornach. On December 9, Steiner begins the serialization of his *Autobiography: The Course of My Life* (CW 28) in *Das Goetheanum*. It will continue to appear weekly, without a break, until his death. Late December–early January: Rudolf Steiner re-founds the Anthroposophical Society (about 12,000 members internationally) and takes over its leadership. The new board members are: Marie Steiner, Ita Wegman, Albert Steffen, Elisabeth Vreede, and Gunther Wachsmuth. (See *The Christmas Meeting for the Founding of the General Anthroposophical Society*, CW 260.) Accompanying lectures: *Mystery Knowledge and Mystery Centres* (CW 232); *World History in the Light of Anthroposophy* (CW 233). December 25: the Foundation Stone is laid (in the hearts of members) in the form of the 'Foundation Stone Meditation.'

1924: January 1: having founded the Anthroposophical Society and taken over its leadership, Rudolf Steiner has the task of 'reforming' it. The process begins with a weekly newssheet ('What's Happening in the Anthroposophical Society') in which Rudolf Steiner's 'Letters to Members' and 'Anthroposophical Leading Thoughts' appear (CW 26). The next step is the creation of a new esoteric class, the 'first class' of the 'University of Spiritual Science' (which was to have been followed, had Rudolf Steiner lived longer, by two more advanced classes). Then comes a new language for

Anthroposophy—practical, phenomenological, and direct; and Rudolf Steiner creates the model for the second Goetheanum. He begins the series of extensive 'karma' lectures (CW 235–40); and finally, responding to needs, he creates two new initiatives: biodynamic agriculture and curative education. After the middle of the year, rumours begin to circulate regarding Steiner's health. Lectures: January–February, *Anthroposophy* (CW 234); February: *Tone Eurythmy* (CW 278); June: *The Agriculture Course* (CW 327); June–July: *Speech Eurythmy* (CW 279); *Curative Education* (CW 317); August: (England, 'Second International Summer School'), *Initiation Consciousness: True and False Paths in Spiritual Investigation* (CW 243); September: *Pastoral Medicine* (CW 318). On September 26, for the first time, Rudolf Steiner cancels a lecture. On September 28, he gives his last lecture. On September 29, he withdraws to his studio in the carpenter's shop; now he is definitively ill. Cared for by Ita Wegman, he continues working, however, and writing the weekly installments of his *Autobiography* and *Letters to the Members/Leading Thoughts* (CW 26).

1925: Rudolf Steiner, while continuing to work, continues to weaken. He finishes *Extending Practical Medicine* (CW 27) with Ita Wegman. On March 30, around ten in the morning, Rudolf Steiner dies.

INDEX

A NOTE FROM RUDOLF STEINER PRESS

We are an independent publisher and registered charity (non-profit organisation) dedicated to making available the work of Rudolf Steiner in English translation. We care a great deal about the content of our books and have hundreds of titles available – as printed books, ebooks and in audio formats.

As a publisher devoted to anthroposophy...

🔄 We continually commission translations of previously unpublished works by Rudolf Steiner and invest in re-translating, editing and improving our editions.

🔄 We are committed to making anthroposophy available to all by publishing introductory books as well as contemporary research.

🔄 Our new print editions and ebooks are carefully checked and proofread for accuracy, and converted into all formats for all platforms.

🔄 Our translations are officially authorised by Rudolf Steiner's estate in Dornach, Switzerland, to whom we pay royalties on sales, thus assisting their critical work.

So, look out for Rudolf Steiner Press as a mark of quality and support us today by buying our books, or contact us should you wish to sponsor specific titles or to support the charity with a gift or legacy.

office@rudolfsteinerpress.com
Join our e-mailing list at www.rudolfsteinerpress.com

🔄 RUDOLF STEINER PRESS